53rd Man

53rd Man

Fighting to Make It in the NFL

John Vampatella

ROWMAN & LITTLEFIELD
Lanham • Boulder • New York • London

Published by Rowman & Littlefield
An imprint of The Rowman & Littlefield Publishing Group, Inc.
4501 Forbes Boulevard, Suite 200, Lanham, Maryland 20706
www.rowman.com

86-90 Paul Street, London EC2A 4NE, United Kingdom

British Library Cataloguing in Publication Information Available

Library of Congress Cataloging-in-Publication Data

Names: Vampatella, John author.
Title: 53rd man: fighting to make it in the NFL / John Vampatella.
Other titles: Fifty-third man
Description: Lanham, Maryland: Rowman & Littlefield, [2023] | Summary: "53rd Man
    tells the inspiring stories of the often-overlooked players trying to make it in the
    NFL-the men who are essentially 53rd on rosters of 53-who toil in obscurity in the
    hopes of seeing their professional football dreams come true"—Provided by publisher.
Identifiers: LCCN 2022061813 (print) | LCCN 2022061814 (ebook) | ISBN
    9781538181492 (cloth) | ISBN 9781538181508 (epub)
Subjects: LCSH: Football players—United States—Biography. | Football—Training.
Classification: LCC GV939.A1 .V28 2023 (print) | LCC GV939.A1 (ebook) | DDC
    796.332092—dc23/eng/20230126
LC record available at https://lccn.loc.gov/2022061813
LC ebook record available at https://lccn.loc.gov/2022061814

Contents

Acknowledgments

It is difficult to adequately convey the challenge of seeing what begins with just an idea in your head become a published book. There are so many steps involved, each one a hurdle of one size or another that must be overcome. The fact is, publishing a book is a total team effort, and I want to take a moment to thank various people for their part in making this a reality.

First, to my wife, Diane—thank you for your encouragement and patience as you gave me space to write and edit and research and conduct interviews. It took an enormous amount of time, and you graciously let me pursue this project.

To my agent, Amanda Luedeke—thank you for taking me on several years ago and guiding me through this process once again. I'm so grateful for the ten minutes we talked at the Chicago Writer's Conference in 2019 and for the interest you showed in my writing. You've been a steady hand at the tiller for me as you've opened up the world of book publishing to me. None of this would have been possible without you.

To my author friends who I've talked with about this and other projects—thank you for giving me advice and feedback and for sharing your own experience with me. It's been invaluable for me as I've learned this craft and this industry. This work is as much yours as it is mine.

To Christen Karniski of Rowman & Littlefield—thank you for resonating with this subject. Your experience in the world of professional soccer as a "53rd Man" in your own sport drew you to this book, and it's been so encouraging having someone so eager to see these stories told.

To Geremy Davis, Matthew Slater, Marcell Ateman, and Austin Carr—thank you for giving so much of your time to talk with me about your experiences. Your stories take center stage in this book, and your insight into the world of pro football gave me the raw material for this project. I hope you are happy with the end result. Your stories were so worth telling, and it's been an absolute privilege to bring them to the public.

And finally, to God—thank you for giving me a passion for writing and telling stories. Thank you for opening doors for me in ways I never thought possible. I don't always see a way, but I'm grateful that you do.

Preface

The National Football League (NFL) is America's most popular professional league by a wide margin. Major League Baseball (MLB), known as "America's Game," boasted an audience of 68 million in 2021, while the National Basketball Association (NBA) had an audience of 17 million. But the NFL in 2021 had an estimated audience of 114 million, some 68 percent higher than MLB.[1]

Of the thirty-two most-watched television broadcasts in American history, thirty of them are the NFL's championship game, the Super Bowl.[2]

Currently, the NFL is about a $9 billion industry, and college football is not far behind, at $6 billion annually. A recent Associated Press poll found that nearly half the country (49%) claim to be avid football fans.[3] According to the Fantasy Sports Gaming Commission, of the sixty million people that play fantasy sports, 70 percent of those (about forty-two million) play fantasy football.[4]

Even preseason NFL games—when players are essentially trying out for pro clubs—draw huge crowds. The New England Patriots, for example, had one home preseason game in 2021 and drew 65,878 fans, filling every seat in Gillette Stadium. Football is a year-round sport these days as well, as events like the NFL Combine and NFL Draft draw huge audiences and fan interest.

Even marginal NFL fans know the great players by name and even by sight. Every NFL fan would recognize Tom Brady or Patrick Mahomes or Aaron Rodgers. Their stories and accomplishments are well known across America. But how well do people know players that are fighting for roster spots and are battling every day just to make it in the league?

53rd Man tells the story of the men trying to make it in the NFL. Each team has fifty-three players on the roster, and this book is the story of life at the bottom of the NFL. It is about the men who toil largely in obscurity, hoping to see their dream of being NFL players come true.

The book tells stories of dozens of players, but there are a few "main characters" whose stories are woven throughout the book: Geremy Davis from the University of Connecticut, Matthew Slater of UCLA, and Austin Carr from Northwestern University. Each man's journey is unique and compelling. Each man made it to the NFL in a different way, and each man's career took a different path.

NFL fans know the story of Peyton Manning, but they don't know the stories of these men, whose journeys represent dedication, grit, determination, disappointment, elation, resilience, heartbreak, and joy. Every NFL fan should hear the stories of "the 53rd man" and with them, gain a greater appreciation for the sport and the men who play it.

A sizeable amount of this book comes from personal interviews I have done with the key figures in the story, and when I quote them from an interview, I use the present tense. Any stories drawn from other publications are cited in the endnotes, and quotes from these sources will be in the past tense.

I hope that these stories give you insight into life in the NFL and that you come to appreciate the journey each of these men have been on in their pursuit of an NFL career. There are some lessons in what you should not do and many more lessons on what you ought to do that can apply to your own pursuits, whether they be athletic or not. I hope you find the characters compelling and their stories interesting and inspiring.

Chapter 1

A Dream Come True

"With the one-hundred-eighty-fifth pick in the 2015 NFL draft, the Minnesota Vikings select Tyrus Thompson, tackle, Oklahoma. The New York Giants are now on the clock."

With that announcement from the podium in front of a packed house in the Auditorium Theater in Chicago, the Giants' brain trust went to work. A crowd of tens of thousands gathered in Grant Park in what was known as "Draft Town." For three days, fans from every team in the league had gathered in the NFL's first outdoor draft event, hoping to see their team pick the next great superstar. The NFL had made the sport a year-round spectacle, with the draft being one of the keystone events—a time when thirty-two franchises would add young talent from the college ranks into their organizations, sometimes to the glee of their fan base and sometimes to their dismay.

Meanwhile, the fortunes of hundreds of young men, all with dreams of making it to the NFL, hung in the balance.

Some 725 miles from Draft Town, in Norcross, Georgia, sat a twenty-three-year-old with long, braided hair; warm brown eyes; and a huge, engaging smile. Geremy Davis had recently finished up his career at the University of Connecticut, having set records at the wide receiver position, and now he waited with nervous anticipation to see what his future might hold.

Born in Memphis, Davis's family had moved to Georgia before he reached the second grade. They moved again and he attended fourth and fifth grade in another school, moved into middle school for sixth into seventh grade, then moved again and finished seventh and eighth grades in another middle school. All that moving made it difficult to develop friendships and maintain them.

Like many American boys, Davis dreamed of becoming a pro athlete. In Geremy's case, football specifically was his passion. But his football experience got off to a rocky start. His mother coached the cheer squad for a local youth team, and Geremy fell in love with the sport by age four. He wanted to play as early as possible, but his mother held him out for a few more years. She waited until he was a little older or more "age appropriate" to give him permission to play.

His favorite wide receiver was Randy Moss, and he hoped to be just like him when he grew up. But when he got his first opportunity, it was nothing like what he had hoped.

"When I first went out there when I was seven, it was trial and error," Davis said. "I was thinking every catch was going to be this phenomenal Randy Moss–type catch. I was trying to figure it out when I was seven."

His biological father was not in the picture, and his mother had married Rodney Redmond, who took Geremy in as his own son. Redmond saw that Geremy was a little too soft on the football field, and used stern tactics to change Davis's approach.

"When I turned eight, he said, 'We're not gonna have it be like last year with you playing soft.' He made me tough. He was hard on me in ways that some parents might think was a little much, but it definitely made me tough. He also had a little pride, like this is my son, he's not going to be the soft kid on the team. It was literally night and day how I switched from age seven to eight, and he had a lot to do with that. When people ask me, I give him credit for how he helped me in football."

It wasn't just about the toughness. It was about the mental side of the game. Redmond played Madden football with Davis, and when they played, Redmond made Geremy understand what he was seeing on his screen.

In his youth football experience, everyone played man-to-man defense, but by the time Davis reached high school, the game became more complex. Teams started using zone defenses and mixing up coverages. Thanks to Redmond's teaching and Geremy's Madden playing, he was able to diagnose coverages. It got to the point where he would tell his quarterback what coverage the defense was in.

As an eight-year-old, Davis's improvement on the football field was dramatic. By this time, he was a third grader, and he had a solid grasp of the game. Three years and a couple of moves later, Geremy met a boy named Max Garcia. Even though Geremy would move several more times, he and Max would become, and remain, the best of friends.

In seventh grade, Geremy's circle of friends grew. He met Jose Morales, and Arius Wright, two other exceptionally talented athletes in the community who all loved football. The group entered their freshman year at Norcross High School with high hopes and dreams. In the summer after his junior year, he met Delino DeShields, another terrific athlete, and the group of friends called themselves "The Five."

Norcross at the time was a community of around nine thousand, and diverse. Forty percent of the community was white, nearly 20 percent was Black, and 40 percent identified as Hispanic or Latino. It was also big into sports, and Norcross High School provided the community with high-level athletic entertainment.

Davis understood that as he entered Norcross. It was a football town, and the local stores would be invested in the success of the program. But Norcross did well in other sports too. The boys' basketball team won state championships in 2006, 2007, 2008, 2011, and 2013. The girls' basketball team had their own success, winning states in 2010 and 2011. In the years leading up to their arrival in the fall of 2006, Norcross football had been to the state tournament many years in a row and had been a powerhouse. That didn't change when "The Five" showed up. They assumed that a state title was in their grasp.

Max had become one of the most popular kids at Norcross. "He could go back and be the governor of Norcross," Geremy says, "because he played youth football in Norcross, and he grew up there. He's probably our [Norcross's] head coach's favorite person ever. I know we have Alvin Kamara, who's a star, but Max Garcia is like a different breed to that coach. We signed together and the head coach spoke about him and started crying. It's funny because my friends and I tease him about it."

Garcia was well liked due to his personality and character. He always loved to sing—something he would continue to enjoy even as an NFL player. And his home was always buzzing with activity—a hub for this group of friends. When they were seniors, Garcia won the "Mr. Norcross" contest and was named homecoming king and team captain. He was popular with his schoolmates, teammates, teachers, coaches, and the community.

Garcia was so popular that they had to rig awards; otherwise he was going to win them all. For prom, they couldn't put Max on the court, out of fear that he'd automatically be voted king. "My buddy Arius and I were on it," Geremy says, "and another friend, Ryan King, who played soccer, and everyone thought it was going to be me or Arius [for prom king]. And Ryan ended up winning. But that's how Max was. To say you can't be on the court because you'll automatically win?" Davis shakes his head and chuckles.

Garcia was also really good at football. He was the fifty-third ranked offensive line prospect in the country, the sixty-first ranked player in Georgia (a football-rich state), and a three-star recruit. The University of Maryland recruited him hard, and he would sign a letter of intent to play for the Terrapins.

The other boys in "The Five" were also gifted athletes. Morales and Wright became high school football coaches, and DeShields got drafted by the Houston Astros in the first round of the 2010 amateur draft. The son of Major League all-star Delino DeShields, he was gifted in several sports. His sister, Diamond, would become an elite athlete in her own right, playing college basketball at North Carolina before making it to the WNBA.

Their senior season came, and the five friends had the state championship in sight. DeShields played running back, and as great an athlete as he was, a sophomore by the name of Alvin Kamara[1] waited in the wings. The team was loaded with talent. But unfortunately, that talent did not materialize on the football field that year, as the Blue Devils went 5–5 and missed the playoffs. "Which is crazy," Davis says. "Probably the last fifteen years, we made the playoffs every year except my senior year. And we were talented. It's like, how is this not working? Skill-wise, that wasn't in question. We had the talent, but I don't know, we just weren't able to put it together."

Their disappointing senior year ended, but Garcia and Davis still had football waiting for them. Garcia signed with Maryland, and Davis was being recruited by Maryland and the University of Connecticut, coached by Randy Edsall. The two of them talked every day, and of course the recruiting process was a major subject of their conversation. The problem for Geremy was that Maryland was also recruiting star wide receiver Brandon Coleman, who was himself trying to decide between the Terrapins and the Scarlet Knights of Rutgers. Davis knew that Coleman was their top recruiting target. The deeper they got into the process with Coleman, the less interest they showed in Geremy. In fact, the communication between Maryland recruiters and Davis diminished to the point of virtual silence.

That silence made Geremy worry that Maryland wasn't the place for him. Coleman at the last minute decided on Rutgers, and Maryland, now in a scramble for a top wide receiver, reignited the conversation with Geremy.

He told Max, who lit up.

"Yo, let's go to the same school!" Max said, dreaming of playing college ball with his best friend.

But for Geremy, it was too late. Maryland's attempt to hold Davis in one hand while reaching for something better with the other ended up costing them both. Coleman became a Scarlet Knight, and Davis became a University of Connecticut Husky.

"Sorry bro. I'm going to UConn," Geremy said.

"UCONN!?" Max couldn't believe his ears.

"Yeah, I just think it's the best fit for me."

"You're kidding. Dude."

"Yeah. They just wanted me more."

For the first time in their relationship, Max didn't speak to Geremy for two whole days.

They went their separate ways, but resumed talking nearly every single day, supporting one another, encouraging one another, listening to one another, and strengthening one another.

Davis sat out his first year as a redshirt, while Garcia played right away for Maryland. While he was a redshirting freshman, Davis's UConn Huskies won the Big East conference and advanced to the Fiesta Bowl for the first time in school history. Oklahoma blew them out, but UConn football was on the rise. Then Edsall left the team following the game and took the job coaching Maryland, of all places.

Garcia, meanwhile, ran into some personal struggles in College Park, and looked to transfer. Will Muschamp of the University of Florida showed the most initial interest, and though other schools got involved, Max transferred to Florida and became a Gator. He began the process of righting the ship.

Meanwhile, Davis got on the field, and after a slow first year began to put up big numbers. In the 2012 season, which his buddy Max was sitting out due to his transfer, Geremy caught forty-four passes for 613 yards. Coach Paul Pasqualoni viewed Davis as a valuable member of the receiving corps. The next year, Davis lit up the Big East conference, catching seventy-one passes for 1,085 yards and a 15.3 yards per reception average. Scouts began to take notice, and at this point, his dreams of reaching the NFL seemed to be a possibility.

"It wasn't till my redshirt sophomore year when I played well that year for a UConn receiver," Davis says. "I got some buzz as a thousand-yard receiver. I started seeing scouts on the sideline, and I was like, dang, everything I prayed for and hoped for is attainable now."

Davis had gotten involved in Athletes in Action at UConn. He had grown up as a Christian, but it wasn't until college that he really began to put the pieces together. He considers these years to be the key time when he decided to become a fully devoted follower of Christ.

Garcia was following a similar path at Florida. He got involved in AIA at Florida, and his faith began to take off. Now Davis and Garcia had more to talk about besides the good old days at Norcross and their current college experiences with school and football. They had a common faith, which only helped their friendship grow even deeper. They would both participate in Athletes in Action's Ultimate Training Camp, which helped them grow even more in their faith and gave them tools to apply their faith to their sport.

Garcia moved from tackle to guard and eventually to center, and during his senior year he was placed on the Rimington Trophy watch list as one of the best centers in college football. Both men earned the distinction of being team captains, as their peers and coaches recognized the character and leadership they brought to their respective teams.

Davis's senior year, however, was marred by an ankle injury that forced him to miss several games, and that, combined with poor quarterback play, led to a decline in his production. He struggled and caught just forty-four passes for 521 yards as a senior. Still, he was good enough to earn an invitation to a college all-star game after his senior year, the NFLPA Bowl. There he suffered a hamstring injury. Davis wondered what that might do to his draft stock.

His agent at the time, Ed Wasielewski, had spoken with enough teams to give Davis a sense of where he might get drafted. It was looking like somewhere in the fifth or sixth round. Wasielewski let Geremy know how teams worked. One team could have him as high as a third-round player, while another could have him off their draft board entirely. But things were fluid, and Geremy never really knew where he stood. He nonetheless went into the draft with his eye toward a possible selection in the fifth or sixth round.

Garcia's draft stock was a little higher, but as the 2015 draft arrived, both men were anxious. Garcia and his family gathered around their television to watch the draft, while Davis and his family did the same. Neither was picked on day one.[2] That didn't worry either Davis or Garcia, as neither had any expectation of being drafted in the first round. Even day two was unlikely, and neither got chosen in rounds two or three either.

Davis recalls, "Once day two went by [when rounds two and three were picked], I wasn't like, 'Dang it.' I'm like, day three, alright, I want to hear my name now."

Geremy and Max exchanged nervous and excited texts as day three of the draft arrived. This is what they both realistically had anticipated as being *their* day.

Earlier in the month, DeShields, who had been selected by the Texas Rangers in the Rule 5 draft from Houston, made his major league debut— a huge moment for "The Five." Now it was Garcia and Davis's turn.

With DeShields in Texas, the other two members of the group split up to watch the draft with their friends. Jose went to Geremy's house while Arius went to be with Max. Garcia was selected in the fourth round by Denver, with the 133rd overall pick.

Geremy and Jose jumped up and down for Max.

"Oh shoot—Max just got drafted!" Geremy cried at the announcement. Obviously, Geremy was elated for his friend, but that also added to his own nervousness. He texted his agent, but Ed was too busy talking with teams, trying to get a sense of what was going on, and also preparing for the possibility that Geremy wouldn't get drafted at all, and Ed wanted to make sure he could get Geremy a free agent deal and an invite to a team's camp. Geremy tried not to blow up his agent's phone, but he was getting antsy.

Finally, the agency responded: "Relax, you're gonna get drafted."

That put Geremy more at ease.

The fourth round ended and the fifth round came, but still Geremy's name wasn't called. Geremy paced around the room. Was this going to happen or not?

The sixth round arrived, and Geremy couldn't even hold his phone anymore. The Vikings selected Thompson, and Geremy turned to Jose.

"Yo, you gotta hold my phone. I can't handle it," Geremy said. Jose took the phone and within seconds, it rang. Jose looked at Geremy, and handed him back the phone. Though Geremy's hands were as steady as they came from being a high-level college wide receiver, they were shaking as he took the phone from his friend.

Jerry Reese, the general manager of the New York Giants, was on the phone.

"We are about to take you with the next pick in the draft," he said. Geremy couldn't believe it.

Next on the line was head coach Tom Coughlin, followed by the offensive coordinator Ben McAdoo, and the special teams coordinator Tom

Quinn. Strangely, even though Davis was a wide receiver, he didn't hear from the receivers coach.

Coughlin put it to him straight. "The only way you're going to make this team is special teams," he said. "Here's the special teams coordinator."

At Davis's house, they did what anyone would expect them to do. They grabbed the remote to turn up the volume so they could watch the pick be made. Most fans understand that NFL teams call their draft picks to tell them before those picks get announced by the NFL on television. So Davis knew he was getting picked before the announcement was made. Jose went to turn up the volume but, as Davis recalls, "Jose messed up and turned the TV off instead. We just rewound our TiVo and saw it come across the screen, and we celebrated."

Ryan, another high school friend who won prom king when Garcia was kept out of the competition, timed all of this perfectly. He went to Max's house first, wearing his Florida shirt, and was there when Garcia got picked. He celebrated with his friend and then quickly drove to Geremy's house, changed into a UConn shirt, and was there when the Giants selected him. From there, they all went back to Garcia's house to celebrate together as a group.

He smiles. "I always say, 'Jose, you're the reason I got drafted. If you didn't touch my phone . . . I should have given you the phone two rounds ago.'"

For Davis, this was more fun than even their college signing day, put on by Norcross High School. "Yeah," he says, "because as you get older, the pool gets smaller, the number of guys who make it. Me and my best friend, getting drafted the same day, in the same year that Delino gets to the majors. We all got to the pros the same time. It's crazy how God worked it out that way, for us to be able to celebrate all this together."

Geremy Davis's dream had come true.

Chapter 2

Like Father, Like Son

When Geremy Davis was figuring out life as a Norcross High School sophomore, Matthew Slater was preparing for a possible NFL future. But it was a future that Slater was not really sure was possible.

Being the son of NFL Hall of Famer Jackie Slater sure had its perks. For Matthew, growing up in Southern California with a dad who played for the Rams brought opportunities to be around the game that most kids could only dream of. He got to go to the stadium and watch Jackie practice and work out. He got to hang around the locker room after games and see players like Jim Everett, Henry Ellard, Kevin Greene, Todd Lyght, and Jerome Bettis. He even got to be a water boy on the sidelines at Anaheim Stadium during games.

"We just had neat experiences that I don't think we realized weren't normal," he says. "But I certainly have a great appreciation for it now. These are memories that I'll hold on to for a lifetime."

It is understandable when a son looks to follow in his father's footsteps, especially if there's a good relationship between the two. That was surely the case for Matthew. He grew up in a football household, raised by a supportive and loving mother and a father who was a star in the NFL. If Jackie were a scientist, Matthew probably would have wanted to be a scientist too. But Jackie was an All-Pro football player, so Matthew naturally gravitated toward the game.

Jackie had a passion for everything related to football. He loved playing, the camaraderie, even the grind. His love for football was contagious and was easily passed on to his sons. Because Jackie loved every aspect of the sport, Matthew and his younger brother fell in love with it too. But ironically, Jackie was hesitant to let Matthew play. In fact, he did everything in his power to keep Matthew from playing. Even when his son's friends started playing Pop Warner in second or third grade, Jackie said no.

"I was like, 'Dad, I want to play!'" Matthew says. "And every year it was, 'No, I don't think it's safe for you to be playing right now. You need to get a little bit bigger.'"

Matthew played other sports but nonetheless persisted, drawn more and more to the game. Finally, Jackie relented, telling Matthew that he could play when he got to high school. But there were conditions. Namely, Jackie insisted that Matthew be fully invested in conditioning, strength training, and the physical work to build up his body. He was rightly concerned about injury, as his son wasn't the biggest kid on the team.

Matthew's first coach in flag football (non-contact) was Vince Ferragamo, who played quarterback for the Rams. He brought Jackie on as an assistant. On the high school team, Jackie reverted to being a parent. Instead of using his fame to push his way, he sat back and was simply "Matthew's dad."

Servite High School, an all-boys Catholic school in Anaheim, had won league championships in 1996 and 1998. As a freshman at Servite, Matthew was allowed to play, but "it couldn't have gone worse. I was probably 125 pounds soaking wet, had never used pads or tackled anyone. Had no idea how to use my body. It was awful. People were like, are you sure you're Jackie Slater's kid?"

Jackie's perspective was that his son had to earn everything, just like everyone else. He let the coaches coach and generally stayed in the background. Matthew, meanwhile, began to enjoy every aspect of the game, just like Jackie did. Rehab, lifting, conditioning, practicing—it all suited Matthew's personality. He saw all of it as a way to improve.

But progress was slow, and he didn't make the varsity team until the end of his sophomore year. Those first two years were a time of growth and development, and he learned a lot about the game. Larry Toner, the head coach, understood his role not just as a teacher of football but as a developer of young men. He constantly talked about helping these boys to become leaders of men. While in high school, Matthew didn't necessarily grasp everything that Toner tried to do, but looking back years later, he appreciated his coach's vision.

"I think some of the lessons I learned in terms of leadership, accountability, discipline," Matthew says, "they started there at Servite, how intentional they were about forming and shaping young men the right way . . . faith-filled leaders. It was really fantastic."

By his junior year he was a starting receiver on the varsity team. The team was successful, and he was enjoying his time on the field. After that season, he received his first scholarship offer, from Colorado. Slater continued to develop, and worked his way to the Division 1 level, receiving a football scholarship to UCLA. A tremendous athlete, he had opportunities to play football or run track.

There were two main groups of schools recruiting Slater. In the first group were Pac-10 schools like Oregon, Arizona, Arizona State, and UCLA. At USC, he was recruited to run track and offered the chance to walk on to the football team. In the second group were Ivy League schools like Penn, Brown, and Dartmouth. The Ivy schools, of course, don't offer athletic scholarships, and education is primary. The Slaters valued Matthew's education, and with the Ivies interested, they narrowed their choices down to Brown and Dartmouth.

Matthew initially preferred Dartmouth, but after assessing the situation more thoroughly, his father, a seven-time NFL Pro-Bowler, didn't feel it was a good fit. Simply put, he didn't think Matthew was mature enough to succeed at an Ivy League school across the country. It was a difficult parental decision, but one made without regret. The call to Dartmouth was short and to the point.

"Matthew won't be coming to Dartmouth," Jackie told the coach.

"Why not?"

"To be honest, he's not ready for it. He needs to grow up a little more."

And with that, Matthew's future changed.

They looked at the two local Los Angeles schools, and when faced with the option of a track scholarship and walking on to the football team at USC, or playing football as a scholarship player at UCLA, the choice was easy. Slater became a Bruin.

"I'm so glad I chose correctly," Slater says, chuckling.

But football at the high Division 1 level was not all sunshine and roses for Matthew. While his father was a six-foot-five, three-hundred-pound offensive lineman, Matthew was six feet tall and not even two hundred pounds. Recruited originally to play wide receiver, Slater found the road to success much harder than anticipated, despite his sprinter's speed.

In fact, his college career got off to a terrible start, right out of the gate. On the very first day of camp, he suffered a nasty turf toe injury and the doctors put him in a boot for six weeks. Unable to participate in any on-field activities, he fell behind, and the next thing he knew, he was redshirting. For Matthew, it was his first real taste of adversity, and it would help shape the rest of his college career. Thus began the character-building process that Jackie knew Matthew needed. As is so often the case, hardship proved to be a great teacher.

Instead of playing wide receiver as a freshman, Matthew spent the year recovering from an injury. It was a trying time, but he used it to focus on other things besides football. He developed other interests and found himself connected to the local chapter of the Fellowship of Christian Athletes. Raised in a Christian home, Slater had adopted the faith of his parents, but it took the adversity he faced in college to spark his own faith journey.

"My faith in that experience, well, my faith up till then was really my parents,'" Slater says. "But here I am in that situation, having to navigate all this, and it was really a time for me to grow and develop in my faith. So the Lord was working on me off the field, and on the field it was challenging. Lots of injuries. I was a skinny kid and needed to build my frame up."

His sophomore year was equally challenging, as he played in just three games and never had a single pass sent his way. Still, he grew physically, mentally, and spiritually. But the struggle was real, and Matthew thought about taking another path, one that might lead him away from UCLA.

He considered transferring. While the academics at UCLA were a bright spot, the football challenge created inner turmoil for him. He had received dozens of scholarship offers, but his college career wasn't playing out in any way like he had envisioned. He also had a lot of personal maturing to do. Jackie's main reason for withdrawing Matthew from Dartmouth was Matthew's lack of maturity. He just needed to grow up a little more, and these struggles exposed that immaturity.

Even as football fell short of expectations, Matthew's interests expanded. As he grew in his faith, his eyes turned toward life after college, and he found himself fascinated with the idea of going into the ministry. He had met people from all over the world at UCLA. Though part of the California public university system, UCLA truly was a global school, with more than thirty thousand students hailing from more than 115 nations; one out of every ten Bruins was from outside the United States. This provided Slater with exposure to other cultures and languages and perspectives on the world. Moreover, it demonstrated to him that the need for Christ was truly a worldwide phenomenon.

"But there was a common theme with all of them," Slater recalls. "All these people need Christ. In all their situations, I felt like there was a need for Jesus. I thought, maybe the Lord is calling me to ministry. Felt as plain as the nose on my face. I thought, they have a need and I have the thing that meets that need (Jesus). I became passionate about people, about talking to people, building relationships, sharing the gospel with folks."

His faith was encouraged not only through these interactions but also by his fellow FCA students, one in particular. Emma Tautola played on the UCLA women's basketball team, and she and Matthew became fast friends. "Having friends like her that I met my freshman year, they were such an encouragement to me. More than anyone else during my college years, she showed what it meant to put Christ first and pursue him to the fullest."

In fact, he developed deep relationships at the church he was attending, and he had even arranged to possibly serve the church after graduation as a ministry intern. Post-college plans were starting to take shape, none of which had anything to do with football.

Nonetheless, Matthew thought about transferring. Maybe there was a better opportunity elsewhere to get more playing time, especially on the offensive side of the ball. But he had two other thoughts as well. The first thought was possibly ditching football and turning into strictly a track athlete. Then he could still be a college athlete and focus on his studies and future ministry. But he loved football too much for that, which led him to his second thought.

At Servite High School, he played defensive back as well as wide receiver. Perhaps there could be more snaps available if he switched to defense. In any case, playing defense could allow him to play special teams if nothing else. Bruin head coach Karl Dorrell's philosophy was to play only defensive players on special teams. Slater figured he could still make something of his college career even if all he did was participate in the kicking game.

He approached Coach Dorrell with the idea of changing positions. Dorrell understood Slater's situation, and when Matthew asked him for the chance to talk, Dorrell immediately thought this might be bad news. To his relief, the news wasn't bad at all. "Good," he told Slater, "because I thought you were going to come in here and ask me if you could transfer, and I wasn't going to let you go."

For Matthew, this was a relief. It told him that he still had a place on the team, and that Coach Dorrell still saw him as having an important role, though Slater didn't know what it was or could be. Just having the coach express that kind of confidence in him was itself encouraging. He decided to stay. The next two years would change the course of his life.

"It was part of the Lord's plan," Slater says. "There was no way they were going to let me play special teams unless I was a defensive player. So this switch not only opened up the possibility of me getting on the field defensively, but in the least, I could get on the field in the kicking game. I could at least have somewhat of a college football experience."

He did manage to play some on special teams his junior year, but it still wasn't a full-time role. The NFL seemed like a total pipe dream at this point, as he was a wide receiver that never got targeted, a defensive player that hardly saw the field, and a special teams player that had made just nine tackles in three years at UCLA. NFL careers were not made of such things.

Matthew and Jackie understood his reality. "I'm a realist. My dad's a realist. Guys just don't go to the NFL who played receiver in college but who never caught a ball or never started a game. We were realistic about what my options for pro ball were. We were just focused on my final year in college."

Then came his senior year. Which started out terribly. He was coming off surgery and wasn't even healthy to start the year. Nonetheless, he asked Assistant Head Coach Dino Babers about the possibility of returning kickoffs. Babers worried about Slater's injured shoulder. Would it hold up taking the kind of hits that happen on kickoff returns? He wasn't sure. But he allowed Matthew the opportunity to compete for the job.

"In camp there were like ten guys trying to be kickoff returner," Slater recalls. "I had a good showing, and by the end of camp I had the return job."

He was good at it. Really good. By the end of his senior season, Slater had twenty-five special teams tackles, and had returned three kickoffs for touchdowns, which set a UCLA record. He made first team All Pac-10 as a kick returner because his three touchdowns and 29.0-yard average led the league. Furthermore, he made the All-American team for his special teams excellence.

It was then that he knew he maybe had a chance. A scout for the New England Patriots spoke to him and told him that he should prepare for the UCLA Pro Day, because he had a shot at perhaps doing this at the next level. For Matthew that was a revelation. He wasn't invited to the NFL combine, but there were other opportunities to make himself visible to NFL executives.

"I was an All-American at the end of the year, and I thought that I owed it to myself to train for Pro Day and see how it goes, and maybe get into a camp and be competitive," Slater says.

That meant putting ministry plans on hold to see where football could take him. He told the pastor at his church that he wanted to pursue football for the time being. No problem, he was told. The ministry would be here waiting.

"Funny enough," Matthew says, "they're still waiting."

Being a track athlete, Slater had good speed, even by NFL standards. He possessed 4.40 speed, a mark that always gives a player a chance. He was just hoping by this point to get an invite to an NFL camp. He figured that being drafted was still a longshot, but he understood that there might be a pathway through the route of undrafted free agency.

His mother, Annie, however, had loftier visions.

"I believe you're going to get drafted," she told him. "I believe the Lord is going to do some things."

Through four rounds of the 2008 NFL draft, there was nothing but silence. It was looking more and more, with each passing moment, like the only route to the NFL was by receiving a camp invitation as a free agent.

Then Matthew's life changed forever.

"My phone rings. It's the fifth round of the draft. Surely this isn't someone calling to draft me. It's probably a team trying to get the jump on free agency. I remember looking at the phone—Boston number. I don't know anyone from Boston."

The voice on the other end of the line was unfamiliar. But the words spoken were ones that Matthew would never forget.

"This is Berj Najarian of the New England Patriots, here with Robert Kraft and Bill Belichick. We're going to draft you with the 153rd pick. I'll put you on with Mr. Kraft and Bill."

Matthew was speechless. "I sat there with my dad, we just looked at each other, not saying anything. This can't be happening. It just felt surreal."

Najarian passed the phone around and soon Slater found himself talking with Belichick. Brown University—a school Slater considered attending—is not far from Foxboro, Massachusetts, where the Patriots' facility resides. Instead, Matthew went to UCLA—some three thousand miles from 1 Patriots Place. And seemingly out of nowhere, he was on the line with the legendary head coach.

"We're gonna take you here with this pick," Belichick said. "And look, I don't know what position you're gonna play, so if the media's asking you, don't tell them anything. You don't know what you're gonna do, but the reason I'm bringing you here is to help us in the kicking game. That's what your role is gonna be. We'll figure out a position. Don't worry about that."

"I'll never forget that first conversation with Bill," Slater says. "I'm thinking, this is a team, with this pedigree, drafting someone who never started a game in college, a receiver who never caught a pass, and they're telling this kid we're going to draft you to help us in the kicking game."

Slater smiles, recalling the almost absurdity of it all.

"I'm thinking, this makes no sense to me. My dad has been around pro football for forty years and had never seen anything like that happen. For us it was like our parting-of-the-Red-Sea moment, because we know what I had gone through on and off the field, and to see God's unmerited favor in our lives. When I think about it, I still get chills. It was strictly God's grace in my life. I get that call and I'm super excited, not really knowing what to expect."

The moment he got off the phone and witnessed the selection being made on television, he turned to his father, and the two of them, true to character, spent the first minutes following this life changing event in prayer together, thanking God for His goodness in their lives.

Matthew Slater, son of Football Hall of Famer Jackie Slater, had seen his dream come true. Like father, like son.

Chapter 3

After Mr. Irrelevant

Not all paths to the NFL look the same. Some players, like Geremy and Matthew, get there through the draft. But everyone's journey is different.

Sitting in the northeast corner of San Pablo Bay, the city of Benecia, California, is roughly twenty-five miles north of Oakland. Home to more than twenty-six thousand residents, Benicia was founded in 1849 on a Mexican land grant of Mariano Guadalupe Vallejo, a statesman and general in the mid-1800s, and in 1853 Benicia became the third capital of California.

Austin Carr called Benicia home for much of his childhood, and it was there that he fell in love with the sport of football, thanks to his father and his first crack at youth football.

A typical day in the Carr household would feature young Austin and his younger brother in their living room with their father, Evan, playing pretend football. At five feet, nine inches and 230 pounds, Evan was a little heavier than in his earlier days as a defensive back. A diehard football fan, Evan instilled a love for the game into Austin.

If football was a virus, he gave it to his son. If it was hereditary, Austin got that gene.

Evan would do what most dads would do—toss his boys around the room, bouncing them off the couch, tackling them to the floor—essentially making the living room their own indoor football stadium. They'd watch games together, reenact the plays, and just have a blast together, with football as the focus.

That led Austin to want to play the game for real. Evan signed Austin up for youth football when Austin hit second grade. From ages six to twelve, Austin competed for the Vallejo Raiders, with Evan as one of his coaches. His first experience, however, gave no indication that pro football could be in Austin's future.

"I was terrible. I didn't know what I was doing. I was on the offensive line, which in youth football, that's where you put the guys who don't know what they're doing, who are not athletic, that kind of thing. And I remember I tackled a guy. I was playing offense and I tackled someone. That's my first memory on the field. Thinking back, that's pretty embarrassing."

But improvement came quickly for Carr. By his second season he had begun to play both running back—his "dream position"—and quarterback. His time in Vallejo was formative for Austin. As he viewed it even back then, Vallejo was a lower-income area with fewer resources. That built a certain toughness.

"Rougher kids, let me just put it that way," Austin says, noting that they had to play despite their disadvantages.

This created a culture for Carr that gave him a competitive edge that would serve him later. "In Vallejo youth football, we would roll into places like Petaluma or San Ramon and play these nicer areas in the Bay area. These kids had everything. It wasn't like hatred or anything, but it was like dang, they've really got a lot given to them, or at least they're blessed with resources. I wonder what that would be like. But then we'd compete with them and oftentimes beat them. I'd probably say over five years at Vallejo playing these teams, we went something like 45–10 against them. My experience in Vallejo formed what you might call the 'dog' in me. Playing with some 'dogs'—the gritty, rough, take-no-prisoners mentality."

The "dog" in Carr led him to the middle linebacker position. He loved to hit, and wasn't afraid of contact. Playing both ways, he was able to take the defensive mentality of being the hitter and apply it to his roles on offense, where he learned to deliver blows to defenders instead of being the one absorbing the hit. He developed a toughness and a willingness—almost an eagerness—to play a physical style of football that would become his hallmark throughout his career.

Born into a multiracial family,[1] Austin enjoyed a diverse upbringing, even when it came to football. He transitioned from the Vallejo Raiders to the program in Benicia, a wealthier (and whiter) environment.

"I have two cultures, two backgrounds, two different experiences that formed me into who I am today," he says. "I look back and there's so many times where I'm like, man, I'm so blessed."

Playing with Vallejo, he often played against programs with far greater resources. Now with Benicia, he was on the other end of the spectrum.

He had nicer facilities, nicer equipment, nicer fields on which to play. He learned a different approach to football as well.

"My youth experience was great," he says. "I learned so much. I had a diversity of athleticism around me that pushed me. I'd say that Vallejo put the dog in me, and Benicia put the football IQ in me."

His freshman year of high school, he chose to play one last year with Benicia rather than for his high school team. That was a decision that led to Austin receiving a lot of grief from his schoolmates. That was considered "playing down" and his friends at school brought the heat, especially when Benecia, the number 1 seed, lost in the first round of the state playoffs to the number 8 seed, a defeat that still stings.

His high school career began the following year, and it was clear that Austin could play. By this point he had played all over, but mainly linebacker on defense and running back on offense. The time at linebacker was instrumental in shaping his approach on offense. He had learned how to deliver hits, not just receive them. Be the hammer, not the nail. That translated to when he was a ball carrier.

His coach once told him, "Austin, you never get tackled going backward. You're always moving forward."

A turning point for Austin was when he scored on a seventy-five-yard touchdown run his last year in Vallejo.

"When I started to experience paydirt, making it into the end zone, it was like, oh man, that feels good."

He grew into a successful high school player and started receiving interest from colleges. It wasn't Alabama or Ohio State but rather D2 and D3 schools that began inquiring about him. But for Austin, these opportunities held little interest. He had other passions and was not a "football or bust" kind of guy. Simply put, football wasn't his whole life.

"Sometimes I feel bad saying that," he says, "because there's a lot of guys who are that way and don't get to see their dream come true. So I'll say it this way: D1 and the NFL were always a dream, but I always had different interests. I didn't see football as central to the essence of Austin Carr. There was always something else I was interested in, another path for me, that would be just fine."

So he turned down the offers from the D2, D3, and junior college programs and applied to Northwestern University as a regular student. He got accepted, and once "in," considered the possibility of walking onto the Northwestern team. He sent in his high school tape and had his high school coach talk with recruiters at Northwestern, and to his pleasant surprise, they showed interest.

"My high school tape was good," Austin says. "I wasn't blazing fast but I was scoring a lot, I was impressive catching the ball down the field, and I could run the ball with authority. I had potential. I mean, every single guy on the field in a Big Ten or Division 1 game has potential and could become something. My high school tape clearly showed that, and they wanted to extend an invitation to me to try and walk on."

Austin made the team, and suddenly was a Division 1 athlete in a Big Ten program. But, of course, the work was just beginning. The time commitment for walk-ons is no different than for scholarship players, but usually without the payoff of getting actual playing time. A typical Division 1 depth chart goes at least four deep at each position, which leaves very little room for walk-ons to play, even in blowouts. There are just too many scholarship athletes on the roster to afford giving snaps to walk-ons.

But Austin was undeterred by any of that. He was determined to give it a good effort and see where it led.

Where it led initially, however, was a hospital.

During his early high school years, Austin worked as part of a family construction crew over the summer. On one particular job, he was in an attic doing electrical work with his father. He had had plenty of experience on such jobs, but on this one day he took a false step in the attic and stepped between the joists, plunging through the "floor," which was really the ceiling of the level below. He landed with a thud, breaking his back—his vertebrae shifted upon impact—and while he would recover, it was an injury that would from time to time flare up in his life.

A few days into camp, his back started acting up. The trainer wrapped his back in ice, using a standard cellophane wrap. He had ventured into the cafeteria when he realized he was about to be late for a meeting. He tried to rip through the plastic wrap but because it had rolled up, it proved to be too strong for him.

Carr felt the immediate need to get it off. "I'm in such a rush that I grab the closest sharp object, which was a butter knife. I held the blade away from me because I knew to be safe, I start sawing the plastic wrap. I saw through finally, but I feel something funny in my pinky. I had severed the tendon in my right pinky finger. It was quite the way to walk onto the Northwestern football team and be ridiculed and teased literally for the next five years. My nickname became A.C. Butter."

Austin wanted to play through the injury, but his mother was having none of it. She insisted that he have surgery, and to Austin's surprise—and gratitude—Northwestern paid for the procedure. Pat Fitzgerald, who in 2006 had become the youngest head coach in the Big Ten and all of Division 1 football, took care of Austin.

"Coach Fitz called me on my drive back to the facility and just checked in on me," Carr says. "I mean, I was a walk-on, had not contributed one play, and Coach Fitz made me feel really valued and kept me on the team."

Austin would sit out his freshman year, taking the time to learn football, focus on studies, and pursue other interests, like music. He even won the student athlete talent show, playing a rendition of "Ordinary People" by John Legend on piano.

He knew he had a lot of growing to do when it came to football. It was one thing to make the team as a walk-on. It was another thing entirely to get to the point where he could get on the field for real. He knew he had potential, but it was a long way from being realized, especially at this level.

"When you saw my tape from high school, maybe I should have gotten D1 offers. But when you look at my first year at Northwestern, I certainly wasn't going to play my freshman year. I was still kind of a boy. I had a boy body. I needed that time for development."

Sitting out his freshman year may have been a blessing in disguise. He worked hard in the weight room and in the classroom, building himself up to be the best collegiate student athlete he could be.

He began to see progress. Slow and incremental but, nonetheless, progress. The coaching staff didn't see him as a running back or linebacker but rather as a wide receiver. Carr didn't see things the way they did, but they insisted that was his best position with the most potential.

Wide receivers coach Dennis Springer played a formative role in Austin's football life.

"Coach Springer molded me, and I wouldn't have gotten to the NFL if it wasn't for him. I was raw. I was an athletic kid who played running back in high school, but they [Northwestern] wanted me to play wide receiver. I pushed back pretty hard, and they were like, OK, we'll see when you get here. I ran some slot routes in high school, but I wasn't a receiver. The ball still scared me when they threw it to me. Coach Springer got a raw, athletic, underdeveloped eighteen-year-old kid that had a lot to work on. It would be over two years before I was in a place to play in a Big Ten game."

His second year at Northwestern, he saw his first action on the field, and it was then that he realized he could hang with players at this level. Like so many athletes, Austin was a big fish in a little pond in high school, then he arrived at a highly competitive college program and realized that there were loads of elite athletes. The adjustment was hard, and it took a few years for him to get to the point where he felt like he could compete on fairly equal terms with even the scholarship players.

In his fourth year (third year playing), he experienced one of the great moments of his life.

"After my third year [second year playing]," he explains, "I got a partial scholarship. Then, going into my senior year [third year playing], right before the game against Stanford, coach brought me and two other guys up front and announced to the team that we got scholarships. The team went nuts, and they ran up and tackled all of us. It was awesome."

He called home with the great news—the best part of which was that "I don't have to pay for college anymore!" Given that tuition, room, and board at Northwestern was around $64,000 a year at that time, the Carr family experienced considerable savings from Austin's scholarship.

He played regularly and caught sixteen passes in the season and felt like a real contributor. He had earned his scholarship and enjoyed the experience of going to a bowl game.

"My career at Northwestern was like a staircase. I'm taking like one step. Imagine you're walking up the Supreme Court staircase, and there's a hundred steps. First year, I took one step. Second year, maybe I took two steps. Third year, I took five steps. Fourth year, I took ten steps."

At this point, the NFL was nothing more than a dream. But if you're going to play Big Ten football, you might as well dream, right?

"My dad is big on dreaming," Austin says. "I never felt pressure to perform for him, so that made his love of football even more contagious for me. One of the values that he emphasized for us kids was to never stop dreaming. Whatever dream you have, do that. And who knows? There's going to be a window of opportunity that if you get into the window, the sky's the limit."

Evan encouraged Austin to dream big. But for Austin, it just didn't seem realistic. He had developed a perspective on his future that was consistent with the "I'm not all or nothing with football" mentality.

"My head space was not like, draft day, 2017," he says. "My head space was like, OK, I'm going to go for my master's degree, and it's going to be a pretty competitive spring camp, so we'll see what the coaches think. And I'm dating this girl now too, so there's like all these things I'm thinking about, and the dream of the NFL, it's not that it didn't exist, it's just that it didn't seem super viable at that point, and I was OK with that. I was going to get a master's from one of the most prestigious business schools in the country."

Then came the fifth year. The year that Austin Carr rose to Big Ten stardom. And everything changed.

"My fifth year, I took all the rest of the steps in one jump. All Big Ten, Big Ten receiver of the year, all the accolades just kind of poured in. There was this foundation of four years, as I got better and better, waiting for my chance and not getting it, finally getting on the field my junior year, then my senior year I did enough to play and be a contributor, but then my fifth year, it blew up."

Austin played better than any wide receiver in the Big Ten—something he couldn't have imagined was possible when he sent in his high school game tape years before. His best performance came against Ohio State, where, after just six hours of sleep the night before, he caught eight passes for 158 yards.

"I remember walking off the field after that game and all I could think of was that this is the grace of God. I can't take credit for that performance. How I got through that without tearing an ACL or pulling a hamstring as my body was so fatigued—the grace of God."

Now one might think that the Big Ten receiver of the year would be a lock to be drafted, but NFL scouts and executives don't draft based on collegiate accolades. They draft based on talent, physical tools, and projectability—what they think a player can be at the next level. They understand better than anyone how much more difficult and different the NFL game is from college.

He got invited to play in the East-West Shrine Game, an all-star game for college players looking to play at the next level. It wasn't his best performance, as he didn't give full effort on the special teams snaps he was asked to play. His rationale was a concern of getting injured on what he considered to be less important plays.

"I had tired legs," he says. "I didn't try that hard on special teams. In hindsight I should have tried way harder on special teams."

Gifted with good but not elite speed, Austin wasn't a great NFL prospect from the standpoint of athleticism. And though he stands six feet tall, he isn't overly large for a receiver. As a result, despite his stellar last season at Northwestern, he wasn't seen as a dynamic NFL prospect.

"I was projected to be a fifth- or sixth-round pick," Carr says. "Speed was the biggest question mark on my resumé. I didn't get invited to the combine, which was such a big letdown. I had had such a good year that I thought they'd invite me, and my agent did everything he could to get me there."

Perhaps that snub was a godsend. He knew he needed to work on his physical tools, so he spent time with Tommy Christian of TCBoost. From 2000 to 2002, Christian was the assistant director of strength and conditioning at Northwestern after having played linebacker for the school. After establishing TCBoost to help other athletes increase speed, strength, and explosiveness, he became one of the top sports performance coaches in the country. Austin was eager to get to work with Tommy.

"He got me down to a 4.5, which didn't amaze everyone, but which is still pretty good. In hindsight, I was too big. As a wide receiver in the Big Ten, there are running plays where you're expected to block a linebacker. Sometimes the Mike [middle linebacker]. That is laughable in the NFL. I was going from the Big Ten where I was expected to be strong enough to block middle linebackers, to the NFL where everything is a track meet. I bench-pressed 225 sixteen times in my pro day, and I haven't done that since then. It wasn't until my second year in the league when I realized that I don't really need to have that kind of upper-body strength. I realized that in the NFL, unless you're a freak, you need to be a track star. You need to be a 100-meter runner who can cut and who knows the playbook."

He ended up running a 4.54 at his Pro Day at Northwestern, which represented an improvement. But his speed wasn't the only question mark scouts were concerned about. Twenty-nine teams sent scouts to Northwestern that day, and Patriots college scouting director Monti Ossenfort sat Austin down for an interview. He spent a long time with Carr going over his game tape, asking questions like, "Why did you go there?" and, "What was the purpose of that?"

When the NFL draft came around, Austin still thought he had a chance to be selected. He didn't expect to be taken on the first day (round 1) or even the second day (rounds 2 and 3), so Saturday, April 29 was the key for him.

He had flown out to Santa Monica to be with family and his fiancée, Erica. By this time, he had signed with Carter Chow, an agent with Yee and Dubin, the agency that represented such NFL luminaries as Tom Brady and Julian Edelman.

Austin was given some pre-draft instructions from Chow.

"Don't track the draft, because you're just going to be stressed," Chow told him. "You're going to watch receivers go off the board and think, 'Oh I'm better than that dude!' Go do something, have fun, and keep your phone close so if they call, you're ready."

Thursday turned to Friday, which turned to Saturday, and Austin knew his time was coming. The fourth round came and went, and the fifth round arrived. Chow called Carr to let him know that the Patriots had interest, but unfortunately, they didn't have the draft capital to select him. That year, in fact, New England made only four draft picks. Following several trades and the forfeit of a fourth-round pick due to the Deflategate controversy, the Patriots were left with two third-round picks, a different fourth-round pick, and a sixth-rounder.[2]

When they called Chow, they only had the sixth-rounder left to go. That meant that the Patriots were letting Chow know that they wanted Carr, but as an undrafted free agent, not as a sixth-round pick. Still, as much as Austin liked the thought of playing in New England, he still wanted to hear his name called as an NFL draft pick.

It was not to be. The fifth round passed. Then the sixth. And finally, the seventh. When the last pick was made—"Mr. Irrelevant" Chad Kelly at number 253 by the Broncos—Austin's dream of being drafted was officially over. To say he was disappointed would be an understatement. But that didn't mean his dream of becoming an NFL player was over. He quickly signed a deal with New England as a UDFA.

"The Patriots offered me a $30,000 signing bonus, so that was nice. I thought, 'OK, they're not signing me for nickels and dimes.' I was happy, because I ended up signing with the team I wanted anyway, but I definitely had a chip on my shoulder."

The Big Ten receiver of the year, a *Sports Illustrated* second team All-American, had been bypassed by NFL teams some 253 times in the draft, but Austin Carr was still going to an NFL camp. He still had his chance to be a pro football player.

All he needed was a chance, and the Patriots had given that to him. He quickly packed his things to report to rookie minicamp. He was on his way.

Chapter 4

An NFL Draft Prospect

By the time the Giants were on the clock for the 186th pick in the 2015 NFL draft, the team had already made numerous moves to reshape the organization. They had taken four players already in the draft: In the first round, they selected Ereck Flowers, a six-six, 330-pound tackle out of Miami. They then traded three picks to Tennessee—their second-rounder (number 40 overall), their fourth-rounder (number 108), and their seventh-rounder (number 245) in order to move up seven spots in the second round. With their newly acquired number 33 overall pick, they drafted Landon Collins, an All-American safety from Nick Saban's powerhouse Alabama Crimson Tide.

The Giants were in need of defensive help. During their disappointing 2014 season in which they finished 6–10, they were ranked twenty-second in points allowed, and a disastrous twenty-ninth in yards allowed. Not many people saw Collins falling to the second round. Jerry Reese, the Giants' GM, quickly put together a deal with Tennessee and snapped up Collins, filling one of their most pressing needs.

With their third-round pick, the Giants added Owamagbe Odighizuwa, a defensive end who racked up six sacks for UCLA. In 2014 the Giants had managed only twenty-three quarterback sacks, third-worst in the entire league. They hoped that Odighizuwa would be part of the solution there. Their fourth-round pick was lost as part of the trade up to select Collins, and with their fifth-round pick they took another defensive player, Mykkele Thompson, a six-foot-two safety out of Texas.

That brought them to their sixth-round pick, number 186 overall. Prior to the draft, the Giants had stocked up at the wide receiver position, and by the time the draft came around, they had eleven receivers under contract. But still, Reese looked at his draft board and wanted more. He would say after the draft, when asked about the wide receiver position, "First of all, as soon as you say you have a lot of depth at any position, you don't have depth. I know better than to say that."[1]

He noted the name of Geremy Davis from the University of Connecticut. UConn had already seen star cornerback Byron Jones go in the first round to Dallas, following one of the most incredible efforts ever produced at the NFL draft combine. Jones actually broke the world record in the standing long jump at twelve feet, three inches, displaying freakish athleticism. As a result, Jones's draft stock rose dramatically, resulting in a first-round selection.

Davis, a college teammate, did not have Jones's athleticism. In fact, by NFL standards, he was considered to have average speed at best for a wide receiver, with scouts estimating from his game film that he had 4.58 speed in the forty-yard dash. But Davis had excellent size for a receiver, at six feet, three inches and 216 pounds. Moreover, he had terrific hands. During his career with the Huskies, Davis finished with 165 receptions and 2,292 yards, putting him sixth on the school's list for both career receptions and receiving yards. During Davis's junior year, he had an incredible seventy-one catches for 1,085 yards, including a fifteen-catch, 207-yard performance against Memphis. He had also managed a reception in every single game he played in during his time at UConn, a span of thirty-six straight games. His size and catching ability made him a potentially useful possession receiver in the NFL.

Before the draft, Davis shared a self-scouting report: "From a receiving standpoint, I am a big, physical guy. I am not afraid to open up big blocks for running backs and other receivers. I am not afraid to go across the middle. I have great hands."[2]

Davis understood that his strengths were in his size and his huge, strong, soft hands. CBS offered these thoughts on Davis: "Good size and is a really skilled receiver, particularly in the middle of the field. Lacks the speed to make an impact on the outside but an underrated prospect."[3] Dane Bruger declared that Davis "is a strong athlete at the catch point, playing like a power forward to locate, attack, and finish with his hands. . . . Davis is an intriguing possession target."[4] Another scouting report said that Davis "will need to make an impact as a special teamer to stick around."[5]

Davis was eager for this moment. At his UConn pro day workout, a reporter asked him, "Everyone dreams of playing in the NFL. Is it starting to sink in to you, how close [you are]?"

Davis replied, "You know, it's so surreal man, because obviously growing up, I can't wait to get to this moment. You know, praise God I got to the combine . . . that was so surreal for me. In reality, I've been doing this since freshman year. I always come out here and run routes, and I just have to keep telling myself, you've been doing this since freshman year. I'm just happy I did well out here today."[6]

When asked how he felt during his pro day workout. Davis said, "I was only nervous for the forty. After that I was like, man I do this all the time. Just have fun and run routes."

But Davis knew that his pro day was crucial to his draft prospects. He had seen teammates in previous years go through the process, some with good success. UConn did not have the advantage of being a football juggernaut like Alabama or Ohio State, so players like Davis faced inferior competition. During Davis's last two seasons the Huskies played as members of the American Athletic Conference following their departure from the Big East, going 3–9 and 2–10 against mid-level opponents. That did not do much for his draft stock. It didn't hurt Byron Jones, who had world-class athleticism, but for someone like Davis, it was a problem.

For NFL prospects like Davis, the forty-yard dash time could be the difference between being a mid-round pick or not being drafted at all. The forty is thought to have originated as a test of sorts in Cleveland, where legendary Browns coach Paul Brown timed his players running forty yards—about the distance of a typical punt at the time.

Zach Kruse, writing for *Bleacher Report*, explained the significance of the forty for NFL scouts: "No event at the NFL Scouting Combine is more heavily weighed or anticipated than the 40-yard dash," he wrote in a 2013 article. And why? Because, he explained, "team decision-makers use the results as a measure of an athlete's true speed. These scouts want to see explosion, burst, and speed—both in a short area (10 yards from a still start) and over a long distance (40 yards)."[7]

Davis's projected 4.58 speed wasn't very fast for a receiver, and that concerned scouts. Davis would have trouble getting separation from NFL-caliber defensive backs, and if you can't get open, you won't get the ball thrown to you. Davis knew he needed to improve his forty time if he wanted to get drafted, so he set as a goal getting below 4.50. Dropping nearly a tenth of a second off one's forty-yard dash time would represent a significant improvement, and Davis, knowing how important his forty time would be for his NFL future, put in a great deal of work simply becoming a better short-distance sprinter. He worked with both football and track coaches to cut crucial hundredths of a second off his time. It worked. During his pro day at UConn, he ran the forty in 4.47, improving by eleven hundredths of a second. His speed was now considered average for an NFL receiver, a vast improvement from where he was before. No wonder he was relieved to see his time during his pro day.

Having improved his speed, Davis now had everything Jerry Reese was looking for as he sought to provide help at the WR position. Davis even had experience working from the slot, a position the injured Victor Cruz had played as his primary position. Needing someone to take Cruz's snaps, Davis fit the Giants' plans perfectly.

But there were warnings bubbling up below the surface. For some players, those warnings came in the form of character issues. That wasn't a problem for Davis, who was a superlative citizen and team leader, having been a captain on the Huskies squad and a leader in his campus's AIA movement.[8] For Davis, his on-field issue was his struggle to beat tight man-to-man coverage. His off-field issue was his health. He had lost three games his senior season due to an ankle injury, and in the NFLPA Bowl (a college all-star game) he suffered a hamstring injury. Scouts didn't see this as much of a problem, so long as the injury didn't resurface. But the Giants had seen firsthand what persistent injuries could do to a player's career, having experienced wide receiver Hakeem Nicks's production drop off significantly following a lower-body injury.

After averaging sixty-six receptions and 958 yards from 2010 to 2013 with the Giants, Nicks played only six games in 2014 for the Indianapolis Colts, catching just thirty-eight passes for 405 yards. In 2015, back with the Giants, he would play just two games and catch seven passes before injuries ended his career. His promising NFL career was derailed by ongoing lower-body injuries.

Not everyone was sold on Davis's ability to make it in the NFL as a receiver, despite his size, strength (an amazing twenty-three reps of 225 pounds in the bench press at the NFL combine, an incredible mark for a receiver), hands, and improved speed. Special teams seemed like it might end up being his ticket to the fifty-three-man roster, something Davis was ready for. He said, "I am going to run down there and make tackles. I can be an in man on punt protecting for the punt. Front line on kickoff return. I am going to use all those traits that I have as a receiver on special teams."[9]

Now here's the thing. Usually the more highly regarded players get picked in the early rounds of the draft. The more "upside" a prospect has, with the fewest weaknesses, the earlier he will be selected. But the more problem areas scouts see in a prospect, the further they will drop in the draft. Of course, the vast majority—even those that are excellent college players—don't get drafted at all. In 2019, more than a million kids participated in high school football. A total of 73,712 athletes played college football at some level, meaning that just 7.3 percent of high school football players manage to play college ball. The overwhelming preponderance of players drafted by the NFL come from the division 1 level (249 out of 254 in the 2019 draft), and of the million or so high school football players, just 2.9 percent of those make it to the D1 college level. In 2019 the NFL selected 254 players, which means that just 1.6 percent of all college players are picked by an NFL team. So out of a pool of over a million high school football players, that gets reduced to just under 74,000 college players, and gets further reduced to just 254 pros.

The further down the draft you go, the less likely it is that a player will succeed in the NFL. The biggest exception in the history of the sport was drafted in 2000, when, in the sixth round, the Patriots selected Tom Brady with the 199th pick. Brady, as any football fan would know, has produced the greatest career in the history of the league. That just isn't expected out of late-round picks. As a comparison, from 2000 to 2020, there were twenty-one number 5 and number 186 overall draft picks. The twenty-one number 5 overall picks combined to total 125 years as starting players, made sixteen All-Pro teams, made thirty-nine Pro Bowls, and played in 2,012 games as a group. Meanwhile, the twenty-one number 186 picks have fourteen years combined as starting players, one All-Pro team, two Pro Bowls, and 619 total games played as a group.

This isn't to say that sixth-round picks can't become great players; Brady is obviously an exception to every NFL rule. But it is relatively rare for a sixth-rounder to make a real impact in the NFL. Of the forty-one players taken in the sixth round in the 2015 draft,[10] none have made an All-Pro team, only two made the Pro Bowl,[11] and only six players were still in the league for the 2022 season.

Approximately 99.7 percent of first-round picks make it their first year in the NFL, compared to just 70.2 percent of sixth-round picks. Naturally, for every round, a player's staying power in the NFL decreases the further out you project; by year five, 71.0 percent of first-round picks are still in the league, while only 10.6 percent of sixth-round picks survive to year five.

Why does this matter? Well, first, when a team makes that kind of investment in a player, both in terms of draft capital and actual money, they are going to give that player a lot more leeway than a sixth-rounder making league minimum. The investment alone means they will give a first-round pick more chances to "get it," but if you're a sixth- or seventh-round pick, the team loses nearly nothing by cutting you if you aren't working hard or picking up the plays or producing on the field. Second, the NFL operates under team salary caps, meaning they can only spend so much money on player salaries. The way the NFL structures salaries means that cutting a player can lead to what are called "dead cap hits"—money that the team has on the books with respect to the team's salary cap. Because the cap in the NFL is a hard cap—meaning there's no way around it and teams cannot, under any circumstances, go over it—these dead cap hits are albatrosses around their necks. Paying a player millions of dollars to not play for them (and in many cases to play—and maybe even play well—for another team) is generally not how teams want to go about their business. Faced with this reality, teams will tend to give players in whom they've made greater investments a much longer leash to produce than they will players in whom they've made much smaller investments.

Furthermore, it is assumed that players selected higher in the draft simply have more talent than those selected later. At most levels of sports, players with greater talent are given more of a chance than players with lesser talent. The reason is obvious. Even if a highly talented player comes with all kinds of problems, teams and coaches often believe that if they can only reach this player somehow, the potential payoff is enormous given their abundant talent. But if a player with lesser talent also comes with issues, why would a team bother making the effort to keep them around? It's much easier to find another lesser-talented player that doesn't have warts than to find a highly talented player that also doesn't have warts. In fact, teams will often choose a highly talented player with lots of red flags over a lesser-talented player who checks all the character and leadership boxes. The belief is simply that the upside of great talent is too much to give up on so quickly. This is why so many great but troubled players get chance after chance.

Geremy Davis didn't have that luxury. He knew he needed to do everything right in order to stick in the NFL. All he wanted was a shot, and when his phone rang on Saturday, May 2, 2015, and the Giants were on the phone making him the 186th selection in the NFL draft, he knew he had the opportunity he had been waiting and working for his whole life. He also knew that one slip up could end his dream. He would have to impress people right away, and never stop impressing them or his career could end in an instant.

Chapter 5

Camp

Players call it "the grind." It's five grueling weeks from the start of summer camp until the start of the season. During that time, a team will whittle their roster down from ninety players to fifty-three plus a ten-man practice squad. No matter where teams hold camp, it's hot and the days are long and it feels like forever before the season begins.

Practice squad players are real NFL players, but they are held in reserve in case the team needs another player for their fifty-three-man roster. Ryan Spadola, who spent time with several organizations before landing on the Detroit Lions' practice squad, explained what it's like: "When you think of the NFL you think of the guys in uniform playing Sundays, but there are 10 guys below the radar who get forgotten about. What a practice squad player goes through and what an active roster player goes through are immensely different. I personally think what a practice squad player is put through is a lot more mentally and physically during a week. You're taking way more reps and you're getting beat up a heck of a lot more; the only difference is you don't play for those three hours Sunday."[1]

And of course, the pay is vastly different. In 2017 the minimum rookie contract for a player with a full NFL contract was more than $450,000. But practice squad players like Spadola earned just $6,900 per week during the season—and practice squad players are only paid during the regular season weeks, not before or after. For the 2022 season, that number had climbed to $11,500 per week, which would come to $207,000 for an entire eighteen-week regular season. Still excellent pay, but far short of the more than $700,000 league minimum.

Rookies are the first to arrive. The Raiders required their first-year players to show up at their 2022 camp at Raiders Headquarters and Intermountain Healthcare Performance Center in Henderson, Nevada, a dozen miles north of the Las Vegas Strip, straight up Interstate 15. The new players arrived on Monday, July 18, with veterans checking in two days later on July 20.

When rookies show up, the scene is both unfamiliar and familiar. All of it is new. They have never been to a summer NFL training camp before. They don't yet know the ropes. In many cases they have never even been to the facility where the team holds camp. Yet the familiarity comes in the sense that it's not too unlike college. The players live in housing provided by the team—whether it be a hotel or a dorm-style arrangement. They check in and are given keys and a schedule, and they take the time to move into their rooms, meeting their roommates along the way.

At that point, the players must pass physicals. For most players, this is a relatively smooth process. They have dreamed of this their entire lives and come to camp ready to go. But every year there are players who fail their physical. This could be due to an injury from the previous season that isn't yet fully healed or some lingering issue that cropped up in the offseason. A player who fails a physical may be put on one of several PUP (Physically Unable to Perform) lists and not be able to participate in practice, but if a player clears the initial physical, he may begin team workouts and practices immediately.

Gone is the time when teams did "two-a-days"—two physical practices a day. The 2011 collective bargaining agreement reduced not only the number of practices but also the number of times a team can practice with full contact. This has come with numerous consequences. On the positive side, it has meant less wear and tear on the players' bodies. On the negative side, players don't get enough physical skills practice, and fundamentals like tackling suffer.

Ryan Riddle, who played with Oakland and the New York Jets over two seasons in the NFL, said about the reduced practice time, "This is why we've seen such a significant downgrade in quality tackling among NFL players. It's becoming a lost art just as the league's public relations machine is force-feeding this Heads Up Certified concept to the parents and children across the country. The message to the public is clear—the NFL prioritizes proper technique for tackling. But the reality is much different. Coaches are scared stiff to have their players tackling each other in practice."[2]

Just because players have fewer full-contact practices doesn't mean camp is easy. It's not.

A typical day in training camp begins with a 6:00 or 6:30 a.m. breakfast in the team facility. Treatment follows, then a team meeting, and finally, the players dress and report to practice by 8:30 or 9:00. Given that camp takes place at the end of July through August—the two hottest months of the year—teams in warm weather climates try to get practice out of the way before the blazing heat of the day. Other teams stationed in the north might wait until the afternoon to get on the field.

A two-hour practice follows, where the team works on all sorts of situations. Many teams begin practice with special teams work like kickoffs, punts, and returns. From there, the organized chaos—it's really a ballet featuring more than 120 people between players, coaches, and staff—morphs into the installation of the team's offensive and defensive plays, ranging from core staples of the team to specialty plays used for specific circumstances.

At times, players will practice without pads, running through the plays in simulated fashion. Other times they will be fully padded, hitting and tackling—all except the quarterbacks, who wear special red jerseys to signify that they aren't to be hit.

That makes sense, as a team's quarterbacks may well represent the biggest investment it has from a financial standpoint. To lose one of the most important players on the team because of a tackle during training camp practice would be unconscionable.

Included in practices are seven-on-seven drills, full eleven-on-eleven scrimmaging, individual drills specific to each position, and one-on-one matchups between offensive and defensive linemen, wide receivers, and defensive backs, for example. Conditioning is also part of practice, and each team handles that differently. Running, of course, is a foundational part of every team's core workout program.

After practice, it's time for more treatment, and then come the meetings. Meeting after meeting. Team meetings. Offensive meetings. Defensive meetings. Positional meetings. Special teams meetings. All this time in the classroom makes camp feel like an intense college course load. Outside of meetings, the amount of reading and studying players have to do is substantial—and crucial if a player wants to make the team.

Former NFL offensive lineman Geoff Schwartz explained his camp experience: "I've done camp multiple ways, with meetings followed by practice and an afternoon walk through, or meetings followed by a walk through, lunch and then a practice. The night is always the same. Dinner and more meetings. Treatment and rehab is sprinkled in throughout the day. Every other day you find time to lift."[3]

When Marcell Ateman reported to his first training camp with Oakland in 2018, Jon Gruden was beginning his second stint coaching the Raiders. Gruden had been with Oakland from 1998 to 2001 before moving on to coach the Tampa Bay Buccaneers to a Super Bowl title in 2002. Following back-to-back 9–7 seasons with the Bucs, Gruden found himself out of a job after the 2008 season. He went into the media, becoming one of the most popular commentators on television.

In 2018 the Raiders, in desperate need of a shakeup coming off a 6–10 season in 2017, rehired Gruden.

Rookies like Ateman reported to camp several days before the veterans. It was crucial to get them up to speed for life in an NFL training camp. Though every player at camp has years of experience playing football, nothing can adequately prepare rookies for what life is like in the NFL.

"There's so much to learn," Ateman says. "That's why they do OTAs. It's why they want everyone to go to OTAs. It's like a preview for what's going to go on in camp. Ramp you up, get you to know what to expect. Because when you're in camp, it's easy to get lost. It's why they bring the rookies in early, to get them oriented. They know how fast-paced camp is going to be."

On the first day of camp, Gruden stood before the team and outlined the vision and values of the Oakland Raiders. Historically, the team motto had been "Just win, baby," coined by former owner Al Davis. Gruden obviously wanted to continue the Raiders' winning tradition, but he needed to turn things around. In six of the previous seven seasons, the Raiders had done a lot more losing than winning. That included three straight seasons from 2012 to 2014 where they had only won four, four, and three games.

Being an offensive-minded coach—he had worked as an offensive assistant in stints with the 49ers, Packers, and Eagles—Gruden personally oversaw the offensive side of the ball with the Raiders. He took charge of offensive unit meetings before turning things over to the positional coaches and offensive coordinator, Greg Olson.

Meetings were very much like college classrooms. Each player received a tablet with all the team's plays, organized and cataloged. While each player took notes on their tablet, the plays were simultaneously projected on a screen in the front of the meeting room. Each coach would go over the plays, with specific intentions for his particular position. Tom Cable, for example, was the offensive line coach, and he would begin his session explaining the responsibility for each offensive lineman during a specific play.

"Hey, this motion, this person's going to come down, you need to block in the C gap.[4] You're going to hear this call," he would explain.

After going over the plays, the coaches would run through a film of practice to show them what went right and what went wrong. Even on a play that ultimately succeeded, there was a good chance that someone did something wrong, and coaches would always be quick to point out those mistakes. Players were given the chance to ask questions, and the coaches would clarify.

It was an awful lot of learning, especially for players new to the team—whether as rookies or veterans coming over from another team. Maybe the team's philosophy was similar to elsewhere, but usually the terminology was different, and it was like learning a new language.

"That's what camp is for," Marcell explains. "To help you learn every aspect of your responsibilities. You have to be able to go out on the field and put it all together instantly. So there's constant, constant repetition, in the meetings, and then on the field."

For the Raiders' veterans, it was a challenge, as Gruden sought to implement an entirely new system. It was like starting from scratch. Fortunately for the players, Gruden ran a relatively light camp when it came to the physical side of things. The Raiders practiced in Napa, California, with regular temperatures in the mid-eighties in August. He did not want to wear his guys down before the season started.

"Coach Gruden did a good job taking care of us in practice," says Marcell. "Our practices weren't nearly as brutal as some other places in the league, where they're constantly hitting."

Camp was the time for players to learn the ropes, get familiar with the Raiders' system, and put their best foot forward. The physical toll was one thing; the mental toll was another thing entirely. Every day brought the stress of knowing that it could be your last with the team. Star players obviously had less to worry about in that regard, but even they sometimes found themselves getting a visit from the Turk and being asked to turn in their playbook. It was much worse for fifty-third-man types like Marcell. It was essentially a five-week tryout for his position, knowing that they could bring in someone else the next day to replace him.

"It's more mental than anything," Marcell says. "Making sure you're ready for whatever they throw at you. Because, you know, they cut people in camp. You mess up? They'll cut you. There were a bunch of players in my class that, if they messed up, don't know the plays, don't know what you're doing, they're going to release you. It's not like college, where they help you get acclimated. You're not on scholarship. They'll cut you and find someone else to bring in. It's a cutthroat business."

Schwartz pointed out that for veterans who were already familiar with the system, and whose bodies were more prone to breaking down, camp is probably the least fun aspect of the job.

"Camp isn't as physical as in the past, but it's still a mental grind. The hours spent in the facility and focused on football can be tough on younger players. Older players just can't wait to get camp over. I've spoken with a few veterans so far in camp and their answer to the question 'How's camp going' is always 'good, just can't wait to get it over with.'"[5]

But that doesn't mean that camp can't also be enjoyable. In 2018, the Raiders did several fun team activities. Gruden brought in comedian Frank Caliendo to give the team a performance. Another night, the team went bowling. Twice, the team broke up by position group, and the wide receivers got the chance to explore Napa Valley and the vineyards. Those kinds of things built camaraderie and relationships that have staying power beyond football.

For Marcell, this bonding represented the best part of camp with the Raiders.

"The most important part of camp is that you're together with these guys every single day," he says. "You just get to know your different teammates. You're around each other all the time, and you get to create great relationships. The competing stuff—we're always going to love that, but the best part is building relationships with these guys."

Getting cut at the end of camp, however, was *not* Marcell's favorite camp experience. But after the Raiders released him, he was fortunate enough to make the team's practice squad, where he remained until the Raiders finally called him up to the fifty-three-man roster before week eight. For three games, he was inactive, but he would get his chance in week eleven.

He had joined a team with a loaded receiving corps, headlined by veterans Jordy Nelson, Amari Cooper, and Martavis Bryant. Despite positive reviews from the Raiders' coaching staff, Atemen found it difficult to crack the main roster, and he had spent numerous weeks working and improving on the practice squad. But, as so often happens in the NFL, doors of opportunity open for players when others suffer misfortune.

First, the Raiders released Bryant, just four months after trading for him. Bryant was facing a suspension by the league for violating the substance-abuse policy. He had missed the entire 2016 season for violating the same policy multiple times but had been conditionally reinstated by the league. His 2017 season was on-the-field redemption, as he caught fifty passes for 603 yards for the Steelers. They then turned around and dealt Bryant to Oakland for the number 79 pick in the 2018 draft, and he became a Raider. Four months later, he was gone.

Oakland got off to a terrible start in 2018 on the heels of a 6–10 record in 2017. The Raiders lost their first three games to the Rams, Broncos, and Dolphins. After winning a thrilling 45–42 game against the Browns in overtime, they lost back-to-back games to the Chargers and Seahawks.

At 1–6, the season was on the brink, and the Raiders decided to make a move, trading Cooper to the Cowboys for a 2019 first-round draft pick.

That left a hole in the team's wide receiving corps, and Ateman got the call. But he was held out as an inactive for three weeks until Nelson suffered a bone bruise on his knee that would keep him out of their week-eleven matchup at Arizona.

The Raiders activated Marcell, who describes the situation: "In the middle of the season, week six or seven, all these guys gone, and they activated me."

The Raiders had picked up former Patriot Brandon LaFell, but early in the game he got hurt, and in the blink of an eye, Marcell was playing wide receiver. He was not only getting his chance to play, he was getting his chance to play against one of the best in the business: All Pro cornerback Patrick Peterson.

"Suddenly, I was in the game," Marcell says, his voice rising with excitement even as he tells the story. "Hadn't played all game, wasn't stretched. First play, I line up, and Patrick Peterson was opposite me. I knew the game plan, having learned a ton while on the practice squad. And in that game, I caught a pass against Patrick Peterson. I was like, alright, come on now!"

His first reception of the game—and the first of his NFL career—was in the second quarter with just under three minutes left and the score tied at 14. Not a huge catch—just a nine-yard reception—but it was real, and it put Ateman in the box score. He wouldn't make another catch until midway through the fourth quarter, a short catch that netted no gain. His big moment, however, would come with less than two minutes to go in the game.

Oakland trailed, 21–20, and had the ball with 1:53 left. Derek Carr hoped to mount a game-winning drive. On the first play of the drive, he hit Ateman for nine more yards. Peterson was in coverage, so for Marcell, to catch a pass against an All Pro was enormous. But a few plays later, with the Raiders facing second and ten from their own thirty-one, Carr lofted a beautiful pass down the left sideline toward Ateman. The pass drifted over Marcell's outside shoulder, and he hauled it in, tiptoeing down the sideline for a fantastic thirty-two-yard reception.

The catch put the ball at the Arizona thirty-seven, and a few plays later, with just two seconds left on the clock, Daniel Carlson booted a thirty-five-yard field goal to give Oakland a 23–21 win. Ateman ended up the team's leading receiver on the day, with four catches for fifty yards, including two on the game-winning drive.

Not bad for a guy who hadn't even been stretched out before entering the game.

"I'm all happy because I contributed to the win," Marcell says. "Coach gave me a game ball and everything. You just never know when God is going to do something and a door opens for you. I had been cut after having a good camp, but I hung in there and got my chance and made the most of it."

Success in the NFL can be fleeting, going from game to game. The next week, he played poorly, catching three passes for a mere sixteen yards in a 34–17 loss to Baltimore.

"Of course the next game I was terrible," he says. "Marlon Humphries of the Ravens, along with Jimmy Smith, man those guys beat on me all day. They're big, tall, long, strong corners. They locked me up bad."

The following week he posted just two catches for sixteen yards, but caught his first NFL touchdown—a beautiful back shoulder fade in the left edge of the end zone. The early success in his first game set the table for some unrealistic expectations.

"After that first game, I felt a lot of pressure to play well because the team needed me, so when I didn't play well the next game, it was hard. I did score a touchdown the following week against Kansas City. That was a good moment. I ran around all excited."

His fourth game was solid, with three receptions for forty-five yards in a three-point victory over Pittsburgh. He would finish the season with modest numbers: fifteen catches for 154 yards and the single touchdown. But Marcell Ateman had made it out of camp and into the NFL.

Chapter 6

From #bleedblue to Big Blue

The post-draft celebration lasted several days, but on May 8, 2015, the Giants opened rookie minicamp and it was back to work for Geremy Davis. The Giants' training center and headquarters, just a few hundred yards due west of MetLife Stadium, features four outdoor fields and a ninety-eight-thousand-square-foot indoor practice facility, along with a massive complex that serves as team headquarters.

After his flight took him to the Newark, New Jersey, airport, and a cab ride brought him to the facility, he walked in the building, trying to find his way around. A team official—Geremy doesn't remember who it was, being a little starstruck—grabbed him by the arm.

"This is one of our draft picks, right here," he said.

Geremy beamed. "That felt so great to hear," he says. "I was like, wow, I feel important."

A few minutes later, he saw something that hit him hard.

"I remember walking in and I see Eli chatting with Odell [Beckham]. I was like, oh shoot, that's Eli. It gave me a real feeling like, 'I made it.' Who would have thought that I'd be in the same room as Eli Manning, who's won the Super Bowl two times? I wasn't star struck, but I was a little bit in awe of the fact that I was here."

He found the locker room and found his jersey hanging in the locker. Number nine. Geremy had known that getting a single digit at that time meant that you weren't a lock to make the team.[1] But the good news was that his number was the same as his favorite player, Tony Romo, quarterback of the Dallas Cowboys.

"I thought, oh man, now I have to do something with this," he says. He felt a responsibility to represent the number well.

Above his locker was the nameplate, but as Geremy looked at it, he realized something was wrong. It said *Geramy*, not *Geremy*. On Saturday May 9, the nameplate was missing, as the Giants realized their mistake.

Ironically, while misspelling *Geremy*, they did manage to spell the name on the locker right next to Davis's perfectly: Owamagbe Odighizuwa.

In camp, the team took their time with the rookies. Geremy worked hard to learn the playbook, wanting to pick it up as fast as possible. He was catching on quickly, learning the signals and play calls. Each rookie was trying to impress the coaching staff, particularly Head Coach Tom Coughlin.

"They have to make plays," Tom Coughlin said. "They have to look and react like they are asked to do. Every one of them is evaluated. It is not like we don't know anything about them."[2]

The first day of minicamp went well for Geremy. Former Rutgers quarterback Gary Nova, who had set school records for touchdown passes and passing yards, was invited as a tryout player. He connected with Geremy on the first long pass completion of camp, which generated some oohs and aahs from onlookers.

Over the course of minicamp, the Giants had him working both as a receiver and in special teams, which is how he figured he'd most likely make a difference.

"Any opportunity to help the team," Davis said. "I just want to fit in a role right now and that role would be as a special teams guy and eventually rotate in with the wide receivers. I just want to take advantage of the skill set, the talent, size, and use it to the best of my ability on special teams."[3]

His camp went so well that Giants' beat writers made note of him in their articles. Geremy had decided to stay away from the internet during those few days, but his mom sent along one article, saying he was a rookie minicamp standout. Geremy had been written about in college, but this was different. He was a pro now.

Organized Team Activities (OTAs) came next, in late May. The whole team showed up for these, and it was here that Geremy really got to share space with some of the stars on the team.

"I got in there with the big guys," he says. "Eli, Ryan Nassib, the two quarterbacks. Odell, Victor Cruz, Rueben Randle. And I'm just trying to make the best of the situation I'm in with those guys."

He started off with the threes, which he had expected. As a sixth-round pick, he understood his place on the team. As the days went on, he got some snaps with the starters as well. He made numerous high-level plays—not superstar plays, but good enough to demonstrate that he belonged in the league.

He didn't consider OTAs to be super demanding, all things considered, but the Giants required all the rookies to stay longer and attend more meetings in order to get more up to speed on the playbook. Moreover, there were additional player development classes to help them navigate other aspects of life in the NFL, including finances and how to navigate outside factors such as family and fans. They wanted to prepare the players for success amid the pro football chaos.

In many respects, it was similar to his time at UConn. Meetings, practice, learning the playbook. Football is football in one sense.

"I went through four different offensive coordinators in college," he says. "So I had to keep learning new playbooks. So I practiced good habits of really working hard to learn the playbook. I really put in my due diligence to avoid making errors on the field."

As a senior in college, he was the star receiver, and the UConn offense made a concerted effort to get him the ball. But as a rookie on a team with Super Bowl–winning players, he had a completely different role. He knew he had to make the right blocks and be a decoy on offense, and on special teams, he had to make the unheralded plays that would help the team. He had gone from a star to a complementary player.

"I need to do these things to get other people the ball, so the offense flows well," he says. "So I don't get fired."

For rookies like Geremy, there were many things he could not control. But those things he could control—his effort, his attitude, his work ethic—he tried to maximize. Learning the playbook was one of those things. His play on the field showcased what he could do, even among the rookies.

Columnist Chris Pflum, writing for *Big Blue Review*, commented on Davis following OTAs: "So what kind of player are the Giants getting in Geremy Davis? I think they're getting one who is going to be very hard to cut. He likely won't be a sensational receiver. He doesn't have the raw athleticism or 'wiggle' to really burn NFL defensive backs or break big plays. But what he does have are strong, reliable hands, a very physical style of play, surprisingly decent—both as a rookie receiver overall and in light of UConn's quarterbacking situation—route running, and a willingness to do the down and dirty things."[4]

But it wasn't all roses. For the first time in his short professional career, his hamstrings tightened. He went to the training room to get them checked out. They weren't pulled; he just wanted to stay ahead of things. His hamstrings had been an issue in the weeks and months leading up to the draft, and it concerned him that they were cropping up again.

Coughlin heard about his visit to the trainer. During the stretching period at the next practice, Coughlin walked over to Davis.

"What's this I hear about your hamstring?" he asked in his no-nonsense manner.

"Just getting looked at," Geremy replied.

"Well," Coughlin said, his eyes boring holes into Geremy, "you'd better get that fixed, or else."

Or else what? Geremy thought as Coughlin walked away. There was no further clarification, and Davis didn't ask. It was just left hanging. Was it a threat? Was it a warning? Geremy had no idea. But that short, twenty-second conversation put fear into Geremy's heart.

"I was like, I'm never going to see the trainer again," he says. "I had no idea what he meant by 'or else.' I thought if I went back to the training room for anything other than a serious injury, they might cut me right there."

In fact, this stuck with Geremy his entire NFL career—never again would he visit the team trainer unless he knew he had pulled something for real.

"I didn't want to give them any reason to get rid of me," he says. "I did all my maintenance outside the building, or with the strength and conditioning people."

Such is life for a fifty-third man in the NFL—if the coaches suspect you are injury prone, or if little nagging injuries keep you from performing at your best, it could mean unemployment in the blink of an eye.

OTAs ended and Geremy went to his new apartment in Tampa, Florida, to work out and train. There he studied the playbook more. He also made sure to stay in constant communication with high school buddy Max Garcia and former UConn teammate Byron Jones. All three were going through the same process together, each with his own team. They encouraged one another and compared notes.

Finally training camp arrived, and, as usual, rookies showed up first. In college, he had experienced the grueling camp of coach Paul Pasqualoni, who put his players through old-school two-a-days. In 2011, the NFL outlawed two-a-days, and in 2017, the NCAA followed suit. When Geremy began his first camp, he was grateful to no longer have to endure such a punishing regimen.

But Tom Coughlin was an old-school coach, and he didn't go easy on the players. Every day in camp was a long one, between extended practices and meetings. Players needed to push through an awful lot, both physically and mentally.

The first two days, Geremy stood out as a wide receiver but struggled on special teams, which he knew was where his chance to make the team lay. He teamed up with backup QB Ryan Nassib for several long completions, but covering punts was a new skill for him, and one he didn't adjust to right away. He put in the effort, but it wasn't easy and didn't come naturally to him.

Nevertheless, he had made an indelible mark right away. Wide receivers coach Sean Ryan praised Davis for his early camp performance.

"I think he's come a long way," Ryan said. "The thing I really like about him is that he's really serious. I mean, for a rookie he's serious about his business. And he's been that way since day one—he's a note taker, he pays attention to everything, he's detailed, he is as good of a worker as you can ask for with a maturity level, for a rookie, that is outstanding. And that is really what's been most impressive to me."[5]

As camp went on, he showed marked improvement as a gunner on special teams. In college, the star offensive players rarely played on special teams at all, but in the pros, those same guys were expected to contribute significantly to the kicking game. Davis proved to be a fast learner though.

"He's progressing," special teams coordinator Tom Quinn said. "He really works hard at it [and] he really has a lot of upside. He didn't do a lot of it in college, so a lot of it is new to him, but he has really taken to the coaching and he tries hard and works hard, so we've been pleased with him."[6]

"I stood out as a receiver," Geremy says. "Special teams—at that time, it was so new to me, I really struggled at first as a rookie. Conceptually, I had a hard time with it. I didn't know what I was doing. I'd never been a gunner. I didn't know where the vulnerabilities were on this kickoff return, what have you. But that was how I was going to play. I showed glimpses, but I for sure wasn't a dog in special teams like I became later in my career."

Geremy's study habits helped him as a receiver, but they were less important when it came to the kicking game.

"Special teams is 'want to,'" he says. "Effort. Nobody grows up and thinks, man, I want to be a great special teams player. So when that's your opportunity to make it, it really has to be something you want to get after."

He gave it the old college try, however. He would find himself sprinting down the field on a kickoff coverage, but, he says, "I wouldn't know what I'm sprinting down there for. I didn't understand gaps and leverage at the time. Matthew Slater can look at it and immediately recognize what's going on. It's experience. He's done it. He would know this trap block is coming, but I'd run down and have no idea the trap block is coming, and it would just kill me."

Geremy's roommate in camp, Juron Criner, was a fifth-round pick of the Raiders in 2012. He played in thirteen games in two seasons for Oakland before finding himself on the outs. The Raiders released him at the end of camp in 2014, and a month later, the Giants signed him to the practice squad, where he spent the entire season. He came into camp in 2015 just hoping to make a roster spot.

He was in a battle with Geremy, Corey Washington, Preston Parker, Marcus Harris, and undrafted free agents Ben Edwards, Chris Harper, and Julian Tilley for the last wide receiver spot. At six-feet, three inches, he was the same height as Davis, but a little thicker at 225 pounds.

Competition would be intense, even between Geremy and his roommate.

Despite the fact that the players were competing with one another for jobs, there was still a sense of camaraderie. Naturally, that came with hijinks. One might call it hazing, but not in the old-school way. More like in the practical joke way.

It was the night of a scheduled walkthrough prior to a preseason game. Veteran players sneaked into the locker room and stole the rookies' jerseys. In the other room was a cold tub—a tub filled with forty-degree water. It was used to help players recover from the brutal workouts that NFL players endure. Bags of ice were dumped into the tub, and a player would lower himself in—usually in one moment rather than in small, slow increments—and feel the sharp pain of frigid water. The idea is to cool the body's core temperature, aiding and speeding up recovery.

But the veterans weren't using the cold tub for recovery. They were using it to prank the rookies. They dunked the jerseys in the cold water, and then hung them back up in the rookies' locker rooms. As rookies put their jerseys on, the shock was instant and most unpleasant. Geremy, however, had gotten wind of the prank.

"I figured out what they were doing," he says. "I took my jersey and put it in the hot tub for a minute, then threw it in a drying machine. So I was fine, but a lot of the other rookies had to wear freezing cold jerseys in the walkthrough."

On another occasion, they stole the rookies' luggage, which was filled with their clothes, and brought it out into the hallway of the hotel. Landon Collins and Ereck Flowers were exceptions because their luggage remained in their off-site apartment. Players drafted high already had their place to stay, having some security as high-round draft picks. Not so for Geremy and other later-round picks and UDFAs. For them, a frustrating discovery awaited. The veterans had emptied the luggage and had mixed up all the rookies' clothing. The rooks spent hours digging through the clothes, trying to make sure they all had their own shirts and shorts and socks. Harmless, but a royal pain.

The cuts started coming. Some players were cut at seemingly random times, but most cuts came at the two appointed dates. Per NFL rules, the ninety players had to be trimmed down to seventy-five by September 1, and then four days later, the seventy-five had to be cut down to fifty-three. From there the team could select players for their practice squad. A host of decisions needed to take place during that time, and every player's fate rested in these decisions.

September 1 was a bad day for Geremy's roommate, Juron. During the first round of cuts, he received his pink slip. Geremy heard, and came over to offer his condolences.

"Hey man," he said. "I'm sorry."

"Thanks," Juron replied. "But why are you sorry? This is the NFL. This is how this works."

This is the NFL? Geremy thought. *Oh man.*

And just like that, the Giants' sixth-round draft pick had a room all to himself.

September 5, however, was a day to be nervous. He had a good camp, and thought that he impressed as a receiver. But it was special teams that concerned him. It just felt like a struggle. He noticed that defensive players tended to adapt to special teams much more quickly than offensive players.

"Defensive players already know how to hit someone," he says. "Our job [on offense] is to avoid being tackled. For defensive guys, it's see ball, get ball. I had to actually think about tackling someone. Just wasn't natural for me."

As cut day arrived, the players were told that they were about to be kicked out of the hotels. Geremy knew he would need to find another place to stay, but he didn't even know if he was going to make the team.

"I went to all these places, but said to them, 'Hey, I'd like an apartment, but can you wait like four more days so I can figure out if I'm going to make the team?'" The apartment owners understood the situation, of course, but for Davis, it was stressful. The manager at the Station at Lyndhurst, just three miles from the Giants' facility, reserved a one-bedroom for Geremy and told him to call her if he made the team.

Geremy found out by mistake.

"I thought that in order to find out if you made the team, you came to the facility. I was like, man, I don't want to wait around all day [till 4:00 EST, which was when cuts needed to be finalized]. So I went there and just started looking around, and I don't see anything. No list. Nobody called me."

He ran into an equipment manager, who recognized Davis.

"Hey, do you want to change your number?" he asked.

"What do you mean?" Geremy replied.

"You have to change it to an eligible number," he said, knowing that while a receiver at that time could wear a single digit in camp, he couldn't during the regular season.[7]

Confused, Geremy asked what numbers were available. The manager told him.

"I'll take 18," Davis said, not sure if any of this meant anything at all. So he called his agent.

"How do you know if you made the team?" Geremy asked.

"You don't want to get a call before 4:00," came the reply.

"Dang, that's a long time."

For players on the West Coast, however, cuts need to be in by 1:00 p.m., meaning they have three fewer hours in the day to await their fate.

"One o'clock—man, the deadline for cuts is a lot shorter out there," Geremy says with a laugh.

He was antsy and spent the rest of the time just roaming the facility. Finally, team officials told him he made the team, and he breathed a sigh of relief.

He called his family and his friends, Byron and Max, both of whom had made their respective teams—Dallas and Denver.

His last call was to the folks at Lyndhurst, and he got the apartment. His new uniform said "Davis" and "18." Geremy had gone from being a Husky to a Giant, and blue still looked good on him.

Chapter 7

The Patriot Way

Matthew Slater calls it the "imposter syndrome." The word *imposter* suggests a fraud or a pretender. For Matthew, the imposter syndrome was the feeling that he just didn't quite belong in the NFL. He had earned his way to the Patriots by being drafted in the fifth round, but he was still a long way from making the roster. He had made it through rookie minicamp following the draft, as well as OTAs in the spring, and he reported to camp without a position and without any assurances of opening the season on the fifty-three-man squad.

The 2008 Patriots were loaded. They had come off the greatest regular season in NFL history, winning all sixteen games, by an average margin of nearly twenty points a contest. In fact, in only four games during the season were the scores even within a touchdown. Nobody had ever gone 16–0 before. The 1972 Miami Dolphins famously went 14–0 during the regular season and then won three playoff games to complete a 17–0 championship season. But since the NFL had gone to a sixteen-game schedule, nobody had run the table. The Patriots did, and marched into the playoffs the overwhelming favorite to win the Super Bowl.

Two somewhat close victories in the AFC playoffs propelled the team to Arizona for the Super Bowl against the New York Giants, a team the Patriots had faced just a month before in the last game of the regular season. New England had won 38–35 in a game that showed that the Giants could compete with the Patriot juggernaut. In Super Bowl XLII, they did just that, holding the explosive Patriots' offense to just fourteen points in a dramatic 17–14 win, the single biggest upset in Super Bowl history. In the process, they denied the Patriots an undefeated championship season.

Most everyone from that dominant team returned to camp for the 2008 season. Widely regarded as still having the best team in football, the Patriots were primed to take out their revenge on the rest of the NFL. The bitterness of the Super Bowl loss could be felt all over New England, no more so than at One Patriot Place, the home of Gillette Stadium.

As the team gathered for training camp, the son of NFL Hall of Famer Jackie Slater arrived, wondering if he was even in the right place. Three recent Super Bowl championship banners hung in Gillette Stadium. Of the eight Pro Bowl players—five of whom were also All-Pro—from the 2007 roster, only one, cornerback Asante Samuel, had not returned. It was, for Matthew, a little overwhelming.

"You look at our team," he says, "having just gone undefeated in the regular season the year prior, and I was like, where do I fit in, what's my role here? I see Randy Moss, Wes Welker, Tom Brady, Tedy Bruschi, Mike Vrabel, Rodney Harrison, the list goes on. I say to myself, I'm not these guys."

Where, indeed, would a rookie wide receiver with no receptions in college fit in on a team with superstars all over the place and a thirst for vengeance on the rest of the league? This was not a rebuilding program. This was a team at the peak of its powers ready to run roughshod over thirty-one other franchises.

Camp opened with ninety men competing for fifty-three spots on the main roster, plus ten more on the practice squad. That meant that the Patriots would need to send thirty-seven players home by August 31. Slater had about five weeks' time to show that he had what it took to play in the NFL. No pressure.

But first things first. He had to find a place to live. For Matthew, finding the proper housing near Gillette Stadium in Foxboro, Massachusetts, was an exercise in prudence. He stayed in a hotel room near the stadium during camp with fellow rookie Kevin O'Connell.[1]

Though money was an issue, he discovered that he would get paid for training camp, which came as a surprise—and a help. He had no idea how long he would last, and he wasn't drawing a serious NFL paycheck. He had learned how important it was to take care of his money, and even though he was putting on a professional football uniform, that perspective carried over.

When it came time to perform on the field, Slater put every ounce of effort into every single rep. After being drafted, he told reporters that he was willing to do anything Coach Belichick asked of him.

"I'm just excited to have an opportunity to keep playing football," he said. "I don't have a preference where I play; I just want to be able to help that football team out in whatever way possible. For me, it's doing whatever it takes. Obviously, I look forward to contributing on special teams.

That's kind of where I made my mark at UCLA, so I know that will be probably my primary focus right away. Wherever they want to use me, I'm flexible, I don't mind, I'm just ready to work hard for this organization and continue to the great reputation they have around the league for being one of the best teams in the league."[2]

As a late round pick, he knew that special teams would be critical for his success. But this was right up his alley, being a special teams standout at UCLA. He figured the transition to the pros might even be easier given what he expected the Patriots would ask of him, and given his college experience.

He was a little starstruck sitting in the same locker room as Tom Brady and Randy Moss. But he also had experience with that as well. Growing up the son of an NFL player, he had spent years hanging around such NFL luminaries as Eric Dickerson and Isaac Bruce.

It was clear that he was no longer at UCLA. Bill Belichick was a different kind of coach. Nobody at UCLA was as successful as various members of these Patriots were. The work was different. It was still just football, and Matthew had been through numerous camps, but there were aspects of the professional life that were markedly different.

For example, in college, scholarship players didn't have to worry about getting cut. But in the pros, a release could come any day. "Guys who were in rookie minicamp with you get cut a day or two into camp, constant turnover on the roster," Matthew says. "It's not something you're used to or are prepared for."

As such, "My first training camp was really about survival." Every day he wasn't called into Belichick's office was another day he had survived. Every day he survived was another opportunity to prove himself the next day. It was a challenge he relished, as he had adopted his father's love for the grind. Whether it was lifting, studying the playbook, or performing on the field, Matthew savored every moment of his pro experience.

The relationships were difficult, however. Seeing friends get cut was a painful experience for him. "I had to get over that shock of 'Oh man this guy's gone, I may never see that guy again,'" he says.

As the days and weeks passed, and the roster churned, he continued to survive in his first NFL camp. Every day the Patriots put more on his plate, and he had concerns. "I'm thinking I was going to get cut every day. There was just so much that I didn't know and understand about playing in this league. I didn't know what my future looked like in this league. There was a lot of angst as far as what's today going to look like, what's this period going to look like, can I handle what's being thrown at me."[3]

He needed encouragement. And he got it from numerous men. Tight end Benjamin Watson, entering his fifth season with New England, took Matthew under his wing and began to give him little nuggets of information. He set the example for Slater in both word and deed, teaching him what it meant to be a professional football player and how to make it in the Patriots' organization.

Matthew also bonded with several others in his rookie class. Linebacker Gary Guyton had been a stalwart at Georgia Tech, and had gone undrafted by all thirty-two NFL teams. He nearly signed with the San Francisco 49ers as an undrafted free agent but reached a deal with the Patriots instead. Guyton had marveled at the differences between the college and pro games. It was much faster even in training camp, and he likened the difference in schemes to the difference between a graduate level calculus class and high school algebra.[4]

Ryan Wendell had played center at Fresno State, and, like Guyton, had gone undrafted. As the seventh round came and went, he wondered if his dream was over. Then he got a call from the New England Patriots. "They put me on the line with Coach Bill Belichick," he said. "The fact that Bill Belichick, Super Bowl champion, Hall of Fame coach one day, gave me a call and took the time to ask me to come and sign as an undrafted free agent, was all it took for me to come out here [to New England]."[5] He couldn't believe his good fortune to come to a team as successful as the Patriots.

Bo Ruud, a linebacker out of Nebraska, had an amazing NFL heritage. His father, Tom Ruud, was drafted by Buffalo in the first round of the 1975 draft, and his brother Barrett was heading into his fourth season with the Tampa Bay Buccaneers. The Patriots made Bo their sixth-round pick in 2008, following their selection of Slater. In two successive picks, New England had drafted second-generation NFL players.

Guyton, Wendell, Ruud, and Slater became fast friends. Each of them had arrived in a different fashion, and they all knew they were the low men on the totem pole. They all were well aware that they were fighting an uphill battle just to make the final roster. During the five grueling weeks of camp, these men supported one another, prayed for one another, and encouraged one another. They shared laughs and they shared their struggles. It was a brotherhood and camaraderie that Matthew would never forget.

Matthew's roommate, O'Connell, had impressed the coaches, but like Matthew, he was concerned about where he stood.

"I don't think I'm going to make it," he confided in Matthew.

O'Connell's career at San Diego State was highly successful, and he knew what it was like to play in a quarterback friendly system. During camp he noted how the offense favored a player like him.

"The offense here is definitely built for the quarterback," he said. "You make decisions and try to put the team in the best possible situations. That's what you've got to learn as a young player, you've got to know what to do and when to do it."[6]

Still, with Matt Cassel of USC and Matt Gutierrez of Idaho State seemingly in line to back up Tom Brady, O'Connell figured his prospects were dim. Matthew didn't see it that way.

"You're a third-round pick," Matthew replied. "You're gonna be fine. You're gonna make the team."

As camp began, Matthew, like most rookies, made a lot of mistakes. Some of them were physical and some were mental. Belichick liked neither kind. Slater describes it as being like a chicken with its head cut off. The effort was there, even if the performance wasn't. But the Patriots kept him on, and slowly, steadily, he made improvements. He showed he could compete, was a hard worker, and was coachable.

August 30 arrived, and it was the day the Patriots, like every team in the NFL, had to pare their roster down to just fifty-three players. Final-cut day. After rookie minicamp, OTAs, and five weeks of summer camp, Matthew felt like he had made significant progress. "I felt at the end of camp like, alright, at least I represented myself in a good way and hopefully left a good impression on our staff and maybe they'd keep me around in some capacity."

Would it be enough to make the team?

"I'll never forget the day of final cuts," he says. "I sat in the hotel room all day. I didn't want to go to the facility and have someone tell me they had to cut Slater. So I literally stayed out of the facility. We had the day off, so I just didn't go in. The way it was explained to me was that if they didn't call you, you just showed up for work the next day, and you keep working."

Wendell made the team. In a surprise to many, the Patriots cut Gutierrez and kept O'Connell as their third quarterback. Ruud did not get cut, but due to an injury, he was placed on IR. He was thrilled.

"Man, they didn't cut me!" he exclaimed to Matthew.

And for Slater, the call he feared would come never did.

"For me to not get the call was fantastic," he recalls.

The Patriots announced their final cuts and their final roster. Matthew's name was on it. The first call he made was to his parents. The three of them celebrated Matthew's success. Jackie, of course, knew what this felt like, but it hit differently when it was his son involved.

Jackie did have some words of wisdom for Matthew, however.

"Remember, son, the work is just beginning," he said.

Back at the hotel, Matthew whooped it up with other teammates who made the final roster. They knew some friends had been cut, but they had also just seen their dream come true. Yet the night was filled with angst as well.

"Now it really counts," he says. "The evaluation continues, and you have to perform every week for your job."

Chapter 8

The Road to New Orleans

Austin Carr settled into his chair in the wide receivers meeting room in the bowels of Gillette Stadium. It was June 1, 2017, and Austin, who had signed with the Patriots following the draft and had made it through rookie minicamp, looked around the room. The Patriots had come off another Super Bowl victory, this time a 34–28 victory over the Atlanta Falcons, as New England came back from a 28–3 deficit late in the third quarter to record the largest comeback victory in Super Bowl history. The team was looking to build on this success, and Austin believed he was going to be a part of it.

Next to him sat Cody Hollister out of Arkansas, another undrafted free agent that the Patriots had picked up less than a month earlier. Hollister's brother Jacob was a tight end out of Montana that was also trying to make the Patriots' roster that year. Malcolm Mitchell, a rookie in 2016 and hero of the previous Super Bowl, was there but was struggling with a bad knee. Mitchell had had an injury-plagued career, starting with a broken leg in seventh grade, and continuing with several meniscus injuries, an ACL tear, and even a fractured hip. He had played a great game in the Super Bowl, but his knee issues had flared up. Still, he was present. Danny Amendola, a stalwart receiver for the Patriots for several years, sat a few rows away.

Chad O'Shea, in his ninth year as the Patriots' wide receivers coach, prepared to start the meeting when the door opened up. In came Julian Edelman, one of the best players on the team. He was dressed in regular clothes and had a backpack slung over his shoulder.

Clearly, Austin thought, *he's not here for this meeting.*

He was right. Edelman was under the weather, but he came to deliver a message to the rookies. After saying hello to O'Shea, he turned to the room.

"Hey rooks," he said, tapping the table in the front of the room. "Have some wintergreen [chewing tobacco] ready for me on this table every day. And have some in your backpack for when I ask for some. You can get some at Sunoco [a gas station nearby]."

With that, he bid O'Shea adieu and left the room. Austin and Cody looked at each other and smiled.

"We had heard about this," Austin says, "so we knew we were going to be alright. We knew we'd make sure to have this."

Austin had been well prepared by Northwestern for life in the NFL, but he perhaps overestimated his level of ability to learn the NFL playbook. He figured that he would take things one day at a time, and whatever the coaches covered that day, being a quick learner, he would simply apply it to that afternoon's on-field workout.

He was wrong.

The Patriots wanted much more out of their players than that. The coaches would go over certain plays and material during the meetings, but on the field, they'd also call out formations and plays that weren't covered in the meetings. Austin found out quickly that the coaches expected the players to do lots of homework, to learn everything. Austin figured he would just keep pace day by day, but he realized that he was already falling behind due to his lack of diligence.

The coaches noticed.

In one session, Jacoby Brissett, the third-string quarterback, called a play in the huddle. Austin wasn't sure where to go. Consequently, he lined up wrong. Offensive Coordinator Josh McDaniels yelled from the sidelines.

"Where the fuck do you belong, Carr?" he shouted.

There was nothing like being singled out by the coaches for not knowing your place on the field.

"You were expected to be studying that on your own," Austin says. "Because I didn't, there would be some calls where I'd be in the huddle and I'd have no clue where to go. That is the number one issue in training camp for rookies, is if you break the huddle and don't know where to go."

It wasn't a one-time thing either. Austin believed he could absorb the material effectively without all the homework. After all, he had been successful in college, and why wouldn't that translate to the pros?

"Looking back, I'm kind of embarrassed, because I didn't apply myself like I should have in those two areas," he says. "I wasn't the go-getter I was in college. So much had come naturally to me at Northwestern."

That did not endear Austin to the Patriots' coaches, who took to making fun of him for being a poor student of football despite having an elite college pedigree.

McDaniels and Belichick laid it on thick.

"Didn't you go to Northwestern, you dummy?" Belichick smirked with an edge to his voice. "How do you not know where to line up?"

Physically, Austin did well. He ran with power and quickness. His hands were good. He was strong in the weight room and was in good health. But his laissez-faire attitude toward the playbook homework came back to bite him.

Conversely, Cody Hollister worked diligently on his football studies and picked up everything the coaches threw at him. Despite having a lesser college season than Austin had the year before, Cody seemed ahead of the curve when it came to picking up the playbook.

Both men found themselves working with Brissett and the "threes"— the third-string unit. Austin did manage to catch passes from Tom Brady, and one in particular still resonates with him. Running a corner route, to the back of the end zone, Austin won the one-on-one rep when Brady lofted a perfect spiral, placed beautifully where only Austin could catch it.

"I'm not sure I've caught a prettier pass in my whole life," Austin says.

They got their work in and tried to follow along as best they could, but the expectations the Patriots put on them were very different from what they had experienced in college.

Belichick had stressed the importance of being on time.

"If you see that there's a storm coming," he told the team, "make your preparations ahead of time and leave early. There is no excuse to be late. No excuse."

Nonetheless, on two occasions, Austin showed up late to workouts.

"Alarm clock issues," Austin told the coaches.

Maybe so, but that didn't stop strength and conditioning coach Moses Cabrera from chewing him out.

"Austin, that's not an excuse," he said. "You have to find out what works for you to get here on time. Can I use that excuse? I have children and have to wake up earlier than you guys. Can I just tell coach, sorry, my alarm clock didn't go off?"

The message was delivered and received, but the demerits began to pile up for Austin. Nobody could be late, and there were no excuses for not being on time for any aspect of camp.

"It was militaristic in a way," Austin explains. "But that's the ship that Belichick runs."

Belichick also routinely quizzed players about the history of the Patriots organization. On the walls of the team facility hung photos of past Patriots greats like Willie McGinest, Adam Vinatieri, and Tedy Bruschi. Statistics and information accompanied the photos.

"These aren't just up for decoration," Belichick explained. "You'd better know who these guys are and what they mean to this organization."

It wasn't just football either. Belichick, whose father, Steve, coached at the US Naval Academy for thirty-three years, expected them to know the difference between Veterans Day and Memorial Day.

"When Memorial Day comes around, I'm going to ask you rookies, and you better not give me the Veterans Day explanation, or I'm going to make you run," he told the team.

Austin's struggles went beyond the playbook. His work on special teams lacked the kind of effort the Patriots' staff wanted to see. He did not have experience on special teams at Northwestern, and his chance to impress coaches in the kicking game during his college all-star performance did not go well. He was a wide receiver, not a gunner on the punt coverage unit. The Patriots saw it differently, of course, expecting players to compete in every phase of the game.

"We're doing these drills," Carr says, "and I wasn't as fast or explosive as I could have been, as maybe I looked on film. I just kind of went through the motions a little bit on these drills. I went the wrong direction on this one drill and Judge[1] ripped me in the special teams meeting. From that moment on, I wasn't worked into the special teams at all."

Discouraged, he needed encouragement. And realistically, a kick in the pants.

During a meal—"The best clam chowder I've ever had"—he sat with Matthew Slater, who spent time trying to lift Austin's spirits.

"Keep at it. You're a good player. Just put in the work," he said.

Running back Rex Burkhead, though he played a different position, offered advice and help with learning the playbook. These men gave Austin what he needed at a crucial juncture of his young career.

In the last full-team practice at OTAs, Austin tweaked a hip flexor. It was painful enough for him to have to sit out some on-field activity. The team had already undergone some depletion at the wide receiver position due to players being banged up, which left fewer guys to take more reps. Edelman, who had come to like Austin, came off the field after running his sixth rep in a row. He was winded, and none too happy.

"I used to like you, A.C.," he said, breathless, his voice with an edge.

At the end of OTAs, Austin stuck around for rookie development. Mitchell was there as well, trying to get more time with the coaches as he struggled with his injuries. In the meeting room, Austin, Mitchell, Cody, and fellow wide receiver Devin Lucien found themselves in a deep spiritual conversation, talking about God and God's expectations for people. O'Shea just sat up front and listened to the men banter. For Austin, this was like his days back at Northwestern, getting into deep spiritual and philosophical conversations with his teammates.

The discussion centered around perceived strict-lifestyle Christians, how much you have to say no to in order to follow Jesus, and whether or not God accepts a person who is living in a way the Bible says is not holy.

The men talked for a while before O'Shea wrapped it up and sent them on their way. Cody and Austin, both strong Christians, spent time debriefing afterward—the "film session" of the conversation, as Austin puts it.

Carr felt like he was in the right place at the right moment, living in the complete fulfillment of God.

"I don't care what happens right now," Austin said to Cody. "I could get cut right this minute. That's so clearly why God wanted us here today. We're living in our purpose right now. God could take me right now."

No matter what happened from that point on, he was content.

Between OTAs and summer training camp, Austin married his sweetheart, Erica, in Chicago. Despite the pressure of providing for another person, he was happy and enjoying his newly married life. It didn't hit him until his honeymoon just how hard OTAs had been on him. It was one of the most stressful experiences of his life.

"It's one thing to be coached hard as a freshman in college, because you know you've got four years still to play," he says. "It's another thing entirely to be coached like that with your job on the line."

And staring at him across the field were people like Bill Belichick and Tom Brady, all-time great football legends. The pressure to perform had never been greater.

He had learned a lot from his OTA experience. He understood what the Patriots expected and how challenging it was. He had somehow survived not being cut after OTAs, and had made it to summer preseason camp. It was a major step in the right direction, one he needed to take if he was to have any NFL career at all. He was, in a real sense, a different athlete heading into camp from what he was during OTAs. He had better study habits, he ran crisper routes, and he caught passes he would not have in OTAs because of his newfound confidence, which came partly from being a married man and partly from what he had learned. Furthermore, he had a newfound confidence in God.

"We walk by faith and not by sight," Austin told himself, choosing to honor God with his play.

As summer camp took off, he found himself running reps against some of the best players in the business: Super Bowl hero Malcolm Butler, All Pro Stephon Gilmore, and starter Eric Rowe.

"These guys are ballers," Austin says. "I'm not by any means saying I'm killing them. But I was dominating my fellow rookies, and I was more than holding my own against the starters. I just believe that I was playing for an audience of one, and that God had me there for a reason. I was making play after play after play."

As the team went through the preseason schedule, Austin's performance picked up. He finished the preseason leading the team—and the league—in receptions and receiving touchdowns. He ran whatever route was called with precision and quickness. His hands caught nearly everything thrown his way. He actually found games to be easier than practice because Belichick's practices were so grueling and demanding.

Fellow receiver Chris Hogan, one of Brady's favorite targets, thought Austin was crushing it in camp. But he also knew there was another gear that Austin could hit.

"Dude, you need to run your routes harder," he said to Carr, noting that it was clear he was running at only about 90 percent speed, which wasn't good for a guy not blessed with 4.3 speed in the first place. For Austin to reach his potential, he needed to light whatever afterburners he had on every play.

The team prepared for the third preseason game of the year, against Detroit. On the opening drive, Edelman tore his ACL, ending his 2017 campaign before it even began. That opened the door for Austin to solidify his place in the wide receiver pecking order. He took full advantage during the last preseason game against the Giants, making several nice catches, including a touchdown.

"I felt like, alright, I'm in, I'm gonna make the team," Austin says.

A couple of days later in practice, the coaching staff made the team run the Hill, a long sloping lawn behind one of the practice fields that the coaches use to condition the team. After making the team run the Hill five or six times, Belichick called them back for an extra round of one-on-one reps. Like everyone else, Austin was not happy, but he took a deep breath and prepared to take his turn.

He figured this was his final test—could he perform at the highest level when exhausted? The coaches wanted to find out. They matched him up against a starting cornerback, veteran Eric Rowe.

"I'm thinking, they're putting me up against Rowe to find out if I'm actually NFL ready as a wide receiver."

He ran four routes and caught passes on three of the four. His session ended and he smiled to himself, thinking that he had just proved himself once and for all against a starting defensive back in the NFL.

In the locker room, players waited to hear from the Turk. Some players—like Amendola or Gilmore—weren't worried at all, but for players like Carr, this was the dreaded moment.

"You see him tap [the] shoulders of different guys in the locker room," Austin says. "You see the guy come back listless and with a trash bag to clean out his locker. You shake your head or comfort him. Guys left and right heading to Coach's office. I'm pretty confident. I scored the other night, and I just beat your starting corner. But you know, anything can happen. I don't *think* I'm gonna get cut today."

Suddenly, he felt a tap on his shoulder, and he turned around. The Turk. His heart sank and he got a pit in his stomach.

Are you serious? Austin wondered.

The Turk led him into the waiting room outside Belichick's office where he sat waiting with fifteen other guys. Austin figured he had to be one of the last guys called into the office. Other players looked at him with surprise. *You too?* their silent eyes asked.

The day before, the Patriots had traded for speedster Philip Dorsett of Indianapolis, but since he played a different kind of wide receiver from Austin, he did not feel that this was of much concern, especially considering how he had performed all summer long.

He was wrong.

Austin was called in. Nick Caserio, the Patriots director of player personnel, sat next to Bill Belichick, opposite Austin. Carr knew what was coming, but expected the delivery to be . . . different. It was not done with malice, but not with warmth either.

"Austin, it's the time of year where we have to trim the roster down to fifty-three," Belichick said, matter-of-factly. "It's never an easy decision. We appreciated how hard you've worked. We thought that you competed and gave great effort, but in the end we have to trim the roster down. We've decided that you're not going to make the final roster. And we don't have room on our practice squad for you, so you can be prepared to leave town soon."

Austin knew that was the signal to stand up and shake Belichick's hand and be on his way. As he considered that for a moment, an odd thing happened. He noticed how blue Belichick's eyes were.

"How random is that?" Austin says, laughing.

But he wasn't about to leave without one question.

"Is there anything else I could have done? Is there something missing from my game?" he asked.

Belichick paused for just a moment before answering.

"I don't think you were competitive in the kicking game at all," he said. "We didn't see you as an asset to us on special teams. And we didn't think you were getting consistent separation from the defensive backs. In the NFL you have to get separation and we didn't see you running routes at that level."

For Austin, the first answer made sense. He knew he had failed in special teams and knew that Belichick valued that. But he still figured he had done enough to make it purely as a wide receiver, which is why Belichick's second reason bothered him.

That's an absolute baloney sandwich, he thought to himself. *I don't accept that. I'm not going to swallow that pill at all.* The insult to injury was that he wasn't even invited to be part of the Patriots' practice squad.

But the decision was made. Austin shook Belichick's hand and made his way back out to the locker room where he found his friend Cody, who had also been cut but had made the practice squad.

"But you're gonna be on the practice squad, right Austin?" he asked.

"No," Austin said, wanting to cry. But there's no crying in football.

Cody was shocked. "Are you serious?"

"Yeah. Looks like I'm moving on."

His wife, Erica, had spent the day at the local church they'd been attending. She was helping out with renovations, and was busy painting a wall. Her phone went off. It was Austin texting.

Looks like I'm getting cut, the text read.

She stopped painting and turned to the pastor.

"Austin is getting cut and we need to move. Sorry."

For someone like Bill Belichick, cut day is among the worst experiences he has as a coach. For as cold as he may have come across to Austin, he has stated numerous times how brutal cut day can be for everyone involved, including the coaching staff.

"The actual process is very difficult for all of us," he said. "Myself, certainly assistant coaches who have established a close relationship with their players and respect for their players because of their effort, work ethic and commitment that they make to the team. But ultimately, 37 of those 90 players can't be with the team."[2]

A couple of days later, Austin heard from the New Orleans Saints, a team that he had considered signing with after the draft. They had shown a high degree of interest in him from the start and had kept an eye on him in case things didn't work out in New England. It didn't take long for Carr to sign a deal and make his way to the Big Easy.

Things were different there, right off the bat. The culture was different and even the way they trained the wide receivers was different.

"When I got to New Orleans, they could tell," Austin says. "I would hop around, because I had a lot of Edelman-isms and Amendola-isms in me that [are] more particular to the Patriots, and it worked there because they have a very specific vision for slot receivers, and I was on track to excel in that. But then I get to the Saints and it's a little more track-and-field, prototypical NFL deal. And it took two years for me to realize that I can't be the Patriots guy here in New Orleans. It's not going to work in this offense."

Austin had made an NFL roster—just not with the team he had anticipated. But he was happy. Instead of catching passes from Tom Brady, he'd be catching them from Drew Brees, another surefire Hall of Famer.

Not bad at all.

Chapter 9

The Playbook

Knowledge is power. This adage is true in football every bit as much as it is in other facets of life. NFL teams want to disseminate knowledge to their players through on-field coaching, film work, and their playbooks. NFL playbooks contain the entire catalog of plays and concepts that teams will use on both sides of the ball. They include the teams' unique "language" that players have to learn.

NFL plays are complicated. Consider this play call in an NFL huddle as shared by former backup quarterback Chris Simms: "West right slot, 72 Z bingo U split, Can it with 58-Lexus, Apple 314 hammer, Dummy snap count on one. Ready, break!"[1] Simms explained what the call meant, breaking it down into four parts. First, there was the formation: "West right slot." Second was the protection: "72." Third was the route concepts the play called for: "Z bingo U split." Last was the snap count, which of course was important if they didn't want to foul up the play before it began.

Simms gave a good idea of how difficult it can be to even get the play right during the frantic moments leading up to the snap. He said, "It's only 40 seconds with a coach screaming in your ear, and then there's only a few really big guys on the other side that want to tear your head off. Other than that, it's a pretty easy job."[2]

In order for a play to work in the NFL, all eleven players on offense (it's the same for the defense) need to know what's going on. They need to be able to recognize what the defense is doing, and they need to understand exactly what the quarterback means by "West right slot" or "Z bingo U split." One miscommunication in the huddle or on the line of scrimmage as the players read the defense can lead to disaster.

For NFL players, learning the playbook is like learning a foreign language. Talented receiver and returner Tavon Austin of the Rams said of his rookie camp in 2013, "I didn't really know what was going on. Everything looked like Spanish and sounded like Spanish to me."[3] Brendan Darby, an offensive lineman out of San Diego State, got a brief cup of coffee in the NFL in 2004 with the Baltimore Ravens during their preseason camp. He described how challenging it is to internalize an NFL playbook: "It's really f***ing hard. I'm not sure many players memorize it per se; it's more about understanding the concepts rather than just knowing every single individual play call. I'd liken it to learning a new language—it's easier to understand the basic structure of it than it is to memorize the dictionary."[4]

Sometimes different teams' playbooks will contain the same language but mean totally different things. It's no different in that respect to human languages. For example, in Spanish, a "burro" is a donkey, but if you ask to ride a "burro" in Italy, you'll get a strange look, since the word means "butter" in Italian. For Peyton Manning, whether with Indianapolis or Denver, "Omaha" meant that they were going to plan B once he surveyed the defense at the line of scrimmage. But other teams use it as a timing mechanism to keep everyone on the same page at the snap.

As Darby pointed out, each team and each coach does things differently. If you play for the same team with the same coaches for several years, it gets easier due to the continuity in the organization. But if you are on a team that sees new coaches come in every year or two, or if you move around to different teams, you have to start over again from scratch. It's not just certain players that needed to know everything in the playbook; it is *every* player's job. And if you don't have it down pat, it could cost you your job. "Everyone needs to know the playbook, not just four positions," Darby said. "I've seen plenty of people get cut on the spot for not knowing assignments."

Over the years players have employed various strategies for learning the playbook. Some players sit and read it, memorizing it page after page. Others need to see it on film or out on the practice field to get a handle on where people are supposed to be. Still others have found it beneficial to have a study partner. Jace Amaro and Josh Tahj Boyd, rookies with the New York Jets in 2014, teamed up to learn the Jets' offense. Ben Shpiegel wrote in the *New York Times* that "Boyd would read a call off a flashcard and Amaro would respond with his responsibilities on the play. They did this over and over again. It took two weeks for Amaro to learn the terminology and the system."[5]

Justin Fields, a 2021 first-round pick of the Bears, has developed his own system. "I think it's just constantly looking over it with flash cards and stuff like that. I've been doing that. Just looking at it. After we meet, going over it 30–45 minutes by myself, kinda just reading over my notes and stuff like that . . . as time goes along I'll get more used to the playbook and I'll eventually know it like the back of my hands. It's just gonna come with time. I used the flash cards for our formations. I just draw up our formations on the flash cards and just look through it."[6]

Eight-year NFL veteran and current quarterback coach Jordan Palmer has offered his advice to players facing the daunting task of memorizing a playbook. He argues that reading it like a novel is a bad way to go; instead, it should be read like a Bible or a cookbook. Learn the material in sequential steps: formations, concepts, protections, and miscellaneous information last. Most importantly, he says, it's crucial that players *own* the information: "A lot of quarterbacks play knowing the system but not owning it," Palmer says. "And if you don't own it, it slows down your process. The ball doesn't come out as quick. You're not as accurate. You're not as sure. When you watch the best quarterbacks play—Brady, Brees, Carson [Palmer]—they're not really reading stuff. They know the offense so well and they know the coverages so well, they're essentially just waiting for defenders to get out of the way so they can throw it."[7]

Fields worked hard to own the Chicago Bears' offense, but he acknowledged that it's quite different from even the complex offense that Ohio State—one of the best teams in college football—runs. "My job of course is to come in here, work hard every day, become the best player and the best quarterback I can be," he said. There were "a few things at Ohio State that we might not have done that multiple teams in the NFL are doing so I'm just kind of getting used to those things and I know the terminology is going to be different here when it comes to different concepts and different protections."[8]

Picking up the playbook came naturally to Geremy Davis. His introduction to the game began as a kid, and between youth football and his games of Madden with his stepfather he was able to see the game clearly right from the beginning. Davis says, "I consider myself to be a smart guy. So the amount of work I had to put in to understand it . . . it wasn't that difficult. Honestly, plays are the same everywhere. Terminology is different. I could show you a play in high school and it could be called 'right P-20 bench,' and in the NFL it's called 'strong right, 300 protection, this, that.' Same play, but more intricate and detailed as you move up the levels."

Every player has his own method for learning the playbook. There were two key elements to Davis's playbook education. "My study habits involved flash cards," he says. "Or I would take the play and I would go outside and just read it and walk what I'm supposed to do. Learning playbooks have never really been a struggle for me because there's one thing for sure: not to say that I'm not athletic, but there's guys more athletic than me. But I've always been like, OK, I'm going to have to beat you in the brains department. I'm going to understand what the X has, the Zebra has, and what the Z has. So now I know all these positions. You might know this one fairly well, but I know the other positions, so if anyone gets hurt, I can play that spot. So that's always been an advantage for me."

In Geremy's football mind, plays are best understood as concepts, not so much by position. Davis understood that he may have been called on to play any number of spots and that learning the entire concept was a critical element to his survival in the league. He says, "I learn plays by concepts. So if I know it's a double slant on this side and a go and an out on the other side, I know what the full field is doing. I think that's what's prolonged my career. There are guys more athletic than me, but coaches know that I'm smart and have a great work ethic and I know all these positions."

Dr. David Redish is a professor of neuroscience at the University of Minnesota, and he has a keen interest in the challenges of learning an NFL playbook, which in some cases can be as thick as a dictionary. Redish specializes in decision-making and information processing, and he has described how difficult it is for a player to take the concept on paper and translate it into action on the field. Essentially, players' brains have two different aspects of thinking that need to work in concert on the football field. First there is the "deliberative system," which people use to make decisions that require a lot of thought, a lot of, well, deliberation. This takes time, and it is the part of the brain that players use to memorize plays and concepts from the playbook. But second, we have the "procedural system," which is a very fast process that people use to make instant, on-the-spot decisions. A quarterback, for example, would engage this system when identifying which defender might be blitzing on a particular play as he sees them in real time.

"The playbook is about memorizing a procedure, but specifically a description of a procedure," he says. "And so the challenge is . . . not only memorizing the playbook but having to translate that memorization into the action on the field. Two different brain systems."[9]

For NFL players, it's much more complicated than simply learning a passage in a textbook. That's because there are eleven players on the other team who are actively trying to trick you, to fool you into thinking you're seeing something that you're really not. Redish puts learning the playbook this way: "It's like trying to play a musical instrument that's scheming against you."

Most NFL teams have all sorts of read-and-react concepts, so even if you have a play memorized on paper, when the other team is acting a certain way in real time, it's much more challenging to decipher. For example, a play might call for what's called an "option route" for a receiver, meaning he can run his route either inside or outside, depending on how the defense is playing him.

If a veteran receiver reads the coverage correctly and runs an inside route against outside leverage, but the rookie quarterback misreads the coverage as outside leverage, and throws a pass to the outside before the receiver actually breaks, the result will be an incompletion at best, and an interception at worst. Of course, sometimes it's the quarterback that reads the defense correctly and the receiver who misreads it, but the result will be the same. Sometimes fans watching the game wonder how a quarterback could throw a pass so badly that only defenders are in the area. Well, this is how.

One key to avoiding these kinds of on-field catastrophes is to have your own team's playbook memorized so you know exactly what everyone is supposed to do. Because of their importance to NFL teams, their playbooks are sacred items. Players are tasked with the responsibility of memorizing them and keeping them safe. NFL teams hope to somehow get a look at their opponents' playbook. Players are expected to keep their playbooks with them and never lose them, or else stiff penalties result. Linebacker Chad Greenway, who played for the Vikings from 2007 to 2016, said, "You always have it with you. That's the one thing that's sacred to football. It has all our secrets."[10]

A typical NFL playbook has far more plays than any team will run in a given game, or maybe even a given season. It contains all the concepts, ideas, and options the team may run at any given point in time. Some playbooks are as much as eight hundred pages, containing everything from basic running plays that get used every week to wild trick plays that a team might pull out once every five seasons. The average team runs between sixty-five and eighty-five plays in a game, but NFL playbooks can have as many as six thousand plays, including all their variations. Moreover, some plays are practiced daily while others are barely ever discussed. Yet players are expected to not only know what they're doing, but also be able to execute it on the field at a moment's notice.

Players will sometimes prank each other with the playbook. A Vikings rookie brought his playbook to the bathroom because losing the playbook constituted an egregious violation of trust. Teammates snuck in and stole it. Michael Bennett, on the Vikings at the time, tells the story: "He laid it down, and they snatched it," he said. "He got up and took off running after those guys with his pants down."[11] And when players are cut from a team, they are expected to bring their playbook with them to the GM's office and turn it in.

For NFL teams, their playbooks contain far more plays than they can possibly use in a game. Teams take their entire selection of plays and select only certain ones to put in that week's game plan for that particular opponent. They will make these choices based on their own personnel (it will matter if they have all three of their tight ends available versus having only one available) and who their opponent is. Weather may be a factor. Any number of variables comes into the equation, and coaching staff put into that week's game plan those things they think will give them the best chance to win that week. So while players are expected to know all the plays, in any given game they are supposed to focus on only those plays in the specific game plan.

It's difficult enough to learn your own team's entire playbook. To learn the playbook of every other team is exponentially more difficult. That's why even though playbooks are sacred and teams want players to turn in their playbooks when they're cut, they understand that their information is going to get out. In 2014, then Cleveland coach Mike Pettine relayed a story of how, when he was the defensive coordinator with the New York Jets, the New England Patriots managed to get the Jets' playbook. Given that it was the Patriots, with all the suspicion surrounding the methods of Bill Belichick, it made national news, giving fans the impression that New England did something underhanded to get information on their opponents.

But Pettine made it clear that he wasn't accusing New England of anything untoward. He said, "It didn't shock me because Rex [then Jets' head coach Rex Ryan] would give them out like candy anyway. He gave one out to [Alabama head coach Nick] Saban, and I was like, 'Don't you know Saban and Bill [Belichick] are pretty good friends? I have a feeling it's going to end up in New England.'"[12] He went on to say, "It's a credit that they have been able to get that information. I didn't mean to imply that it was gathered illegally. . . . To me, it's a sign of a smart team. We're not actively pursuing playbooks, but when they fall into your laps, you'll study it."

Nobody could possibly memorize every other opponent's playbook in its entirety. Moreover, nobody can really know what plays their opponents will put in their game plan for that week. It doesn't mean having the opponent's playbook has no value; of course it does. It may help you learn tendencies, or it may spark ideas for play and concept design that you can incorporate into your own plans. In that sense, it's not unlike one company getting ideas from another. Even if you don't know exactly when they're rolling out their next big product, if you have inside information into their board meetings, you might find they have some great ideas worth using yourself.

Every player, from the star quarterback to the rookie on the practice squad, is held responsible for knowing the playbook. Failing to learn it can result in dire consequences. A top draft pick will of course get more chances to fail than the last guy on the practice squad. For the fifty-third man, the pressure to know the plays is immense, as it could mean the difference between staying on the team and finding oneself suddenly unemployed.

Chapter 10

Opening Night

Players never forget the moment they step onto the field for their first real NFL game. For Geremy Davis, it was with 4:33 left in the first quarter of the first game of the 2015 season. The Giants were at Dallas, and the Cowboys, who had received the opening kickoff, had marched from their eighteen-yard line down to the Giant's 3, where the New York defense managed to stymie Tony Romo and the Cowboys' offense. They had to settle for a short Dan Bailey field goal, and then it was New York's turn to get the ball. The kickoff return team ran out onto the field, and among them was number 18, rookie Geremy Davis from UConn.

The ball was placed at the thirty-five-yard line, and Bailey stood ten yards back, ready to get a running start leading up to his kick. The Giants had positioned their first line of blockers at the 50, and Davis was lined up on New York's far right edge of the first line. His body angled toward the ball, he could see Bailey kick off, but he also had to have an eye on the Cowboy special teamer he was assigned to block. In this case, it was number 57, rookie linebacker Damien Wilson, Dallas's fourth-round pick from Minnesota, who himself had done the hard work to make his first NFL roster.

The Cowboys coverage team got a running start and Bailey boomed the ball high in the air toward wide receiver Dwayne Harris. Immediately, the Giant blockers sprinted all the way back to their thirty-yard line. At that point, Davis spun around and engaged Wilson at the 20 as the kick sailed out of the back of the end zone. Wilson and Davis gently collided, hands pushing out toward each other, but immediately the whistles blew, ending the play. There would be no return, but Davis had just experienced his first play in a regular-season professional football game.

* * *

73

Standing on the opposite sideline were two players that, though they were enemies on this day, were close to Davis's heart. The first was Byron Jones, his teammate at UConn. Jones played four years with Davis in Storrs, Connecticut, and had become one of the better cornerbacks in both the Big East (his first two seasons) and the American Athletic Conference (his last two seasons after UConn switched conferences). He had a well-rounded game and was both a good technician and an elite athlete. But the world didn't quite know the full story on Jones until his remarkable NFL combine, when he ran the forty-yard dash in 4.44 seconds, put up a 44.5 inch vertical, and then broke the world record in the broad jump at 12 feet, 3 inches, besting the previous record by eight full inches.

The Cowboys made Jones their first-round pick in 2015, and now Geremy and Byron were division rivals.

"Byron [Jones] grew up a Giants fan, and I grew up a Cowboys fan, and ironically, we were both on each other's favorite teams," Davis says. "We talked about how our senior year [in college] sucked. I got hurt. He got hurt. And the place where we were living was terrible. I hate to put it this way, but if you're a star player at Alabama or Clemson, your best players are not going to live in the situation like we were in. We were living in a place that was far from campus. Neither one of us had a car. We couldn't talk on the phone inside the house, so when agents would call us, we had to step outside and talk. And it was just kind of a miserable senior year. We were like 2–10. And for us to climb out of that situation and make it and see each other—we both had a sense of gratitude, having come to UConn together, going through all that and making it to the NFL."

The second player on the Dallas sideline that Davis felt a connection with was Tony Romo, Davis's favorite player growing up. Seeing Romo was a priority for Davis. He recalls the minutes before the game, catching a few moments with his former UConn teammate. "So I'm out there warming up, looking for Byron [Jones]. I'm like, 'Yo, bro, we're here, this is crazy.' And . . . I did ask him. I was like, 'So when's Romo coming out?' Because for me personally, him being one of my favorite players, I'm like, on the same field as him. But at the same time, I am locked in. This is my first NFL game. You know, I want to do well."

Romo was an outstanding high school athlete, being an all-state football player for Burlington High School in Burlington, Wisconsin, as well as being a terrific basketball player, averaging 24.3 points, 8.8 rebounds, and 4.7 assists, joining future UConn basketball player and NFL star Caron Butler on the all-county team. The University of Wisconsin–Green Bay recruited Romo to play basketball, but no football scholarships came his way. Yet he chose to play football anyway, at Eastern Illinois.

The Cowboys had signed Romo as a UDFA in 2003, and like other UDFAs, Romo had to earn his spot on the team. He did, but did not get a chance on a real NFL field until the fifth game of the 2006 season, when he threw two passes in a blowout win over Houston. The next week, starting quarterback Drew Bledsoe struggled mightily against the Giants, and at the half, Parcells made the switch to Romo. Down 12–7, Dallas got the ball to start the second half. On the first play from scrimmage, Romo dropped back to pass and promptly threw an interception to Giants' linebacker Antonio Pierce.

Romo would throw for 227 yards, two touchdowns, and three interceptions on that day. It represented the end of the Drew Bledsoe era in Dallas. The Tony Romo era had begun.

Romo would go on to be a superstar, a four-time Pro Bowler. He would have some legendary performances over his career, including a 25–36, 506-yard, five-touchdown performance in 2013 against Denver. He would throw for 300+ yards forty-six times during his career, but in the eight games where he threw for the most yards, he was winless at 0–8. But that ninth game, he won.

It was on opening night against the New York Giants in Geremy Davis's first ever NFL game.

And it was the last great game of Tony Romo's career.

For Davis, it was not only a chance to play in his first NFL game but also his first chance to see his boyhood football idol play in person. Romo had been Davis's favorite player since 2006 when Romo took over for Bledsoe. He appreciated his climb from the bottom of the roster into stardom. He liked how Romo went about his business and made himself into a great quarterback. He loved Romo's confidence combined with his humility. And for nine years, whether he was a young boy, a high school athlete, or a star in college, Geremy Davis rooted for Tony Romo.

And now, in his first NFL game, thirty-four-year- old Tony Romo was about to bury Davis and the Giants.

* * *

The first game for most players is usually a fog. For some, putting on the uniform and walking out onto the field in a preseason game is remarkable enough. But for a regular season game, it's an otherworldly experience. The hours leading up to the game, especially for first-timers like Davis, can feel like an eternity. Required to be there several hours before kickoff, the players arrive at the stadium and begin their pregame routine. Davis had never been in a regular-season NFL game, but he had played in dozens of college, and now NFL preseason, games. He had his own routine to work with. For some players, this involved some treatment by the team's physical training staff. Muscles needed to be massaged, limbs needed to be stretched, ankles needed to be taped. Music was also a key component, and music can be a great unifier or divider in a sports locker room.

For example, on February 14, 2017, the University of Maine campus police were called to handle an incident that took place with some members of the men's basketball team. Senior guard Marko Pirovic had music on in the locker room, and teammate Wes Myers asked Pirovic to turn it down. Pirovic refused, and Myers came over to shut it off himself. That led to a fight between the two, and Myers broke Pirovic's jaw with one punch. The two cooked up a story to try to hide the fact that they were fighting over music, but eventually the truth came out.[1]

But music also has a way of bringing teammates together. Locker rooms may have a designated DJ—a guy who is responsible for the team's mood music. Ryan Riddle, who played two years in the NFL, described it this way: "One of the all-time favorite locker-room prep songs that seemed to pump guys up the most was 'In the Air Tonight' by Phil Collins. Who would have thought Phil Collins would be pumping up NFL locker rooms around the nation? But there is something special about the build-up of the song, which climaxes into an infectious explosion of emotion when the drums kick in."[2]

Everyone has his own routine and habits. Pro Bowl linebacker Brian Urlacher's superstition was to eat two chocolate chip cookies before every game. John Henderson of the Jaguars apparently requested that a staff member slap him before the game. The slap helped him get rid of pregame jitters. Some players would go out and test the field conditions. Others would rest. But eventually, it was go time, and the players came together in the locker room to hear from a captain or a coach.

The NFL has a fifty-three-man roster, but only forty-six are active for any game. Players showing up to the stadium would find out whether they were active or not by looking in their locker. If a uniform was hanging there, they were to suit up and prepare to play. If there was no uniform, obviously they were inactive. Players at the bottom of the roster like Geremy were advised to get there early to find out, because the disappointment of being inactive might be too much for players to bear in front of their teammates.

On September 13, 2015, Geremy Davis stood in front of his locker and saw the white number 18 printed on the back of the blue Giants' uniform. It was his superhero suit. A sign that he had made it. He was active, and tonight would be his first game.

For some players, this was *the* moment when it all seemed real. They were going to put on a real NFL uniform in a real NFL game. All-Pro Chandler Jones recalled the first game he ever played in the NFL, a 1:00 game on September 9, 2012, in Foxboro, as his Patriots hosted the Tennessee Titans. Jones recalled, "I remember touching my jersey. . . . I'm really in the NFL. I grabbed my jersey. . . . I'm an NFL football player. Like . . . this is real."[3]

For Geremy, his first *I really made it in the NFL* moment came on the team bus as it entered the stadium.

"The first thing that comes to mind," he says, thinking about that first moment, "is when I'm on the bus going through that tunnel. I saw the Cowboy fans, and I was like, 'I'm really in the NFL.' And I just took a moment to have gratitude towards the Lord. And I'm not just saying that as a flippant answer. I just really felt like, this is crazy. I'm literally *on* the bus. I'm not outside the bus as a fan or watching on TV. I am like on the bus getting ready to play against the Cowboys."

But then the questions started swirling in his head. Preseason was one thing. This was a *real* NFL game, and he didn't know the routine.

"I just get off the bus, and was like, how does this work? Because it's not the preseason, right? Do I go warm up now? Is it too early? Or do I wait a little bit? So I'm kind of just waiting for the other receivers to get out there. I have a healthy anxiety. I just want to get on the field and move around."

Davis put on his uniform and the team headed out for pregame warmups. The crowd in Dallas's AT&T stadium had already begun filing in. Built in 2009, the stadium was a monumental facility, capable of holding more than ninety-three thousand fans. It also possessed a gigantic screen hanging above the field to help fans view the action. It was a spectacular sight. Davis, of course, had seen it on television many times, cheering for Tony Romo and the Cowboys. But now he was here as a player, as a member of the opposing team.

Davis took in the scene with an appropriate amount of rookie awe: "We come out of the tunnel and people are booing us," he recalls. "And it's another moment where I'm like, I'm really in the NFL, this is crazy."

Just warming up on the field was surreal. Pro Bowler Tyrann Mathieu of the Arizona Cardinals had a similar experience just two years before, and even during warmups found it hard to comprehend what he was going through. "I was nervous before the game," he said. "I actually thought I was going to go out there and choke. I mean, I probably spent the first ten minutes in warmups just, like, looking around the stadium."[4]

On more than one occasion, Davis found himself looking over at the Cowboys' side of the field, watching Romo warm up. He was on the same field as Tony Romo! It was crucial that Geremy go through his warmups properly, but it was difficult to concentrate when his football idol was standing right over there.

As warmups continued, more of the crowd filed into the stadium, and soon it was buzzing with anticipation. This was opening night, week one in the NFL, and the hated Giants were in Dallas to play America's Team. Night games allow for many more hours of tailgating, and in most fan bases this usually means a lot more alcohol has been consumed before kickoff. It was no different in Dallas that night, and as the teams emerged from the locker room following warmups, the crowd was already in a frenzy.

The crowd. It's something you notice, especially if you're not from a big-time football machine like Alabama, Michigan, Clemson, or Ohio State. Seth DeValve, who went to Princeton, made his NFL debut for Cleveland in 2016. He was overwhelmed by the experience of playing in front of nearly seventy thousand people at Lincoln Financial Field, home of the Philadelphia Eagles. DeValve recalled, "My first NFL game ever, whether I was attending as a fan or playing in it as a player. I remember the crowd . . . being just electric. That's what you dream of when you're a little kid. It was a pretty crazy experience, coming from an Ivy League school where you might have a couple thousand people in attendance."[5]

Davis had gone to UConn, which held its games in Rentschler Stadium; it held a maximum of just over forty-two thousand fans. A fine college stadium, it did not come close to rivaling the venues hosting the major programs in college football. So when AT&T stadium was filled to capacity, with ninety-three thousand wild fans screaming at the top of their lungs, Davis was awestruck.

The game itself was a back-and-forth affair. The Giants, on the strength of three Josh Brown field goals and a defensive score by Dominique Rodgers-Cromartie, held a 16–13 lead going into the fourth quarter. They added to it with 8:01 left when Rashad Jennings scored from one yard out, giving New York a 23–13 lead.

Dallas was by this point playing without star wide receiver Dez Bryant, who broke his foot in the second half of the game. Romo needed to engineer a comeback without one of his most formidable weapons. He managed to march Dallas down the field and completed a short touchdown pass to ace tight end Jason Witten, cutting the Giant lead to 23–20 with 5:08 to go, but New York countered with a solid drive of their own, leading to Brown's fourth field goal. And with 1:34 left in the game, Romo and the Cowboys would have one last chance, needing a touchdown to win the game.

Romo had led his team to an amazing twenty-three fourth-quarter comeback victories over his Cowboy career. Davis had seen all twenty-three of them and knew that he had the ability to do it again, even without Dez Bryant available. Davis had played eight snaps on special teams but played no role on defense, so all he could do was stand on the sideline and watch as his favorite football player tried to pin a loss on Davis's team.

"Don't get me wrong," Davis recalls, chuckling. "I wanted to win the game. I wanted to win the game. I did not come there to lose the game. I wanted us to score and put them away. So yes, I wanted to win the game. But as a fan of Romo, and this sounds bad, but I didn't want to win the game at the expense of Romo losing it. So let's say Romo handed the ball off and the guy fumbled. Alright, great. But I was like, I do not want Romo to throw a pick-six or something like that."

After the kickoff, Romo needed to go seventy-two yards and had 1:29 to do it. On the first play, running back Lance Dunbar slipped out to the left and Romo hit him with a short pass. Dunbar, outracing Uani Unga for a twenty-four-yard gain, made it to New York's forty-eight-yard line.

"That's your best receiving back against their middle linebacker," Cris Collinsworth said on the NBC broadcast. "Took advantage."

Romo got the snap on the next play and the Giants' rush nearly got to him. He slipped out of the grasp of a defender and flipped a soft pass to Dunbar again, this time on the right side. Dunbar raced for another sixteen yards, down to the Giant 32. Dallas, out of timeouts, rushed to the line.

He fired the next pass to Jason Witten for another thirteen yards, down to the Giant nineteen-yard line. Romo was cooking. Davis had seen this all before, but now it was happening to his team. And as if he were a fan watching it on television, he was helpless to do anything about it. Except this time, it was happening right in front of him. In person.

Romo threw an incompletion, and then picked up eight yards on a short pass to Terrance Williams on the right sideline, leaving Dallas with thirteen seconds left and eleven yards to gain. Williams managed to get out of bounds so Dallas could at least huddle up. The crowd was in full throat, and Giants defenders were on their heels. Davis was watching a master at work, and he knew it.

Romo barked out signals, and the play clock ticked down, second by second closer to zero. At 0:01, Dallas snapped the ball. It was low and Romo couldn't field it cleanly. He scooped it up, stood in the pocket against the Giant rush, and fired a bullet over the middle to Witten, who reached across the goal line for the go-ahead touchdown. The crowd went berserk. Davis just shook his head on the sideline.

"I'd been a Romo fan for years," he says. "I'm just now on the Giants, and for me, I'm like, 'Wow, I'm watching Romo conduct a fourth-quarter comeback,' which people say he can't do. And when he threw the touchdown to Witten, I was, inside, like 'Bro, that was so sick.' I got to watch that live, right in front of me. I was like, I gotta hide the emotions of being a Romo fan right now. And it's funny because after the game I see Byron and he was like, 'You said it for years that he [Romo] was clutch, and it's crazy—he really does this.' After the game in the locker room I was disappointed because I wanted to win and I wanted to play more, but as a Romo fan, I was happy I got to have that moment to see him conduct a fourth-quarter comeback."

But he still had a job to do. He snapped his chinstrap and headed out on the field for one more play on the kick return unit. But Dan Bailey made sure that there would be no spectacular return, blasting the kick out of the back of the end zone, giving the Giants the ball at their twenty-yard line with seven seconds left. Two plays later, and Dallas was celebrating their first victory of the season. For Tony Romo, it was the last great performance of his career, throwing for 356 yards and three touchdowns. He would get injured the next week against Philadelphia and only play three more games before retiring after the 2016 season.

Meanwhile, for the Giants, it was a disappointing result. After blowing a ten-point lead in the fourth quarter, allowing a last-second touchdown at the end of a seventy-two-yard drive, it would be a long, unhappy flight back to New York, made all the worse by the fact that mechanical issues kept the Giants from leaving until 4:00 in the morning.

But for Geremy Davis, his NFL career had begun. For real.

Chapter 11

First-Game Jitters

For Matthew, the road to the first game began with finding a place to live. After making the team, he quickly had to find suitable housing. He was now drawing a real NFL paycheck and it was time to move on from the hotel. But despite making NFL rookie money—more than he'd ever seen before in his life—he was still aware that his NFL existence was week to week. He knew he needed to be prudent.

Slater describes his situation: "I said, hey, I'm gonna find the cheapest and closest place to the stadium I can, and that's where I'm gonna live." A mile and a half from Gillette, northeast off Route 1 in Walpole, he found a place called the Preserve. It wasn't exactly the Ritz Carlton, but for a rookie just looking to save some money, it worked. It was also close enough to the stadium that it was easy for him to get to and from work.

He rented the bare minimum amount of furniture—a bed, a couch, and a dresser. "It looked like a true bachelor pad," he jokes.

He lived by himself those first couple of years, but even though the league minimum salary for a player on the fifty-three-man roster is much higher than the median yearly pay for American workers, he had no idea how long it would last.

"The reality is, as a rookie, you're doing well, don't get me wrong, you're in the National Football League," he says. "But you're not making Tom Brady money, Patrick Mahomes money, and always in the back of your mind, you realize, hey, my contract is not guaranteed. So if I get cut, I'm not seeing another dime. I don't have any work experience doing anything else, so I need to be as frugal as possible."

Settled in, he began the preparation for his first game.

The New England Patriots opened their 2008 season at home against the Kansas City Chiefs. The Patriots had won nineteen consecutive regular season games, dating back to week fifteen of the 2006 season, when they won their last three contests. Of course in 2007, they went 16–0 in the regular season, becoming the only team in NFL history to accomplish that. But the 2007 season ended in crushing disappointment with the 17–14 loss to the Giants in the Super Bowl. Coming into 2008, however, the team's spirits were high, and they were widely regarded as one of the very best teams in the league again.

The Gillette Stadium crowd was eager for the 2008 campaign to begin. The team had unfinished business ahead of them, and expectations were high.

The Patriots turned the ball over on a Wes Welker fumble on their first possession after driving to the KC thirty-eight-yard line. The defense forced a quick three-and-out by the Chiefs and the Patriots began their second possession on their own sixteen-yard line. Six plays later, New England was right back at the Kansas City 42, with a first-down play coming up.

Brady dropped back to pass, and Chiefs safety Bernard Pollard came in on a blitz. He was picked up by running back Sammy Morris, who took Pollard to the ground. But Pollard fought on, and as Brady stepped up to throw, Pollard dove at Brady's leg. Brady's left foot was planted on the ground as he unleashed a pass downfield to Randy Moss, and Pollard slammed into Brady's left knee. It bent at an awkward angle and Brady let out a scream even as the pass fell into Moss's hands for a twenty-six-yard gain. Moss fumbled and the Chiefs recovered, but that wasn't the story on the play.

Brady lay on the ground, clutching his knee. CBS's Dan Dierdorf made the call: "Kansas City came up with the ball, but that's not the story. Tom Brady took a tremendous hit as he released that ball right on his left leg."

The capacity crowd fell silent. Fans immediately saw their season potentially go up in flames.

It wasn't just the fans, though. The players on the field knew something was wrong. Pollard said after the game, "He was in a lot of pain. When you hear a scream, you know that." Brady came off the field, and though they didn't realize it at the time, he suffered a torn ACL and MCL in his left knee, and he would be done for the season. The promise of a return trip to the Super Bowl was snuffed half a quarter into the season.

For the Patriots, that meant that the game fell into the hands of Matt Cassel, the lightly regarded backup from USC. But it also meant that a lot of veterans had to step up.

For rookie special teams player Matthew Slater, it was a game he'd never forget, for several reasons. The first, of course, was that this was his first ever game as an NFL player. Like anyone, he faced the pregame nerves and anxiety that come with a pro debut. But there were two other reasons why this game was memorable for Slater.

"Most people remember that that's the game that Tom Brady tore his ACL, early in the game," Slater says. "And I've got to be honest with you. I've never played with a player, before or since, with the profile that Tom has. What he meant to the team, what he means to the league, just his overall importance to everyone. For a player like that to suffer a season-ending injury, I was kind of in shock. I was like, what do we do? How do we respond to this?"

He had only been with the team a short time, but he knew how important Brady was to the team and to the NFL as a whole. As a rookie, he had to follow the lead of older players. He, too, had hopes of winning a Super Bowl, and he knew what the injury meant for his team's chances.

But the Patriots weren't a one-man team. They had captains like linebacker Tedy Bruschi, who rallied the team. "Worry about the consequences later," he said. "Whoever's in there, do your job." Leaders like Bruschi helped the Patriots get through the game—a 17–10 victory—but also helped Cassel perform well in a very tough spot. Cassel would finish 13–18 for 152 yards and a touchdown in the win.

"I was thrown into the fire," Cassel explained afterward. "I didn't know what to expect, first quarter of the game of the season, and I'm playing."

Brady's injury opened the door for Cassel to play when it was actually somewhat miraculous that he was even on an NFL roster. He had barely played at USC, being a career backup with the Trojans. His senior year he completed just ten of fourteen passes for ninety-seven yards, with no touchdowns and one interception, backing up future NFL Pro Bowler Carson Palmer. It was unfathomable that his name would be called during the NFL draft, and yet in the seventh round of the 2005 draft, the Patriots selected him with the 230th pick.

When Brady went down, the doctors gave him an examination on the sideline. They were not encouraged by what they found.

"Before the second series," Cassel recalled, "the doctor walks by and says, 'It doesn't look good. I think it's going to be your team for the year.' I was like, uh, could you wait until after the game to tell me this?"[1]

Cassel connected with star receiver Randy Moss on a touchdown that settled him into the game and showed him that he could play at the NFL level. He had sat on the sidelines backing up Tom Brady for three seasons before Brady's knee injury opened the door to give Cassel an opportunity. Thrown into the fire, Cassel handled himself admirably.

Beyond Cassel, the leadership of the Patriots shone brightly, and Slater noticed how effectively guys like Bruschi and others led the team in those dark moments.

"I really saw great leadership on display from the veterans on the team. So that obviously sticks out to me," Matthew says.

But it wasn't just the Brady injury that Slater remembers. In the second quarter, following a KC field goal, they kicked off to New England, and Slater was their kickoff return man posted at their goal line. He received the kick, but he misplayed it and it led to a Patriots' touchback.

"I remember the very first kickoff return that I went back for," Slater recalls. "It was in our end zone by the lighthouse. I fumbled it. The ball hit me in the chest, bounced to the ground. There was a scramble for the ball, so obviously not the way you want to start your career."

It could have been a catastrophe if the Chiefs had recovered in the end zone or deep in New England territory. But the Patriots covered it and ran out the clock to end the half, holding a 7–3 lead. Still, moments like that are terrifying for any player, especially a rookie playing in his first NFL game.

But there was more to it for Slater. He got blown up a couple of times as a blocker on special teams, and on one play trying to cover a kick, he got thrown to the ground. The NFL has no mercy on rookies, and Matthew's first experience on the field almost couldn't have gone worse.

"It was a rough outing, needless to say," he says. "What was even rougher was the following day when Bill [Belichick] had me on film, about four or five clips highlighting my poor play. I'll never forget where I was the off returner, and Ellis Hobbs was deep. I had to go block one of the linebackers and try to open up a run alley. He ran through me like Swiss cheese. And in front of the team, Bill plays the clip. He keeps rewinding it, back and forth, over and over again. He says, 'Here's a tip, Slater. The bigger they are, the harder they hit.' Here I am looking like a grenade went off."

Belichick, of course, is famous for ripping his players in front of the team when reviewing film. He has no mercy, regardless of who is in his crosshairs. That includes Tom Brady. Moss described a time when Belichick tore into Brady in a team film session.

"We were doing two-minute and I was the single receiver," Moss recalled. "Tom Brady gave me the signal to run a 5-yard quick out. Make a long story short, me and Tom didn't connect. For whatever reason, the ball was not caught. The ball was thrown, but it was not caught. Was it his fault or my fault? I don't care; the ball was not completed. So we come in the next day, Bill Belichick puts up the film and basically says, 'Are you kidding me? I have my such and such All-Pro wide receiver, and I have my All-Pro quarterback, and y'all cannot complete a 5-yard out?' He said, 'Tom, I can go down here and get the local high school quarterback to come and complete me a 5-yard out.' And everybody was like, *Oooh*. So basically, when he humiliated Tom, in front of the boys, man, we went out there and put everybody up. I don't care who it was; whoever was on that defense that day, they got it. And that was *practice*."[2]

Chad Ochocinco (Chad Johnson) shared a similar story on FS1's "Undisputed": "Let me tell you what scared me as a player. First day, you know, team meeting. Everybody is coming in. And Belichick, no greeting, no nothing. He puts on the loss to the Jets in the playoffs when they went home early. And he puts it on and rips into Tom. First meeting, no practice. I'm like, is this a joke? From my understanding, you don't chastise your quarterback, and you definitely don't do it in front of everybody. And he laid his [Brady's] you know what out, and I'm like, oh my god. That set the tone right there for me. I was walking on eggshells from that point on."[3]

If Tom Brady didn't escape the wrath of Bill Belichick in film sessions, what hope did a rookie like Matthew Slater have? Still, his memories from that first game are positive, despite these obvious down notes. "Of course," he says, "it was my first real game, and I could always say that I played in an NFL game. My family was there, so that was special."

Matthew's NFL career had begun.

The entire 2008 season was a roller coaster for Slater. In weeks two and three against the Jets and Dolphins, Slater played but did not touch the ball. But in the next three games, he had five kick returns that averaged more than twenty-three yards each. He had slowly begun to figure it out. He credits teammate Larry Izzo for teaching him much about special teams play.

"I just tried to be a sponge and learn as much as I could from a guy like that," Slater said. "I think he's really one of the best players to ever really be a core specialist. I just looked at the way he practiced, the way he mentally approached the game, and I tried to learn as much from him as I could."[4]

But playing in the NFL is not without risk, and Slater ruptured a tendon in his wrist, forcing him to miss two straight games. He wouldn't see the field until week nine, a 20–10 victory over the Bills. In the next game, however, he lost a ball, but the Patriots managed to recover. For a special teams player like Matthew, taking care of the football was job number one. Being careless with it did not sit well with Belichick.

Years later, Julian Edelman would explain Belichick's philosophy when it came to ball security.

"There's a premium for keeping the ball in your hand in New England," Edelman said. "I remember Bill Belichick used to say, 'When you are carrying the football, you're not only carrying the football for the team and everyone in the building, but you're carrying it for everyone in the region. Their fate is in your hands.'"[5]

Mistakes like this were something not to be tolerated even by star players, never mind rookies on a short leash. The Patriots were known for extreme practice habits to reinforce the primacy of ball security.

"Let me just say that my personal coaching philosophy and my mentality has always been to make things as difficult as possible for players in practice," Belichick said in 2015. "With footballs, I'm sure that any current or past player of mine would tell you that the balls we practice with are as bad as they can be—wet, sticky, cold, slippery. However bad we can make them, I make them. I want the players to deal with a harder situation in practice than they'll ever have to deal with in the game. Maybe that's part of our whole ball-security philosophy. I'm trying to coach the team, and that's what I want to do."[6]

Matthew knew the grace period he enjoyed would quickly come to an end if he did not fix this. Not surprisingly, it led to a great deal of stress. Especially when, two weeks later, it happened again.

"I put another ball on the ground against Pittsburgh, and we went on to win that game," he says. "Every week I felt like every Monday after a game, they could be coming to my locker and telling me, 'Hey, Bill wants to see you. Bring your playbook.' That was kind of the way I thought. I thought my spot on the roster was week to week. That's how I was being coached. That's how some of the veterans treated me. I can't say I ever got comfortable that rookie year. I never felt like I could breathe, even if I made a play or two. That was the story of my rookie year. Struggling with confidence, struggling to have a place on the team, struggling to feel like I belong in that locker room. I'd say 95 percent lows, maybe 5 percent highs."

The Patriots played three games in California that year: in San Francisco against the 49ers (a 30–21 win), in San Diego against the Chargers (a 30–10 loss the following week), and later in the season in Oakland against the Raiders (a 49–26 win). Being from Los Angeles, his family got to see him play in person multiple times.

"I don't know how long this is gonna last," he thought, "but my family got to witness me live out my childhood dream and play in the NFL."

Belichick kept him on the team despite his fumble issues, but he removed him from kick return duties and relegated him to coverage units only. Suddenly, Matthew found his stride. The following week against Seattle, he had three special teams tackles, including one with just under three minutes remaining that helped keep the Seahawks in their own end of the field, preventing a last-minute comeback. He would have four more the rest of the season. That allowed him to finish second on the team in special teams tackles with twelve, a point the coaches made sure to make during Slater's year-end exit interview.

The Patriots would finish 11–5, a record that most experts did not believe was possible given the blow they were dealt in the first quarter against the Chiefs. Cassel would go on to throw for 3,693 yards and twenty-one touchdowns, but the Patriots missed the playoffs for the first time since 2002, becoming the first team in NFL history to win eleven games and not make the playoffs.

Matthew recalls that 2008 team with pride. "There were talks that the Patriots should cut Matt Cassel. They should get rid of this guy, just have O'Connell be the backup. But the way he responded when Tom got hurt, and the way the team rallied around him that year, I really saw what a team looked like. That was still one of the best teams I've ever been on. The ability to be selfless and play for each other, and to elevate—you talk about the next man up, the ability of that team to elevate their play under those circumstances, was pretty remarkable."

Chapter 12

Active!

For most players, their first NFL game experience at least takes place in a somewhat "normal" football environment. That is, when flags are thrown and the referee announces the penalty, the crowd typically understands what is happening. The most exciting plays in a normal game are scoring plays—particularly touchdowns. In any NFL stadium with seventy thousand people, of course, some won't understand some of the rules, or won't get what a "down" is. But for the most part, people who spend the money to attend an NFL game have some idea of what is going on. Fans show up wearing jerseys supporting their favorite team and favorite player on that team. Foam fingers signifying their team is number one dot the stadium landscape.

When Austin Carr walked out of the tunnel onto the grass for his first NFL game, he and his New Orleans Saints teammates saw something completely different. The Saints and the Dolphins, their opponent on this cool, damp, October 1 afternoon, looked up at the crowd and saw generic sports jerseys or NFL fan paraphernalia, indicating that the fans were supportive of football and sports, but might not be true fans of either team.

This is really odd, Austin thought. But then he remembered: *Oh right, I'm in London.*

The NFL had been seeking to grow its brand internationally, creating a series of games at historic Wembley Stadium in England. The first game featured the Giants and Dolphins in 2007, and it had become an annual tradition from that point on. American football had become popular enough that in 2013 Wembley hosted two games, and then from 2014 to 2018 that number grew to three. In 2019, the last year before the COVID-19 pandemic, four games were played in London. As with all other things in the world, the pandemic interrupted the NFL world, and no teams traveled to England in 2020. The schedule resumed with two games in 2021.

Earlier in the 2017 season, the Ravens and Jaguars had squared off in London, and the hunger for American football had grown significantly by the time the Saints and Dolphins took to the Wembley pitch in October. There were 84,423 fans packing the stands, cheering every run, throw, and—especially—kick of the ball by NFL players.

The current Wembley Stadium was a 2007 rebuild of the old Wembley, which itself had been built in 1923. Commissioned to host the British Empire Exhibition in 1923–1924, it was—shockingly—completed early, and it quickly became the site of most major outdoor sporting events in England. This included the annual championship match of the famed F.A. Cup final of British soccer, as well as the main stadium for the 1948 London Summer Olympic Games. Soccer great Pelé once said of it, "Wembley is the cathedral of football [soccer]. It is the capital of football and is the heart of football."

The very first event to take place at Wembley was the 1923 F.A. Cup final between Bolton and West Ham. Crowds far exceeded expectations—and Wembley capacity, which then was one hundred twenty-seven thousand—and the fans spilled onto the pitch. Unsure what to do, organizers delayed the start of the match forty-five minutes, until George Scorey, a constable, rode around the grass on a white horse, gently pushing the crowd away from the playing surface. For having saved the day—the match was a 2–0 Bolton victory—the nearby foot bridge near the stadium was named for George and his horse Billy: the White Horse Bridge.

Old Wembley closed in 2000 and was demolished, paving the way for the spectacular new stadium, featuring seating capacity for ninety thousand spectators. In comparison to the £750,000 (about $61 million 2022 USD) cost of building the original, the new Wembley came with a price tag of £798 million ($1.57 billion 2022 USD), making it one of the most expensive stadiums ever built.

Austin had come to New Orleans after being released by the Patriots at the end of training camp, a bitter pill to swallow for a guy who thought he did enough to at least make New England's practice squad. Arriving in the Big Easy, he found himself in the same locker room as another all-time great quarterback, Drew Brees. To Austin's surprise, Brees was approachable and friendly.

But Carr had not gotten off on a good foot with the Saints. When Austin arrived, he immediately immersed himself in the work of the job—staying in shape, learning the playbook, trying to be the best player he could be. He wanted to earn a wide receiver job with the Saints. One thing Austin did not do was take the time to develop relationships with the rest of the

New Orleans' receiving corps. He had not gone through camp with the Saints, and they viewed him as an outsider. Austin failed to make a real effort to get to know his teammates and foster the kind of bonding that is so important in an NFL locker room.

"Looking back, I was like, man, these guys aren't warm to me. Part of it was that I didn't go in trying to win people to who I was. I was more like, OK I'm here now, let's get to work. I wasn't actively trying to make friends, which was my mistake."

Brees was different. Right away, the two had at least a somewhat amicable relationship. Brees was the leader of the team and the face of the franchise. Yet he was humble and cared for his teammates, whether they had been with him for years or just arrived, like Austin. He and Austin shared in common the fact that they both played college ball in the Big Ten Conference, and could relate to one another in the experiences of playing Michigan in the Big House, or going up against perennial powerhouse Ohio State.

One reason the other receivers didn't take too kindly to Carr was because Head Coach Sean Payton immediately schemed up a small handful of special plays designed to get Austin the ball in the red zone. Payton knew that opponents would key in on certain players deep in their own territory, and he wanted to take advantage of what he suspected their focus would be. The first week Austin arrived, plays were drawn up to go to Austin. For other receivers, this was a bit of a slap in the face. *After all,* they thought, *who is this new guy who didn't go through camp with us? Who is this rookie? He's a Patriots' guy even!*

It was well understood that if you were a Saint, you were a Drew Brees guy, not a Tom Brady guy or an Aaron Rodgers guy or a Peyton Manning guy. Austin had spent the summer with Brady and the Patriots, not with Brees and the Saints, and he was not, in a way, one of them. Yet he was going to get touchdown opportunities in the red zone? It didn't compute. Naturally, they weren't exactly enthralled with Austin.

Carr had never been to Europe before, and London represented a brand-new world for him. When NFL teams travel, players room with each other in the hotel, and nobody not associated with the team is allowed to enter the circle. But for this trip, the Saints allowed players' wives to join them. Austin's new wife, Erica, took time off work to fly to England and be with Austin, and in the week before the game, they took in many of the sights and experiences of London.

They spent time in Piccadilly Square. They took photos in front of some of the more than 250 statues scattered throughout the city. They did high tea at the famous Harrod's Tea Room. They ate at a traditional English pub.

Perhaps the highlight of the week, however, was when they visited a church and jumped in with a small group Bible study in the city. It was amazing for them to experience a shared faith with people from another part of the world, to enjoy Christian fellowship with men and women from Great Britain, and to dig into the scriptures together. Erica had been figuring out how a job with Athletes in Action might work as an NFL wife, and she was encouraged by these Christians in London.

Austin wore his Saints gear, of course, and all of London knew that the NFL had come to town. They also knew that the New Orleans Saints were not a British Premier League soccer team, so when they saw Austin, they knew that he was one of those "American footballers." For Austin, this is when he felt most like a pro football player.

"I felt like an NFL player more when I was off the field than when I was on it," he says. "That may sound weird, but my on-field NFL career wasn't exactly one that filled the stat sheet, but when I walked around and people saw me with my Saints gear on, and they knew I was a pro football player, but didn't know that I was the last man on the roster, that's when I most felt like I was a real NFL guy."

On the field on October 1, the Dolphins and Saints went through their pregame warmups. It was a homecoming of sorts for Dolphins' running back Jay Ajayi, who was born on June 15, 1993, in London. He had been injured during his prior visit to Wembley two years earlier. The English crowd, which had grown fond of the Dolphins back in the 1980s when British television began broadcasting NFL games, loved Ajayi. But more than anything, they were just there for the spectacle of professional American football. Austin looked up at the crowd, scanned the field, and realized what he was in for.

"There was that moment warming up in the pregame, and I was like, OK, this is it," Austin says. "In my mind, I was the kind of guy who was focused on my role. Don't make this a big deal. Just go out and do your job—that was ingrained in me by Bill Belichick. My role wasn't a major role, but I still wanted to be laser focused on my responsibility."

Austin's opportunity to play had come—as it does for so many players—due to the misfortune of another player. Willie Snead had been New Orleans's primary slot receiver for the first two years of his NFL career, with sixty-nine receptions for 984 yards and three touchdowns in 2015, and seventy-two receptions for 895 yards and four touchdowns in 2016. But he had broken his foot prior to the 2017 season, and, to make matters much worse, had been suspended for drunk driving back on June 11. He was due to return for the Miami game in London, but tweaked a hamstring, leaving Payton frustrated.

"I hadn't earned anyone's respect yet. I was filling in for Willie Snead, who had been their slot receiver. Coach Payton decided, you know what, I'm gonna go with Austin and see what he can do. His closed door became my open door."

His assignment for the game was primarily special teams and to be ready for those particular red-zone moments when his number would be called—those plays that irked his fellow wide receivers. In terms of special teams, they were asking him to do things he had done very little of in his entire career, like rushing the punter on the punt return team.

"Oh that was weird," he says. "I hadn't done really any of that either at Northwestern or in New England."

Austin felt like he was in over his head. It wasn't about the speed of the game or the knowledge of the playbook, both of which he felt fully prepared for. It was being put in a strange position with little to no experience, and this in his first ever NFL game.

The Saints had lost their first two games of the season in 2017, to Minnesota by ten and New England by sixteen. In their first divisional game in week three, they finally got things in gear and trounced the Carolina Panthers, 34–13. The Miami game would prove to be an important test, especially given where it was played.

Austin stood on the sidelines, in his first NFL game, played on foreign soil in a country he'd never been to, having learned a brand-new playbook, being asked to do things he'd never done before, with no real friends on the team.

But . . . he was about to play.

What he didn't expect was for his back to hurt. He had spondylolisthesis, which is when a vertebra can slip forward, causing intense pain. Typically the condition is solved by fusing the vertebrae together or by removing the part of the bone that causes the pressure. In the third quarter, on a punt return, he aggravated his back, causing sharp pains, the kind that made him think he might be done for the game.

"That was the low point of the day," he says. "Thinking that I had to take myself out. My one shot, my one chance, was being blown because of my back condition flaring up. I was like, I can't play like this. I need to say something."

The next thing he knew, someone handed him two Advil.

"I put that down my gullet," he says, "and I was good. It's funny, because that basically was the solution for me that enabled me to finish the game."

English fans of American football had come to love the sport, but especially the kicking game.

"You know what really gets 'em going?" Austin asks with a smile. "When we punt. Man they LOVE that."

Every time the officials threw a penalty flag and the referee turned his microphone on to explain the call, the Jumbotron flashed with an explanation of what the penalty was and why it was illegal.

In the fourth quarter, with Austin's back in good enough shape to play, the Saints made it down to the Dolphin red zone, up 13–0. It was time for Payton to call Carr's number. It was designed to beat tight man-to-man coverage, and the Dolphins showed that exact defense as the Saints lined up.

"We actually did get to the five-yard line, and we ran my play," he recalls. "And it didn't work at all. The defense swung back to where I was going, switched to zone. My read was completely off."

The play blew up and standout Dolphin defensive end Cameron Wake sacked Brees for a seven-yard loss, pushing the Saints back to the Miami twelve-yard line. On the next play, Brees shoveled a pass to running back Alvin Kamara, who scampered in for a touchdown to put the game away.

In the locker room after the game, the players were jubilant. It was a big win coming in difficult circumstances. For Austin, it was a moment to celebrate.

"I actually played a part in us winning," he says. "It was a big game for us, and I was a part of that. I had finally contributed."

As he saw it, he had, for the first time, made a deposit in the bank account with the organization and—especially—his teammates. He had done his job and helped the Saints get an important win. He rejoiced with his teammates in the aftermath of the victory.

"Obviously those first two weeks weren't what we aspired to be," Brees said to reporters after the game. "We played two real good teams, the Vikings and Patriots. Basically now, two road wins—I felt like we had a great plan coming out here. Obviously it's a tough trip coming across the pond."

While it was a success for the Saints, the feeling from London newspapers wasn't as cheery. Reporter Sean Ingle of the *Guardian* wrote, "For years, Americans have been told that to truly love soccer they must learn to appreciate a 0–0 draw. At Wembley on Sunday the New Orleans

Saints and Miami Dolphins served up the equivalent for British NFL fans—an error-riddled, penalty-strewn, stodgy stinker of a match between two teams the wrong side of average. And yet, curiously, 80,000 people seemed to find it a good enough way to spend three hours as the Saints won the second London match of the season 20–0."[1]

But that didn't matter to Austin or the Saints. A win was a win, and for Austin, he finally felt part of the team and a real part of the NFL.

Chapter 13

The Best Athlete You've
Ever Known

Fans say really dumb things all the time.

"That guy sucks!"

"He can't throw to save his life."

"He's terrible at football."

"I can't watch him anymore. He's absolutely awful."

Fans say these things about actual NFL players, and it should only take a brief moment to realize how ludicrous these statements are. Geremy Davis is not considered fast for an NFL wide receiver, even at his improved forty-yard-dash time of 4.47. But consider just how fast that actually is in real terms. Davis, at top speed, can run 18.3 miles an hour. That may seem slow when you're driving a car, but rest assured, that is incredibly fast for a human to run. Let's put that into perspective.

Eliud Kipchoge holds the world record for fastest marathon run, at 2 hours, 1 minute, 9 seconds, a mark he set in Berlin on September 26, 2022. That means that Kipchoge was averaging 12.9 miles an hour—over 26.2 consecutive miles. He averaged 4.39 minutes per mile. Now to give you some sense of how fast *that* is, a men's Division 1 track and field program likely wouldn't even give a high school runner a look if he can't run faster than 4.25 for a mile. That's for *one* mile. How many regular people can run that speed? If you think you can do that, I'd encourage you to try; 4.25—even 4.39—is incredibly fast for a normal person. That's why these Division 1 programs will only consider male athletes who can post these times. This is elite-level speed. And Kipchoge basically runs that for 26.2 miles.

So when you think about how fast 12.9 miles an hour is, think of it in those terms. You have to have nearly Division 1 speed in order to run one mile at the pace that Kipchoge runs a whole marathon. Now Kipchoge is the fastest ever to run the marathon, so it may seem unfair to compare any-one to him. But just understand how fast he's really moving. For a human being, running 12.9 miles an hour is really fast. He's basically running at what would be the top sprinting speed for 99.9 percent of the human race.

In fact, at the Chicago 2018 marathon, people had the chance to run on a specially designed treadmill that simulated Kipchoge's running speed. Runners were invited to see how long they could keep up Kipchoge's pace.[1] The vast majority of people couldn't even keep it up for two hun-dred yards. Most people fell within seconds because the treadmill swept them away. Forget about the ridiculous stamina needed to run that many miles at that pace and just focus on the speed Kipchoge was running. Most human beings can't keep up Kipchoge's speed for more than a handful of steps. And that's "just" at 12.9 miles an hour.

Geremy Davis, who was drafted in the sixth round and is not considered fast for an NFL wide receiver, ran 18.3 miles an hour. Now Davis, not being a marathon runner or a cyborg, could never keep that speed up for 26.2 miles. He couldn't even keep it up for two hundred yards. But 18.3 miles an hour is so much faster than 12.9 miles an hour, and 99 percent of people can't even do 12.9 miles an hour for more than a handful of steps. Geremy Davis is so much faster than virtually everyone who is reading this book it's not even funny.

Clay Travis is a controversial and outspoken commentator and football gambling guru. He spent three months training for the NFL combine in 2008, in an attempt to learn what these athletes go through. His eyes were opened to just how good these guys are.

He wrote an article in 2014 explaining why these athletes are supe-rior to normal people. Travis wrote, "Now that the NFL combine is here and everyone is glued to the NFL Network watching the combine on television, I always think it's worth bringing some reality to all the couch warriors out there who think they could break a 5.0 in the forty. Newsflash—you can't. Not even close."[2]

He set up a forty-yard dash challenge with his radio show in Nashville, Tennessee, and dozens of people showed up to try to run a sub-5.0 forty. The results? One person—a former college baseball player who was the fastest guy on his team—broke 5.0. Most didn't even break 6.0.

Even big guys in the NFL are fast. Really fast. Travis trained in 2008 with Geoff Schwartz, a six-foot-six, 335-pound offensive lineman from Oregon. Schwartz was drafted by Carolina in the seventh round, and it took him a year before he saw any NFL game action. He started a couple of seasons but mainly served as a backup lineman in the league for four teams (Carolina, Minnesota, Kansas City, and the New York Giants). So by most measures he had a successful NFL career, but he was never "great" by NFL standards.

Schwartz's best forty-yard time was 5.36, which is a speed of 15.3 miles an hour, significantly faster than Kipchoge's marathon pace that most people can't even attain, but it's three miles an hour slower than Geremy Davis's top speed. And Schwartz is an enormous human being. Ninety-eight percent of people in the world are shorter than six feet, two inches, and Schwartz is six-feet-six. In the United States, just 0.1 percent of people weigh more than 300 pounds, and Schwartz is 335, or was when he played in the NFL. He is in the top 1 percent of Americans in terms of overall size. And yet he can run at a speed that would leave the overwhelming majority of people in the dust.

Back to Davis. At six feet, three inches, 216 pounds, he is also a huge man. He's even big by NFL wide receiver standards. Seventy-two percent of Americans weigh less than 200 pounds, so even as sculpted as he is, he's still heavier than most people in the United States. For a man that size to be able to run 18.3 miles an hour is mind-boggling.

Davis isn't just big and fast though. He's incredibly strong. He managed twenty-three reps of 225 pounds in the bench press during pre-draft workouts. To give you an idea how impressive that is, it is estimated that 0.1 percent of the overall population can bench press 225 pounds. Of people who regularly lift weights at the gym, 40 percent can bench press 225 pounds—once.[3] These are the people who are focused on weight training and in many cases have personal trainers and workout programs. In other words, these are very fit people looking to get stronger. And just two out of five can get 225 pounds off their chest.

Fifty-two offensive linemen showed up for the 2015 NFL combine, and thirty-seven did the 225-pound bench press drill. Davis's twenty-three reps was as good as, or better than, fourteen of them. He was also better than ten defensive linemen. In other words, Davis, a wide receiver, was roughly at the lower end of the middle of the pack in terms of strength for the very strongest players in the sport. He wouldn't be considered a strong offensive or defensive lineman, but he certainly is stronger than many at those positions, which require incredible strength to move 300-pound men.

So Davis is bigger than most people. He is much faster than almost anyone you have ever known. And he is also stronger than all but the tiniest percentage of people, even stronger than many players who play the power positions in the NFL. But what about skill? How does his skill translate in real terms?

To give you an idea how hard it is to catch passes from an NFL quarterback, consider the story of Lance Kearse. In 2013, Kearse—cousin of longtime NFL receiver Jevon Kearse—tried out with the Jacksonville Jaguars. Now, Lance was an excellent athlete, having had a highly successful Division 2 basketball career at Eckerd College following a stint at Virginia Commonwealth University. At Eckerd, he made fourth team All-American, averaging 16.2 points a game. Anyone who makes a Division 1 basketball roster and is an All-American at the Division 2 level is an excellent athlete.

Former Florida running back Earnest Graham encouraged Kearse to try out for the NFL. At six feet, six inches, 245 pounds, he had the ideal size to play tight end in the NFL. Some of the more successful tight ends in the league were former basketball players, like Antonio Gates and Tony Gonzalez. One reason for this success crossing over from basketball to football is that to be a good basketball player, you have to have good, soft hands. You have to be able to catch passes of all kinds—low passes at the ankles and high passes over the head, soft arcing passes and bullet passes, passes on the run and passes surrounded by three other players in traffic. You have to be able to catch bad passes too—passes that are thrown way off target that you still need to grab.

Kearse had those good hands. His big, soft hands allowed him to catch all kinds of passes, grab lots of rebounds, and shoot the ball with a feathery touch. But he found catching a football from NFL quarterbacks to be on another level of difficulty.

He described what it's like: "Let me explain this to you. Catching a ball from an NFL quarterback is like catching a rock, a hot lava rock. Like, it burns. When it hits your hand, it hurts. With the gloves on too. As it's coming to you, it sounds like a train. You know how the Nerf ball sounds and it makes that whistle? It has a sound behind it. It's like, oh my god, these guys."[4]

Jeffrey Crampton played college football at Yale University in the 1980s. When asked what it's like to catch a football thrown from an NFL quarterback, this is what he had to say: "It's painful, and you can't do it. . . . You can't imagine what it's like. Having your strongest friend throw to you from 10 feet away won't do it, even if he played QB in high school. It's not close to the velocity or impact from a real NFL quarterback."[5]

In order to throw a football, quarterbacks put immense spin on the ball. This spin allows it to cut through the air accurately, similar to how a rifled barrel (with grooves that make a projectile spin) allows guns to shoot more accurately than smooth-bore barrels. In fact, the development of rifled barrels gave militaries a huge advantage over their enemies because of the greatly improved accuracy. Not only do quarterbacks impart a lot of spin, but they also throw the ball hard. The average NFL quarterback throws a football 54 miles per hour. Imagine standing on the side of the road and a car comes by at 54 mph. It's going to whiz by you. Now imagine a one-pound object whistling through the air at that speed, that is rotating ten times a second—that's as fast as an electric screwdriver. This means you not only have to deal with the straight-line velocity of the football coming right at you, but also the rotational velocity of the ball as it spins. The laces rotating like that can leave players' hands with deep cuts.

During Lance Kearse's tryout, he managed to catch almost all the passes thrown his way. That's because he's a tremendous athlete. But those were in drills, not during live action. Geremy Davis was an outstanding receiver, almost never dropping a pass in college. He didn't have many chances in the NFL regular season to catch passes either, but he converted most of them. In the first game of the 2018 preseason for the Chargers, Davis made a spectacular touchdown catch down the left sideline. NFL veteran Geno Smith threw a high arcing pass to Davis, who was running at top speed. Davis then leapt over the defender, caught the ball at its highest point, and somehow managed to keep both feet in bounds. When he landed, he shook off the defender and went into the end zone for the score.

This singular play demonstrated Davis's elite speed, size, leaping ability, hands, strength, coordination, and awareness. It was a catch that, simply put, almost nobody you know could make.

The reality is that the average person doesn't understand or appreciate just how much better these professional athletes are than the rest of us. Fans watch a football game and see a quarterback throw an errant pass to what looks like a wide-open receiver, and say, "That's terrible. Even *I* could have completed that pass." Or they watch a 94 mph fastball right down the middle of the plate and see the batter swing and miss, and say, "How can you miss *that* pitch?" The unspoken assumption is that of course even average Joes could hit it.

Fans don't have any comprehension of the difficulty of these scenarios.

Andrew Joseph, writing for *USA Today*, drives the point home: "It never ceases to be hilarious whenever a regular person believes they can challenge a professional athlete in their given sport. The answer is always a resounding, *No, you can't.* Pro athletes are so absurdly good at their sports that regular people can take for granted just how amazing those athletes are whenever they miss a shot, strike out, shank a tee shot. The worst player on an NBA team was likely among the best players ever at his college and is a legend at his high school."[6]

To even get recognized as a high school athlete is difficult. There are roughly three hundred thousand seniors playing high school football each year. Of those, just under thirty-six hundred receive any stars (one to five, five being the best) by the various ratings services. That's 1.12 percent. The rest don't receive any stars and cannot even hope to play Division 1 football unless they somehow make it as a walk-on. In the Power 5 conferences, virtually every player playing any real snaps is at a minimum a three-star recruit. Only 1,328 out of 300,000 seniors (0.44%) receive three stars. Only 380 receive four stars (0.13%), and a mere 30 receive five stars (0.01%).[7] Some entire states have never had a four- or five-star player graduate from high school at any point in history. Geremy Davis, from Norcross High School in Norcross, Georgia, was a three-star recruit, the number 166th nationally ranked wide receiver in the class of 2010. He was the 100th ranked prospect coming out of Georgia that year, and was number 1,341 overall in the United States, regardless of position.[8] That put Davis in the top 0.4 percent of all high school seniors playing football in the entire country that year. Since talent tends to not be evenly distributed geographically—some areas have far more Division 1 talent than others—Davis would have been far and away the best football player in the history of the vast majority of high schools in the country. In most high school conferences, he would have been that utterly unstoppable player that just destroyed everyone he faced.

Geremy Davis is far and away a better athlete than any that most people have ever met, or will ever meet, in their lives. Sometimes a little perspective is needed for fans of all pro sports.

Chapter 14

Injuries and Setbacks

Football is an incredibly violent sport, designed for full contact between large men running at incredible speeds. Watching a high school football game up close can open one's eyes to frightening collisions between bodies hurtling through the air. In college, the players are bigger and faster, and thus the force generated when players crash into each other is greatly magnified. And in the NFL, it's far greater still, as the Darwinian process of selection has brought the biggest, strongest, and fastest players to the pro game.

Like so many of his college teammates at the University of Miami, tight end Kevin Everett had dreams of playing in the NFL. He had a modest career at the "U" after transferring from Kilgore Community College in Texas, but he showed enough athleticism that the Buffalo Bills selected him with the 86th overall pick in the third round of the 2005 NFL draft. Everett arrived at rookie minicamp a few days later, not yet having signed his contract. But Everett did sign an agreement with the team protecting him against possible injury during camp.

Buffalo had high hopes for the six-foot-four, 241 pound Everett. During rookie minicamp following the draft, on Friday, April 29, Everett made a reception—Buffalo had hoped to see a lot of that in the years to come—and turned to run. Unfortunately for him, his cleat stuck in the turf, putting a great deal of force on his left knee. The pain from the twisting motion felt to Everett like he had been stabbed with a knife, and he crumpled to the ground in agony. At first, it appeared that the injury might not be as severe as feared, but the team sent him to get X-rays and an MRI. Coach Mike Mularkey announced that the team would wait for those results before making any call on Everett.

But the MRI revealed that Everett had torn his ACL—a common injury among football players, whether from contact or even without it—and surgery was planned for later in the week. Everett's agent, Brian Overstreet, issued a statement: "It's a setback, no doubt," he said, "but Kevin will overcome this. He still has a very bright future in the league. And the Bills have been terrific with him. He is still a big part of their plans."[1]

As it turned out, Everett would miss his entire rookie season, but that didn't keep him down. He rehabbed and got back into playing shape and found his way onto their fifty-three-man roster for the 2006 season. He played in all sixteen games, including four starts, and became a key man on Buffalo's special teams. He entered the 2007 season with high hopes for a significant role with the team.

The first game of the season saw Buffalo hosting the Denver Broncos. At the half, the Bills held a 7–6 lead, and Everett, aside from blocking and playing special teams, contributed one reception for three yards. Denver would receive the second-half kickoff, and Everett lined up in his customary spot on the kick coverage unit.

Rian Lindell, the Bills' kicker, booted the ball to the goal line, and Bronco receiver Domenik Hixon caught the ball and began to run upfield. Everett raced downfield, zeroing in on the Bronco returner. Everett squared Hixon up, and the two elite athletes collided with brutal force. When a two-hundred-pound defender crashes into another player running at 4.56 speed (in the forty-yard dash), it can generate as much as sixteen hundred pounds of tackling force.[2] Football pads and helmets are designed to distribute this force more evenly, hoping to prevent catastrophic injury when players meet like this.

But it wasn't enough.

Everett's helmet struck Hixon between his helmet and shoulder pads. Instantly, Everett was knocked out cold and his body went completely limp. He fell to the turf face first and lay there. The whistles blew and everyone on the field knew right away that something terrible had happened. The crowd at Ralph Wilson Stadium knew it too. They sat quietly, a dull murmur of concern permeating the stadium, waiting for Everett to get up.

He didn't.

Buffalo's medical staff rushed to the field to check on him. Assistant athletic trainer Christopher Fischetti said later, "The initial assessment was that Kevin was not able to voluntarily move his extremities."[3] Medical staff immobilized him and gently put him on a gurney. An ambulance drove out onto the field and Everett was loaded in and taken to the hospital. Doctors determined that he was paralyzed due to his spinal cord being dislocated in his neck, being broken between the third and fourth vertebrae.

"It's probably the hardest thing I'll ever have to go through . . . watch a teammate go through something like that," Bills' punter Brian Moorman said. "You see that happen—it's really tough. I hope it's the last time I ever have to choke back tears on the playing field."[4]

As soon as Everett arrived at Millard Fillmore Hospital, doctors applied a new procedure. They injected his body with a solution of icy saltwater, in hopes that the sudden cold would prevent swelling, fever, and further nerve damage. Their goal was to get his body temperature down to just ninety-two degrees.[5]

It didn't work at first, as Everett's body temperature remained at ninety-eight degrees overnight. They operated on him and tried the cold treatment again, and this time it worked. Doctor Andrew Cappuccino realigned Everett's neck, and a plate and two metal rods were put in place to hold his head steady. Cappuccino announced that it was likely that Everett would be wheelchair-bound for the rest of his life.

Later, Everett explained Cappuccino's position: "He was just going off of past research on the injury. I couldn't expect him to say anything else but what he said because he didn't know the outcome. Nobody did," Everett said. "I was just hoping for the best. We were giving everybody the worst-case scenario."[6]

After the surgery, Everett's mother, Patricia Dugas, sat with him. Everett was on life support, and Dugas reached out her hand and touched Kevin's arm. She asked if he could feel her hand and Everett, to Dugas's stunned amazement, said yes.

"I can't even explain it to you; he's like a miracle," she would tell the *Ledger*.[7] It wasn't long before Everett could wiggle his toes, move his ankles, elevate his leg, and extend his elbows.

Dr. Kevin Gibbons, supervisor of neurosurgery at Millard Fillmore, explained, "The patient's made significant improvement. But no one should think the functions in his legs is close to normal. Not even close. . . . If you ask me, 'Would he walk again?' I would tell you that I wouldn't bet against it. But he has a long way to go."[8]

In fact, Everett would regain partial mobility in his hands, legs, and toes within days after the surgery.

"I have to be honest," Everett would later say. "In the beginning . . . I was like, 'Wow, why did this happen to me?' But I just prayed, and God just calmed me and let me accept it for what it was."[9]

Having already overcome a torn ACL, Everett was determined to attack this rehab with determination. For five months, his mother and Wiande

Moore, then his fiancée and now his wife, encouraged him. His physical therapists pushed him.

A month after surgery, he took his first steps and just two weeks after that, he was able to stand without any assistance.[10]

Cappuccino gave a lot of credit to the revolutionary cold therapy they administered to Everett right away. "I will hang a good portion of my belief in this recovery on cold therapy," Cappuccino said, "because we don't normally see this recovery in people with spinal cord injury."[11]

Years later, Everett is walking, and he and Wiande are parents. But obviously he never played football again. He has been able to reflect on his journey since that time. Everett said: "Sometimes I catch myself lying back in my chair with my eyes closed tight just thinking about playing. It's something I can't get over just quite yet, especially when I'm watching football. I was trying hard to block it out in the beginning, but it's coming stronger now. I was blocking out the whole 'not being able to play again,' but I see it and I just come back to thinking about it. I'm still really in love with the game."[12]

In 2008 author Sam Carchidi worked with Everett on a book titled, *Standing Tall: The Kevin Everett Story*, and Kevin has been an inspiration to so many people who have suffered debilitating injuries.

His time in football ended the moment his head collided with Hixon's. But his career wasn't the only one impacted by his injury. Hixon was never the same either. He harbored massive guilt for what happened, similar to how a soldier can feel guilt for being the only member of his unit to survive combat.

"I was devastated," Hixon said. "It was one of those things that I talked to my parents about giving up football after that happened. I was just like that's not what I want to play for. I just felt so bad that I changed someone's life like that. I wondered about just giving up on football. The next three games after that, it was bad. I was having nightmares."[13] He deteriorated so badly that Denver released him shortly thereafter. The Giants picked him up, and he had the chance to meet Everett on December 23 in a game against Buffalo. Everett had made his return to the stadium to walk publicly for the first time. The two had a chance to talk, and Everett assured Hixon that it wasn't his fault. That meant the world to Hixon, and it changed how he approached the game and life thereafter.

"Being able to meet him when we went up there to play . . . he was a huge influence on me and he changed my life, and just a God fearing man and Christian," said Hixon. "He changed my life then and I finally started . . . I felt like I played like myself."[14]

The Bills would end up releasing Everett, mainly so that he would receive the benefits due him per the collective bargaining agreement between the NFL Players Association and the league itself. The team said the decision was hard but was in the best interest of Everett. "Kevin will always remain a Buffalo Bill in the same way that Jim Kelly, Thurman Thomas and so many others before him are held in the highest regard by our franchise," they said in a statement.[15]

Most players do not suffer the kind of injury that befell Kevin Everett, thankfully. As violent a sport as football is, that is a rare event.[16] But players are prone to all kinds of other injuries. Everett's first major injury, a torn left ACL, was something that's much more common in the NFL. Oftentimes torn ACLs occur as a non-contact injury, the result of a violent action in the knee. The New England Patriots lost star receivers Wes Welker in 2010 and Julian Edelman in 2017 to non-contact ACL tears.

The most common body part to get hurt in football is the knee, followed by the foot and ankle. More than 30 percent of all injuries involve ligaments of some kind—ACL, MCL, PCL in the knee, and lateral ligaments in the ankle. Next comes the head, with concussions making up more than 7 percent of all injuries. Concussions are particularly problematic due to the increased likelihood of chronic traumatic encephalopathy (CTE), which can lead to erratic behavior, increased aggression, and even dementia.

Boston University conducted a major study on the connection between CTE and football. Published in the *Journal of the American Medical Association*, researchers found that CTE existed in 99 percent of all brains of NFL players they studied, 91 percent of college football players, and even 21 percent of high school players.[17] CTE is considered to be a major factor in the Aaron Hernandez murder/suicide tragedy.[18]

While the NFL deals with the serious and potentially life-altering issue of concussions, lesser injuries can still sideline or end careers. Superstars generally don't lose their jobs due to injury, but the same can't be said for fifty-third men. Bill Belichick has said that the most important ability is availability, and if a player on the NFL bubble isn't available, teams generally can find suitable replacements.

That puts tremendous stress on players at the bottom of NFL rosters. If Patrick Mahomes breaks his hand, Kansas City would need to replace him in the short term, but they aren't about to cut him and move to another quarterback. For a player like Marcell Ateman, however, an injury can mean the end.

Largely thanks to the COVID pandemic, 2020 was a hard year for everyone, both in and out of the world of professional sports. Marcell Ateman had a great camp that summer, coming off his 2019 season in which he played eleven games for the Raiders. In the last preseason game, Ateman was on the punt return unit, and his responsibility was as a blocker. As the kick descended to the Raiders' punt returner, Ateman rushed to make a block. His left hand got tangled up on the play, jammed between him and another player. In an instant, he felt a pop and a sharp pain.

He thought he dislocated his finger, but X-rays determined that he broke his hand.

Oh man, I hope I don't have to have surgery, he thought. The doctors told him that surgery was unnecessary, but he would be out for a while as he rehabbed. The team put him on IR.

"That's the game of football," he says. "You never know what's going to happen."

Marcell did the rehab work, went to meetings, studied film and the playbook, and watched practice, everything he was expected to do. He wasn't allowed to travel or stand on the sidelines during games, however. That made him feel like a walk-on back in college.

He got mixed messages from the team. The trainer encouraged him to take his time with rehab. As a receiver, he could only be effective if his hands were functioning properly. The coaches, however, gave him a different vibe.

"When are you coming back?" they'd ask him.

Marcell knew he wasn't a star in the NFL. He was eager to get back and pick up where he left off, but he also knew he would be useless if his hand wasn't healthy. The pressure mounted.

"I didn't have the luxury of waiting," he says. "I was like, the minute I'm good, I will be right back in there playing."

When all was said and done, he missed the entire season, and left his future uncertain. When 2021 opened up, Marcell was finally healthy, but training camp had changed dramatically. The Raiders had brought in John "Smoke" Brown from the Buffalo Bills, and Willie Snead from the Ravens. In Marcell's experience, camp was all about rotating players and giving everyone a chance to prove themselves. Who had improved? Who took the leap forward in development? Who was in or out of shape? Who clicked in the offense? These were all questions camp was designed to answer.

It was immediately clear that this was not the vibe of 2021 Raiders' camp. The Raiders' coaching staff seemed to be working to get everyone on the same page as quarterback Derek Carr. Understandably, they were feeling pressure themselves, having come off a string of unsuccessful seasons. Marcell found himself on the outside looking in.

"I felt like I was behind the eight ball right from the start," he says. Similarly, veterans Brown and Snead, who signed thinking they were going to be regulars in the wide receiver rotation, were restricted to playing with the backups.

After one practice session, Brown said to Marcell, "Man, I've never been through this. I've never experienced a training camp like this, not even getting a chance to compete." It was discouraging for all three players.

After the second preseason game, the Raiders cut Ateman. They brought him in on practice squad but released him shortly thereafter. Then, two weeks later, the Raiders brought him back and activated him for the week-nine game against the Giants. They cut him again and put him back on the practice squad through the end of the year.

Equally frustrated, Brown requested his release, and the Raiders honored that request by cutting him at the end of August. In the middle of the season, Snead requested his own release, and the Raiders let him go on October 26.

Marcell looks back on his situation and smiles while shaking his head. "I was playing well," he says. "It was so tough, but I was trying to see what God had for me in it. Sometimes you question things. I was *this close* to making the team before this happened."

In 2022, the Cardinals suffered numerous injuries in their receiving corps, and called Marcell in to participate in camp. He had wondered if he'd ever get another call from an NFL team, so naturally he was excited. Furthermore, it gave him a chance to be with his son, who lived with his mother in Arizona and was just starting the school year.

Marcell knew they really just needed a "camp body," but he figured, "I'm just gonna give it everything I've got. I've got nothing to lose. Whatever happens, happens. I understand how the business works."

The Cardinals kept him in camp for a couple of weeks, but soon cut him. Marcell realizes his NFL career is likely over, but there's a piece of him that still dreams of playing again.

"I still hope for it," he says. "I still pray for it. I still work for it. God can do anything. It showed me that even when you least expect it, God can make something happen in an instant. And on the flip side, it can be taken from you in an instant too."

His career was on a nice trajectory until his hand injury. After that, it was all downhill. So did the broken hand cost Marcell Ateman his NFL career?

He's not sure. But, he says . . . "It didn't help."

Chapter 15

Hammies

One injury that plagues players is a pulled or torn hamstring. Football is an explosion sport, meaning that players go from dead stops to sudden bursts of speed. Hamstrings act as a sort of brake, working to decelerate knee extension as the lower leg moves forward during a stride. In some athletes, the muscles are too weak to slow this forward movement. In others, the quads (the front muscle of the upper leg) are much too strong for the hamstrings, creating an imbalance. In others still, the glutes—the base of power for running—are underdeveloped and it puts too much strain on the hamstrings.

It's not just football players, of course, that deal with hamstring injuries. Sprinters also suffer from these, which makes sense given the nature of that sport—it is also an explosion sport, as athletes go from being still to accelerating to top speed in a very short space of time. In 2017, Canadian sprinter Andre De Grasse had to pull out of the World Championships because of a hamstring tear. He "felt a pop in his right hamstring," indicating that his muscles tore in lightning-fast fashion.[1] Usain Bolt fell on his leg of the 4x100 meter relay with a hamstring injury and had to be wheeled off the track.

One of the problems with hamstrings is that they take a long time to heal properly. A 2007 study on sprinters with moderate hamstring injuries showed that 20–55 percent of the original injuries had not properly healed even after six full weeks.[2] In sprinting, competitions don't come around all that often, so missing six to ten weeks of training, while problematic, still gives most sprinters (De Grasse being an exception, of course) time to run in the next race.

For NFL players, it's different. There is a lot of pressure to get on the field and stay on the field. "You can't make the club from the tub" is an NFL idiom, meaning you can't stay in the league if you can't manage to fight through injury and play. For practice squad players, or guys at the bottom of the fifty-three-man roster, this pressure to get out on the field is enormous. Their NFL lives depend on their availability.

This means that players often rush back from an injury, or they take shortcuts in order to get "good enough" to play. Studies have shown that 16.2 percent of NFL players who have hamstring injuries reinjure themselves. Teams understand that when players hurt their hamstrings, it's going to be some time before they're ready to go. Former head coach Lovie Smith said, "If a guy has a hamstring injury, he's going to be out a while. I could have come up here and said 'day-to-day,' which most people do with hamstring injuries. It doesn't work like that."[3]

During his senior season in college, Geremy Davis suffered an ankle injury that kept him out several games. But that didn't worry scouts. It was during the NFLPA Bowl that Davis felt that something wasn't right with his hamstring.

He managed to recover and get through his first camp with the Giants. But the injury lurked in the background. During his first season, his last game action came against the Patriots in week ten, a 27–26 loss in which he played thirteen special teams snaps. Following the game, he was put on the inactive list each game for the remainder of the season.

During the Giants' 2016 camp, Davis played regularly with the first unit and was playing well.

"Right now, I'm just having fun," Davis told reporters. "I'm enjoying being back in football. Obviously, I was inactive for the last six games [of 2015], so it feels good to actually put on pads, put on a helmet, and play the game and be around the culture with the players and just play football."[4]

He was working on specific aspects of his game that the coaching staff had pointed out to him. "I think each year I just increase fundamentally and technique-wise," he said. "There's still some tweaks. I'm never going to be perfect. But that's why it's good that we have film and stuff. We go back and learn. Just little things—I'm a tall guy, just staying low, getting in and out of breaks, the position of my body on certain catches. That's what I've been told and what I've been trying to work on."[5]

Davis had several highlight-reel catches during camp, but soon he experienced the pain in his hamstrings. They were hurting and were impacting his performance. By the end of camp, the Giants had made a decision. They couldn't keep Geremy on the fifty-three-man roster, and on September 3, they released him. James Kratch, reporting for *NJ. com*, wrote, "Davis made strides in the offseason program and at the start of training camp, but he was hampered by a hamstring injury for much of the preseason as players like [Tavarres] King and [Roger] Lewis passed him by."[6]

Even his final preseason performance (three receptions for thirty yards against the Patriots) wasn't enough. The Giants, needing healthy bodies, cut him and shortly thereafter placed him on the team's practice squad. With that demotion came a loss of status and money. Davis would have to work his way up from the bottom.

The NFL, though, is a land of opportunity. The Giants at this point saw Davis as a practice-squad player, but the Chargers saw him differently. They signed Geremy off New York's practice squad on November 9, 2016, and put him on their fifty-three-man roster. He was inactive for the first four games with the Chargers, but was active and played in the last three games of the year. Now with a new team, he had another chance.

His second season with the now Los Angeles Chargers in 2017 was an up-and-down affair. On September 3, he was waived and signed to their practice squad. On September 11, he was brought up to the fifty-three-man squad and activated for their opening game against Denver. Davis played thirteen snaps against the Broncos, and then five days later was waived and re-signed to the practice squad. A little over a month later, on October 26, he was brought back up to the active roster, but was put on the inactive list for each of the next four games. He was active but didn't see any game action in week thirteen against Cleveland, and then was inactive the rest of the year.

In 2018, Davis had his best year as a pro. By this point, he was healthy and had become a stalwart of special teams. He had finally settled into his role on the team and felt comfortable about his place in the NFL. Of course, he wanted to get more snaps as a receiver, but special teams was a good way to make a living in the league.

He started 2019 the same way, averaging fourteen special teams snaps a game. He even got some action as a receiver. In week four, he caught two passes for twenty-five yards. "It was just fun being out there," Davis said after the game. "Just actually being in the huddle with Phil. Seeing how he orchestrated us from a field standpoint, but ultimately helping him get the win. . . . It was just fun."[7]

But soon he was put on the inactive list, and Geremy knew why. The hamstrings were back, and they were barking. He was inactive for three straight weeks before the Chargers put him on injured reserve before week thirteen. He had been listed as "questionable" with a hamstring injury but didn't recover in time for the game. Needing the roster space, the Chargers elected to end his season due to the injury.

He became a free agent after the 2019 season, and Detroit showed the most interest. On March 30, 2020, he signed a one-year contract with the Lions. Geremy was excited for a fresh start with a team that really seemed to value him.

But it was not to be. Davis's hamstrings continued to plague him, and right before the season, Detroit had no choice but to release him. This was a serious test of Geremy's faith.

"Transparent here. I was annoyed with the Lord, you know?" Davis explains, "Even jumping ahead a little with Detroit—I always felt that with Detroit, I had favor with them. They wanted me there. And my hamstrings were just so messed up. And I remember venting to the Lord, like, 'Lord, Jehova Rapha [the Lord that heals], you have the ability to heal me, but you're choosing not to. Why?' I was drafted by the Giants and played a bit with the Chargers, but I felt like Detroit actually *liked* me, you know? They wanted me there. With the Chargers I felt respected—the coaches knew I was always one of the last ones to leave the building, always doing extra stuff. But liked? I don't know. But Detroit liked me. And I felt like I could establish myself there finally. But God was choosing to not heal me. He's sovereign, right? Romans 9, He's sovereign, but he's choosing not to. But the scripture that he put on my heart was John 13:7, when Jesus told his disciples, 'You don't understand what I'm doing right now, but later you will.' So it gave me a sense of peace because I got cut after that [by Detroit]. And what I'm doing now [talking about his faith in podcasts he produces weekly] it all started in Detroit when my legs were messed up, I was proclaiming the gospel more than I ever did in my life."

Injuries cost Davis several games during his senior year of college. They cost him a spot on the Giants' active roster following camp in his second season. They cost him after he had his best season ever with the Chargers. And once again they cost him a chance to play with the Lions during what may have been his last crack at the NFL. The injuries proved to be too much for Geremy to overcome, even if they did produce other kinds of fruit in his life. The fruit of faithfulness. The fruit of patience. The fruit of trust. The fruit of faith. The fruit of authenticity. Geremy's character was growing, even if his NFL career wasn't.

Of course, injuries are a huge part of life for professional athletes in all sports. Injuries impact superstars and fringe players alike. Star wide receiver Wes Welker tore his ACL on a non-contact play just prior to the playoffs in 2010. NBA star Gordon Hayward suffered a horrific leg injury in the first quarter of his first game with his new team, the Boston Celtics,

on October 17, 2017, dashing his hopes for a great season with the legendary franchise.

But the pressure to be back playing is lessened when you are a star
making guaranteed money. For borderline players like Geremy, being
unavailable due to injury can be the difference between making the team
or not. He often felt the pressure to push through despite knowing that
his hamstrings could pop at any moment. This pressure that Davis—and
others like him—experience often comes with serious mental health
repercussions as well.

Dr. Samantha O'Connell, a Boston-based clinical psychologist, and Dr.
Theo Manschreck, a professor of psychiatry at Harvard Medical School,
published an article in a 2012 issue of *Current Psychiatry* titled "Playing
through the Pain: Psychiatric Risks among Athletes." They pointed out
that while non-injured athletes suffer depression at rates consistent with
the general population, and while participation in sports can help protect
athletes against various forms of emotional and mental distress, "researchers have found that injured athletes experience clinically significant
depression six times as often as non-injured athletes. Injured athletes
also exhibit significantly greater anxiety and lower self-esteem than non-
injured controls immediately after injury and at 2-month follow-up; those
with more severe injuries are more likely to become depressed."[8]

They point out that athletes feel pressure to play despite being injured
because they may have a scholarship (in the case of college athletics) or
paychecks (in the case of professional athletics) on the line. A poll among
Division 1 athletes showed that at least half of them felt pressure to play
while injured.

At the professional level, it's even worse, especially in the NFL. Even
stars can be replaced, but there aren't many players at the top of the food
chain. The number of players in Geremy's situation—borderline fifty-
three-man roster players—is countless. To not play because your hamstring doesn't feel right means to risk your job—maybe even your NFL
career. But to play with injured hamstrings is to potentially suffer a major
injury anyway. It's an incredibly difficult spot to be in.

Davis's injuries were severe enough that he couldn't play. It's not like
he isn't a tough player. During his career, he experienced many major collisions, including one in his rookie year against the Patriots. New England
had gone ahead in the last seconds on a long Stephen Gostkowski field
goal, and, trailing by one point with just the kickoff left to go, the Giants
needed a miracle. The plan was to keep lateraling the ball as long as possible, hoping that a running lane could open for someone—anyone—to

return it for a touchdown. With one second left on the clock, there wasn't time for anything else.

Gostkowski kicked off and after a lateral, a Giants' player fumbled the ball and it rolled near Geremy. He grabbed it and saw Patriots' special teamer Jonathan Bostic bearing down on him. He also spotted teammate James Morris on the other side of the field and, trying to keep the ball alive, threw it across the field to Morris. As he released the ball, he got absolutely lit up by Bostic and was driven to the MetLife Stadium turf. The play would fail, but it was a huge hit that would put many people out.

Davis describes the play this way: "I got crushed. I got crushed. The special teams coach said, 'Whatever you do, don't end the game with the ball in your hands.' So I see the ball [after a lateral and a fumble] and I have to get this ball because we're trying to just some miraculous play to score. I get it and I'm trying to run, trying to not get tackled with the ball, and I throw it, and while I'm in mid-air, boom, I just get hit hard. I didn't feel it, but I *felt* it. That was my last play because I was inactive after that for the last six games."

Geremy Davis was a tough football player, able to absorb enormous hits from huge, fast NFL players. But there was nothing he could do about his hamstrings. No amount of stretching or weight training or therapy could keep them from troubling him. And with the lingering injuries hitting him throughout his career, teams needed to choose other, healthy, players. Davis's hamstrings cost him his NFL career.

And even for a man of great faith, it was a lot to bear.

Chapter 16

Learning the Ropes

Scott O'Brien had spent seventeen years in the NFL. From 1991 to 2001, he served as a special teams coach for three organizations: Cleveland, Baltimore, and Carolina. During that time, he developed a reputation as one of the finest special teams coaches in the league. Following the 2001 season, the Panthers elevated him to assistant head coach in addition to his special teams duties. His 2003 Carolina team faced off against Bill Belichick in the Super Bowl, a tight, dramatic contest won 32–29 by the Patriots on a last-second field goal by Adam Vinatieri.

He spent 2006 in Miami as the assistant to Head Coach Nick Saban, and then in 2007 and 2008 served as Denver's special teams coordinator. Well-traveled, with many years of diverse NFL experience, O'Brien had demonstrated an ability to get the most out of his players.

Following the 2008 season, Patriots special teams coach Brad Seely moved on, and Belichick hired O'Brien to replace him. It was a move that would have a huge impact on Matthew Slater.

The Patriots had been pleased overall with Matthew's rookie season, yet Slater did not at all feel like his place on the team was secure. "I was on pins and needles until probably my tenth year," he says. "So that never changed. My mentality in terms of my role and my comfort level didn't really change a ton." Every year he knew he had to prove his value to the team.

He wasn't even sure that the team believed he was a good player. They knew he had a good work ethic and good physical ability. But could he really be the next special teams ace they were looking for? It was clear he was not going to contribute much, if anything, in the passing game. He was listed as a wide receiver, but that was in name only. He was purely a special teams player, so in order to give them the value they wanted, he needed to be excellent at this unique role.

The year did not start out well for Matthew. He had surgery in the off-season, and then in preseason, he dislocated his elbow. He missed the first two games of the season, finally making his first appearance of the year in week three against Atlanta. By now, Brady was back, having recovered from his ACL injury, and the Patriots were expected to contend. That meant that all three phases of the game had to be high level, and that put a lot of responsibility on Slater. Larry Izzo had departed, and Sam Aiken was the new special teams captain, but O'Brien put more and more on Matthew's plate.

"When we hired Scott," Matthew says, "I had never really had a coach probably since high school that believed in me the way he did, and that was from the beginning. The way he spoke to me, the way he challenged me, and the belief he showed in me. He told me he thought I could become a big-time player."

What he saw in Slater was tremendous leadership potential. Despite his soft-spoken nature, Slater demonstrated the drive and commitment to being the best he could be. He took well to coaching, and showed a passion for all aspects of the game. Not only did Matthew verbally inspire his teammates, but he also demonstrated the qualities the Patriots looked for in their players. O'Brien knew that Matthew could be pushed to higher levels, and he began to work with him to attain it.

"For him to show that belief in me my second year in the league, based on how my rookie year went, really gave me a boost. It was very intentional, you could tell. He saw something in me but knew I needed to be challenged in a unique way. In 2009 he began to bring the best out of me."

When Matthew made it on the field in week three, O'Brien gave him responsibilities he never had as a rookie. Slater was given the freedom to make checks in the kicking game, which required he have a total grasp on what was happening. Checking into a wrong coverage could prove disastrous, and for a team with championship aspirations, those kinds of mistakes were unacceptable. O'Brien—and Belichick by extension—had put a great deal of trust in Matthew.

He began to have a voice on the field that he never had before. His teammates looked to him for leadership, which was not common for a second-year player. O'Brien made it clear to the rest of the team the trust he had in Matthew.

"Slate's going to be one of the leaders of special teams," he told the team. He pushed Matthew to the forefront and coached him in a way to give him a great deal of confidence.

The Patriots ended up with a disappointing 10–6 record, which included a crushing 33–14 loss to the Baltimore Ravens at home in the Wild Card round of the playoffs, marking the fifth straight year that New England had failed to win the Super Bowl following their third title in four years. The pressure began to mount for the entire organization. No longer were the Patriots the plucky underdogs that upset the mighty Rams in Super Bowl XXXVI. They were the premier team in football and carried the weight of lofty expectations year in and year out.

For Matthew, the transition to his third year was the most critical time of his career. Brian Flores was part of the special teams coaching staff, under O'Brien. The special teams lacked a captain, however, with Aiken moving on after the 2009 season. It seemed natural for Matthew to slip into the role, but the Patriots did not name Slater captain. He had all the responsibility that came with captaincy, but not the title. Matthew believed he had grown enough to take that on.

"We didn't have a special teams captain that year, and it kind of bothered me," he says. "Scott was asking me to do everything the past captains had done—lead the players' meetings, become the primary signal caller on the field. But they didn't want to name a special teams captain that year. On a personal note, it kind of hurt because I felt like I was ready to lead."

The Patriots went 6–1 in their first seven games, but Slater got off to a slow start. In weeks four to six he had no special teams tackles, and he was inactive for week seven. Over the next four weeks, he accumulated three tackles, but it was still a struggle. He had grown in his understanding of the game and what he was asked to do, but the results on the field weren't what they could have been.

The coaches, however, continued to see progress in his game, and in week thirteen, the New York Jets came to Foxboro for a Monday Night game. The Patriots blasted the Jets 45–3 and with the win, New England improved to 12–2 and looked once again like the class of the NFL. Slater had one of his best games of his career, totaling three special teams tackles and generally being all over the field in the kicking game.

The next day, Flores pulled Slater aside to talk.

"I watched the film of you play last night," he told Matthew. "That's what we need from you. That's the player you've gotta be. If you can make plays like that consistently, I'm telling you, you can be a Pro Bowl player in this league."

For a player who had just been looking to make the roster every year, this comment blew him away. He was still operating like it was a battle just to make and stay on the roster every year.

"I knew that my standing on the team was the same. I was a special teams player, and I knew I had to earn my roster spot every day. But I can do it! I believe that I can do this."

This belief that he could not only stick in the NFL but actually be a top-tier player began with Flores's comments and grew during the rest of that season.

"I'll be honest with you," he says. "I never thought about being a Pro Bowl player, but it was those two men [O'Brien and Flores] who really instilled that belief in me, that I could maybe do something special in this league."

The Patriots continued to roll through the rest of the regular season, and entered the playoffs as a major threat to win it all. But disaster struck in the Divisional Round as they lost to the same Jets they had blown out a few weeks earlier, 28–21. It was one of the most inexplicable losses in the Belichick/Brady era in New England.

"I'll say to this day," Matthew recalls. "I don't think we were one of the best teams in the league. We were *the* best team in the league. That team in 2010 was one of the best teams I've ever been on, including the ones that won championships. I believed that we were going to win the Super Bowl that year. A lot of us did. To lose to the Jets in the divisional round was painful. It added to the doubt that had been creeping in of whether or not we could ever get back to the level of 2004 and win another championship."

The season suddenly was over, and it was time to take stock of what had happened, both for the team and for Matthew personally. He had accumulated sixteen tackles and had led in every way on the team. It was easily the most productive year of his short career to that point, and one that showed he had the potential to be a star in the league.

"That was when I finally figured out how to play the game," he says. "By the end of 2010 I was a different player than I was when I came into the league in 2008."

After the 2010 season, the NFL experienced a labor dispute, and the owners locked the players out from March 12 through July 25, 2011. Players were forbidden to practice or even work out in team facilities. That put Matthew in a strange spot. He had a decision to make—would he stay in Massachusetts or head back to California. He decided to return home.

"After my third year, we get locked out. I said to myself, I'm not going to pay for an apartment and be locked out. So I put all my stuff in storage, gave up my apartment, and moved back to my parents' house. I spent the entire offseason training and living at home with my mom and dad."

The lockout lasted about eighteen and a half weeks, during which time players like Slater just tried to stay in good shape. When it ended with the two sides agreeing on a new collective bargaining agreement, Matthew had to figure out his living situation.

"Once that lockout was over, I came back and thought, I'm not getting an apartment," he says. "I made a little bit of money, but it wasn't like I could just sail off into the sunset. What I'm going to try to do is see if I make the team, and if I do, figure out my housing situation from there. I make the team, and I have a week, week and a half, to figure out my housing."

Not surprisingly, he made the team and more than that, he was elected captain by his teammates. Given how disappointed he was in 2010 with the team having no special teams captain, he felt fulfilled and honored by his teammates.

Ryan Wendell found a house for rent, just two miles south of Gillette Stadium, on Payson Road in Foxboro, and he talked with Matthew and third-year player Julian Edelman about living together.

"Hey if the three of us split this house," he told them, "we can all have a room and a bathroom."

That sounded like a good plan to Matthew and Julian, and the three of them paid a thousand dollars for a fully furnished house, utilities and cable included.

"I was like, alright—we're in!" Matthew recalls.

Chad Johnson (then Chad Ochocinco), a Pro Bowl wide receiver from Cincinnati, had been acquired via trade in the offseason, as New England sent the Bengals a 2012 fifth-round pick and a 2013 sixth-round pick. Ochocinco had agreed to restructure his contract to accommodate the deal. For Christmas that season, Ochocinco bought Slater a gift card to Best Buy, and he bought a big-screen TV with it.

On the field, Slater grew into an elite player, compiling a whopping twenty-four tackles, most on special teams, including eighteen solo. He also forced a fumble and, to top it off, made the first (and only) catch of his NFL career, a forty-six-yard bomb from Tom Brady in the first game of the year against Miami, helping the Patriots to a 38–24 win over the Dolphins.

During the 2011 season, Matthew received a handwritten letter from Dolphins special teams coordinator Dave Fipp. In it, Fipp praised Slater for his leadership and performance on the field. It was a sign of utmost respect for a rival coach to speak so glowingly and in such a personal way to an opposing player.

"I'll never forget it," Slater said. "Because I've had great conversations with coaches over the years, but he's the only person that's written me a handwritten note. Every time we play Dave, I remember that. And I'm super thankful for men like that, who have encouraged me even if I haven't worked with them directly, but they've been supportive."[1]

By year's end, Matthew had been voted to the Pro Bowl, the first of what would become ten such selections. Two of those (2016 and 2019) would also include All Pro selections. Matthew had gone from fifty-third man to a bona fide NFL superstar.

In 2020, Belichick gushed about Slater.

"I can't think of anybody that's done more than he has and that's done it over a very consistent period of time at an extremely high level, in addition to all the other qualities that he brings off the field—leadership, just doing the right thing, just the person and the human being that he is. But, his competitiveness on the field . . . he's a great teammate, just outstanding in all areas. It would be hard for me to imagine anybody going ahead of him. We've had some great players here and I've had some great players through my career—in Cleveland, going back to the Giants—but, he's certainly the very best that I've ever been around and that we've had to play against, as well. His consistency is outstanding, but he factors in on a lot of plays."[2]

And in 2022, Belichick would elaborate further. "Certainly Matt Slater will go up there, in the kicking game, with Brady on offense and (Lawrence) Taylor on defense. So I feel very, very fortunate to have had the opportunity to coach all these players, but I'd say those three in particular."

In terms of leadership, Slater would become a stalwart captain year in and year out for the Patriots. He had grown from wide-eyed rookie to on-field leader to overall team leader, second maybe only to Tom Brady on the team's leadership pecking order.

Current Patriots' coach and former middle linebacker Jerod Mayo recently spoke about how Slater and teammate Devin McCourty have led so effectively on the team.

"Those guys, they lead by example," he said. "They always have. I would say over the last few years though, they've both become very vocal. And that was because there was a lack of that voice. They've done a great job bridging that gap. They've been through a lot. And they're resourceful with younger guys. I think they've been great helping those guys along."[3]

Matthew had become a star in the league and an indispensable team leader for the Patriots. He didn't yet have a Super Bowl ring, however, and that was something he had in his sights.

Chapter 17

Minnesota Miracle

The Saints returned to the United States after their 20–0 victory over the Dolphins in their 2017 game in London. Upon returning, they enjoyed a bye week, which was much needed given their brutal travel schedule. But after their first two losses of the year, they had now won two straight and were about to face four straight NFC opponents. Having rested up, they proceeded to dominate Detroit (52–38), Green Bay (26–17), Chicago (20–12), and Tampa Bay (30–10), putting them at 6–2 at the halfway point of the season. The defense was playing well, and the offense had begun to click.

In weeks ten and eleven, it was more of the same, as they pounded Buffalo 47–10 and got past a pesky Washington team, 34–31. They finally lost in week twelve, 26–20 against the Rams, but followed that up with a ten-point win over division rival Carolina the next week. Atlanta upended New Orleans 20–17 in week fourteen, but the Saints rebounded with two more straight victories over the Jets and Atlanta in the rematch. Finally, in the last regular season game of the year, they lost to Tampa Bay, 31–24 to put them at 11–5 and firmly in the playoffs.

Over the long, grueling stretch of the NFL regular season, the Saints had proven themselves to be one of the better teams in the league. They had excellent coaching, a formidable defense, a strong running game led by Alvin Kamara of Norcross High School, and a dynamic passing game featuring one of the best receivers in the game in Michael Thomas and an elite quarterback in Drew Brees.

The team prepared for the playoffs, and the entire city of New Orleans was ready.

But Austin Carr had only been a peripheral part of the story.

After his first NFL game experience in London, and after the bye week, the Saints put Austin on the inactive list for their game against Detroit. The next week, he was inactive again. And then again. Week after week went by, and Carr remained inactive. He hadn't done anything wrong per se. He just hadn't done enough right to be made active. For the rest of the regular season, Austin stood on the sidelines holding a clipboard instead of a helmet.

"What the heck," he says, looking back. "I'm not gaining ground with the team or with the league. I was practicing pretty well, and I think that's why I was sticking around. The coaches all knew I could ball, but it wasn't enough to see the field."

On the one hand, all it would take was one injury for Austin to get another chance. On the other hand, all it would take was one injury to Austin for his time with the Saints to be done. Moreover, he wasn't getting a chance to show the rest of the league what he could do, so he faced the real possibility of a release being the end of his short NFL career.

"I'm nervous," he says. "Like, I could get cut any day. I'm asking myself, what's their view of me? Why am I on the roster but inactive? Don't they think I can contribute somehow?"

Like any other position group on every other team in the league, New Orleans's wide receiver room was filled with guys who were banged up. Maybe they weren't "injured"—that is, unavailable to play—but they were certainly beat up and slowed by all the bumps and bruises and nicks that come with being a regular NFL player. Austin figured that he, at 100 percent health, might be a better option than another player at 70 percent health. The coaching staff, however, didn't see it that way.

Every week, Austin practiced with zeal and determination. He was in no-man's land—on the roster, which was better than being on the practice squad, but never active. He knew that any moment he could be activated or released. There was nothing to do but work hard and continue to give his best.

During games, he still had a job to do. The coaches assigned him the task of charting plays, so every game, he stood on the sidelines, clipboard in hand, jotting down each play, each formation, and the result. The wide receivers coach liked to go over the plays on the sideline, and Austin's detailed information proved valuable. While he would of course much rather have contributed on the field, at least he was doing something to help the team. Still, for a competitive athlete, it wasn't easy.

And yet, it was easy.

Austin grew up in a blue-collar home, where hard work and sweat was what you had to put out in order to earn a paycheck. He was the son of an electrical contractor and, as a teenager, learned to get his hands dirty. Nothing had been handed to him, and he needed to earn his way on the

Northwestern roster as a walk-on and then make it in the NFL as an undrafted free agent.

While there is a significant difference in pay being on the fifty-three-man roster versus being on the practice squad, there is no difference in pay if you are on the fifty-three-man roster and active versus being on the fifty-three-man roster and being inactive. Austin was getting paid the same amount per game whether he was active or not, which felt bizarre to him.

"You're collecting a check—a pretty handsome check at that—to be on the fifty-three-man roster and there's no pressure on you in games. In fact, games are pretty chill. You have a front row seat on the sideline for the games, and you're not on the hook for all the game planning and you're not under pressure to perform in the games."

For Austin, his "games" were on Thursday and Friday in practice. That's when he got the chance to "play"—showing the coaches his skills and determination to be better. That's when he went up against the Saints' starting defensive backs and tried to get open. That's when he got to perform as a football player instead of a glorified—and highly paid—team manager.

"On the scout team during the week," he says, "I just got to cut it loose. But on the weekend, it was like, cool, I hope we beat the Packers, but I'm just gonna be here charting plays."

His wife, Erica, took to calling him "Clipboard Boy," a nickname that he both liked and disliked. Of course he would rather play, but it wasn't the worst gig in the world to get paid a real NFL salary and only have to assist the wide receivers coach during the game.

"You're just kind of hanging out on the sideline, talking with the wide receivers coach, going over the plays. I'm wearing an ear bud, standing next to the quarterback, listening to the play call. Hanging there, collecting a good check. I'm getting paid good money to practice for three or four days and then stand on the sideline tracking plays. Now there's more to it than that, of course, but in some ways, it wasn't a bad deal."

To be clear, there *was* much more to it than that. Austin had dedicated himself to football excellence, and that required long hours at the facility, training, learning the playbook, and developing rapport with the quarterbacks and coaches. He lifted regularly and did hard levels of conditioning. He spent countless hours in meetings and practices, all in an effort to stay sharp and get better. This was on top of years of making football a top priority in his life. For many people, this may seem glamorous and hardly like "work," but the reality is, NFL players have put in incredible numbers of hours of hard work just trying to make it in the league.

Nonetheless, Sundays weren't exactly difficult for Austin, given that he was a guy who used to spend his summers crawling in attics or in basements running wire for his father.

Moreover, in the back of his mind, Austin always knew that it was not football or bust. He went to Northwestern and had alternative plans should the NFL not work out. He had received a top education from one of the finest universities in the country. He had numerous skills and abilities that would serve him well beyond the NFL. But at the same time, *this* was his job *now*, and being a competitor, he wanted the chance to play.

It wouldn't come during the rest of the regular season. And that made the regular season grind even harder. As week after week progressed with no change in his status, he felt further apart from his teammates. He knew he hadn't put the work into building the kinds of relationships with his teammates that he should have, and given that he wasn't contributing on the field, that created a real sense of loneliness.

"I'm not going to sugarcoat this," he says. "My relationships with my teammates [weren't] strong. I wasn't building strong relationships with the guys. I'm kind of a guy that's slow to warm up. Plus, I wasn't really a star in any sense, and I wasn't playing much at all. With all that, plus not having a big personality, people didn't interact much with me. It was lonely. Those were some lonely days."

It's a good thing he was married, because he needed someone to be with and process life with. Erica was there for him, and she provided him with the companionship he needed. His friendships with Saints players were just slow to materialize.

Financially, though, Austin understood that he had a good situation. He was making rookie money, which by NFL standards was the bottom of the barrel. But he knew it was still terrific pay by normal standards.

"Even my current financial position, where I am today, I'm still reaping the benefits of a short stint in the NFL in which I played forty or fifty games, and still have my health."

The Saints played division rival Carolina in the Wild Card round of the playoffs and won a closely contested game 31–26; now they would face Minnesota. The Vikings were an NFC powerhouse that year, going 13–3, including an opening-day victory over these same Saints. This would be a true test of the talent and teamwork of the entire New Orleans organization.

Austin prepared for the game like he did every week: hard. He gave every route, every minute in meetings, every snap with the scout team, his very best, knowing that he would once again hold the clipboard on the sideline for Curtis Johnson, the wide receivers coach.

On Tuesday following the Carolina game, Brandon Coleman, who had caught twenty-three passes for 364 yards and three touchdowns during the season, suffered a neck injury, and that led Payton to call Carr's number. All of a sudden, Austin's outlook on the game changed. He would play after all.

The night before the game, the team did a makeshift walk-through in the hotel. Coach Johnson wanted to make sure that Carr was OK.

"Don't be nervous, Austin," he said. "You need to make sure you're not nervous."

"I'm not nervous, coach," Austin replied. "*You* need to be not nervous."

Austin was confident because by this point in the year, he knew the playbook inside and out. He had had a good week of practice. He was ready. Everything was as it should have been, and Austin was excited because there were several plays laid out where he might make a splash in the game.

The game arrived, and the crowd was in full throat. Dressed in purple, cheering frantically, hearing the giant Gjallarhorn blow before the game, the entire building was electric. For Austin, this represented one of the most incredible crowd experiences of his career.

"I would say, of all the places I've played in or been to, that would be [in the] top three. Playoff game in Minnesota, it got loud. That Skol chant, it's funny, but man, it's loud."

The Skol chant harkens back to the heritage of Vikings. The word means "cheers" or "good health" and in 1961, when the organization was founded, James "Red" McLeod composed a fight song for the team. When the team opened up U.S. Bank Stadium in 2016, the chant became an integral part of the fan experience.[1]

The crowd roared, its voice like booming thunder:

SKOL!

SKOL!

SKOL!

The Vikings got out to a 17–0 lead before the Saints mounted a comeback. Brees connected with Alvin Kamara in the corner of the end zone to give New Orleans their first lead of the game at 21–20 with three minutes left in the game.

Austin had been in on nine offensive plays during the game, but didn't catch a pass. He wasn't on the field for Kamara's spectacular catch, but he was still very much in the game, whooping it up on the sideline as the Saints came roaring back.

"If anything felt like I was in the NFL, this was it," he says. "Because now I'm in the playoffs, and now I'm in on key third-down plays. I'm not just a decoy, I'm actually an option."

But the Vikings were not done. Keenum marched Minnesota down the field and, keyed by a twenty-four-yard completion to Adam Thielen, got them in range of a long field goal. Again, kicker Kai Forbath was true, nailing a fifty-three-yarder, and just like that, Minnesota was ahead 23–21.

Now it was Brees's turn. He drove the Saints down to field goal range and Lutz drilled a forty-three-yarder, and with just twenty-five seconds left in the game, the Saints held a 24–23 lead.

The Vikings needed to get to about the Saints' forty to give Forbath a chance. Quarterback Case Keenum completed a nineteen-yarder to Stefon Diggs, but soon faced a third-and-ten situation from the Vikings' thirty-nine with just ten seconds left in the game. They were out of timeouts and didn't have enough time to complete a pass in the middle of the field and spike the ball. This pass needed to be a sideline throw, and everyone in the building knew it.

The Saints' defense was in a quandary, however. They needed to protect against the long touchdown pass, and playing tight coverage, especially on the sidelines, invited a deep ball that stood a decent chance of success. So they would have been content to let Minnesota complete a shorter pass as long as they kept them in bounds. However, they needed to make sure that the Vikings didn't gain fifteen or twenty yards on the play—no easy task given that they just allowed a nineteen-yard completion to Diggs a few moments earlier.

"To save time, Keenum's going to try to work the ball to the boundary [sideline]," Fox analyst Troy Aikman said.

Keenum looked over the defense and saw that the Saints were rushing four and playing fairly deep coverage across the field. He took the shotgun snap and dropped back. Defensive end Cameron Jordan, one of the best pass rushers in the NFL with thirteen sacks in 2017, came barreling in on Keenum's right side. Keenum stepped up in the pocket to avoid Jordan and slung the ball thirty-five yards down the right sideline. Diggs had run a deep out, and as the ball came to him at the Saints thirty-four-yard line—well within Forbath's kicking range—Saints' safety Marcus Williams—who had made a key interception earlier—had a split-second decision to make. If Diggs caught it and stepped out of bounds, there would still be time to kick the winning field goal. If Diggs, however, had the ball knocked out, it would have been fourth and ten back at the Vikings' thirty-nine-yard line with just seconds left. And if Williams managed to tackle Diggs and keep him in bounds, even though they were in field goal range, Minnesota would not have time to get another play off.

As it turned out, Williams did the one thing he could not afford to do.

He missed the tackle completely.

Diving for Diggs's legs, he whiffed, and suddenly Diggs was free on the sideline with nothing but green ahead of him. Well, green and the purple end zone that awaited.

Fox play-by-play announcer Joe Buck made the call.

"Keenum steps into it.... Pass is ... caught! DIGGS ... SIDELINE ... TOUCHDOWN! UNBELIEVABLE! VIKINGS WIN IT!"

Austin stood on the sideline, totally stunned as the crowd erupted.

"Utter heartbreak," Austin says, recalling the scene that unfolded before him. "Oh man, that was heartbreaking. Disbelief. It was so disappointing. I wanted to play in an NFC Championship game. Erica's parents were in the crowd, and it would have been fun to celebrate with them. It was utter disbelief, having come back from seventeen points down."

He shook Keenum's hand after the kneel-down. Austin knew Keenum was a man of faith.

"Hey, go ball for the Lord," Austin said.

"Thanks, man," Keenum replied. "You're a great team." He asked Austin a couple of questions about himself before they parted ways. The brief moments of conversation between the two stuck out to Austin, especially given what Keenum had just accomplished.

For Marcus Williams, it was a dark night. He had gone from hero to goat in one play, and on the ride back to the hotel was nearly inconsolable. In tears the whole way, he felt like the weight of the world was on his shoulders. Due to his missed tackle, Saints fans were furious. Some camped out at his apartment, meaning he couldn't even go home after the game.

"I don't know what they had planned," Austin says, "I don't know what that was about. But all I know is that he had to sleep at a teammate's house that night for that mistake."

For the Saints, the 2017 season was over. But for Austin, it would be just the first of several years of life as a fifty-third man in the NFL.

Chapter 18

Fifty-Third-Man Money

The average NFL career lasts about 2.5 seasons. This is due to the extreme physical nature of the sport and to the fact that salaries are not guaranteed, unlike in other major pro sports. Why does the nature of NFL contracts matter? It's pretty simple, actually. Players that don't produce face the prospect of being cut. Sometimes, due to salary cap rules, a team has to stick with a declining and expensive player for a year or two beyond what they'd like, but nothing like in other sports where teams are on the hook for huge dollars for a long time. Due to salary cap rules, cutting or trading a player may leave a team with "dead money" on their roster—money that counts against a team's salary cap. The bigger the dead money hit, the more difficult it is for a team to cut or trade a nonproductive player.

At the bottom of an NFL roster, there are virtually no salary cap implications for cutting the fifty-third player on a league-minimum contract. If you are at the bottom of the fifty-three-man roster and showing signs of decline, you will almost certainly get a ticket home, because there's someone else out there who can do the job as well as, or better than, you, but for less money than you'll earn the next year.

Thus the competition at the bottom of an NFL roster is intense. Players know their time is limited, and they know that league minimum contracts might only last a couple of years. They also know that life after football, from an income perspective, will likely never be as lucrative.

The average NFL player will earn approximately $7.1 million over the course of his career.[1] This is buoyed, of course, by the top-end contracts, with star quarterbacks making well in excess of $40 million a season. So in reality, the typical player, whose career is three years, earns far less than this. In fact, it's much more like $1.8 million.

Now, the median annual income for a twenty- to twenty-four-year-old in the United States is $640 per week, or $33,280 per year.[2] The 2022 NFL league minimum salary, which is what most players in their first three seasons make (which also represent ages twenty-two to twenty-four), was $705,000. That's eighteen times the median annual earnings for their age group. Thus if a player survives in the NFL for three seasons at league minimum, it would take the average American of the same age nearly sixty-four years to earn what the young NFL player earns in just three years.

In the NFL, the pay disparity among peers can be drastic. Geremy Davis's peers in the 2015 New York Giants' receiving corps included star Odell Beckham Jr.; veteran Rueben Randle; Dwayne Harris, who had just come over from Dallas; Hakeem Nicks, who had returned to the Giants after starting the year in Tennessee; and Myles White.

In the NFL, position groups are like small fraternities. Players, of course, have relationships with teammates who play other positions, but most of a player's time is spent with teammates within his own position group. This makes sense, as there are special coaches for each position. Sean Ryan was the Giants' wide receivers coach, and it was his job to hold meetings with the receivers to walk through their film and oversee their development. This smaller fraternity within the team showed itself in team meals as well. And that often made for interesting experiences.

An NFL tradition is for veterans to go out to dinner with rookies and then stick them with the bill. That's not a problem for a rookie making $600,000 if the meals are reasonable. But sometimes it gets out of control. In 2016, Houston Texans rookie safety K. J. Dillon was stuck with a dinner tab of $16,255, even though Dillon himself only ordered a $13 salad. By far the biggest item on the tab was the alcohol—twenty-two orders of Hennessey Pardis Imperial, which alone came to $7,700. A 20 percent tip added would have brought the total bill to some $19,500—which would have been 4 percent of his year's pay.[3] It would be the equivalent of a twenty-three-year-old making the median salary in the country of $33,280 paying more than $1,300 for a single dinner for his coworkers.

The veteran wide receivers on the Giants were far wealthier than Davis, and it showed in how they approached dinner. For Davis, like K. J. Dillon, it was a time to be frugal. Davis was at the bottom of the roster, and he knew it; he had no illusions about the fact that he was guaranteed nothing in the future. Taking care of his money was of crucial importance. But for Beckham, an emerging megastar, there was a little more financial wiggle room, and he could live a more lavish lifestyle.

When the group would go out for dinner, Davis found it challenging. The veterans would order expensive meals, and Davis knew he couldn't keep up. They even put Geremy through the traditional rookie hazing, much like what Dillon experienced. But it was then that Beckham showed some compassion with Davis.

"The situation with rookie dinners is that they always get the draft pick to pay for the dinner," Davis explains. "There's one thing I'm picky about. If you buy food, please finish your food. It's one of my pet peeves. But they're [the veterans] like buying food to hurt my wallet. And the check comes. Odell [Beckham] was like, bro, I'll pay for half. I was so appreciative of that. He dropped big money to help me out. The other guys were trying to abuse my wallet, and I was like, guys, I'm a sixth-round pick now. I wasn't like Ereck Flowers or Landon Collins who were already millionaires based off their draft status. Odell didn't have to help me out there, but he did, and I've always been appreciative of that."

Davis was frugal by nature, and, like many NFL players, he came from very little means growing up. He moved a lot as a kid, and during his sophomore year in high school, he didn't even live with his mom, who was struggling at the time. His sister lived with her, while Geremy slept on the couch at a friend's house. Eventually, her financial situation improved enough so that she could get a place to stay, and the family was reunited. "It wasn't the best place," he explains, "but eventually I was able to live with them again—this lasted until the end of my junior year. Then my mom and stepdad got reconciled and our financial situation improved."

On the whole, he classifies his upbringing as lower-middle class. Never was he enjoying anything resembling wealth.

"My financial situation growing up had its ups and downs," he recalls. "There were times when we were steady and it was fine, and then there were times when it was a struggle. My mom and stepfather got divorced, and that's where the struggles happened. I guess you could say I was always frugal. Even when I made it to the NFL, I was trying to not spend money. Someone had to convince me that I had earned this money and I could reward myself. My personality is to be very frugal. My mom would tell me that, my closest friends would tell me that. My financial advisor would tell me that, that I'm just very conservative about my money."

The only major purchase he made in his first year was a new car—a Jeep Wrangler Sport. But he wouldn't make that purchase until his place on the fifty-three-man roster was secured. "Before I made that purchase, I made sure that I made the final roster because I didn't want to take a risk. I was like, damn, I have all this money, but I still had a frugal mindset. I was able to send some back home, go to dinner with my girlfriend, but nothing too crazy."

For many young men of modest to little means, football is seen as a way out of a bad situation. Due primarily to the concussion problem in the sport, football participation has dropped 6.6 percent in the past decade in high schools, according to the National Federation of State High School Associations.[4] But the major drop-off has come from primarily white families. In Illinois, for example, high school football rosters are increasingly made up of kids from low-income homes and families of color.

Albert Samaha, a *BuzzFeed* investigative reporter and author of *Never Ran, Never Will: Boyhood and Football in a Changing American Inner City*, isn't surprised by this. He says, "The reason that football is so valuable to them [kids from poor homes] is the fact that it's still the sport that's the most popular in America, that is getting the most money from high schools and colleges in America. At a time when the educational gap continues to widen between low income, particularly black and brown kids, and higher income white kids, football offers a path to upward mobility that is not really available through any other extracurricular activity."[5]

In other words, football is seen as a way out of poverty for many kids from low-income backgrounds. Unfortunately, many of these kids become young men inexperienced at handling money. When they go from poverty to suddenly making hundreds of thousands of dollars in a year, in many—or even most—cases, financial disaster looms.

This isn't just about football, though. It's common in the general population for people coming out of poverty and suddenly finding themselves wealthy to squander that wealth in a short amount of time. According to CNBC, lottery winners are more likely than average Americans to declare bankruptcy within three to five years of winning.[6] Jay Zagorsky, an economist for *U.S. News and World Report*, says, "Studies found that instead of getting people out of financial trouble, winning the lottery got people into more trouble, since bankruptcy rates soared for lottery winners three to five years after winning."[7]

A 2009 *Sports Illustrated* investigation found that 78 percent of NFL players go bankrupt or are under serious financial stress within two years of retiring.[8] Agent Leigh Steinberg explains that many of the reasons are some of the same we've touched on—lack of experience handling money, poor investments, and many people holding out their hands expecting players to give them some. But he also says that football players "forget that the current rate of compensation [as NFL players] is not going to last and can be terminated by injury or skill at any point. Spending habits assume the revenue will be coming in forever."[9] In other words, they make the mistake of thinking that their NFL salary will be coming in for years and years, and they treat money as if it's not going to end.

Given that the average NFL career is less than three years, this seems like especially poor thinking. But understand that these young men feel they are invulnerable. Robert Turner, author of *Not for Long: The Life and Career of the NFL Athlete*, writes, "We have to remember there's something about young people that is the same throughout generations across time. They think they're invincible and whatever has happened to everybody else is not going to happen to me, and so I'm the exception to the rule."[10]

Young athletes tend to believe they are made of steel and are indestructible. A 2012 study published in the American Academy of Pediatrics showed that "despite an increase in media attention, as well as national and local efforts to educate athletes on the potential dangers of traumatic brain injuries . . . many high school football players are not concerned about the long-term effects of concussions and don't report their own concussion symptoms because they fear exclusion from play."[11]

It stands to reason that many NFL players think their careers are going to go on and on, allowing them to rack up millions of dollars in earnings. Steinberg added that, in conjunction with players thinking their NFL careers will last forever, players lacked preparation for a post-NFL career. He writes, "NFL players have long off-seasons they can use to lay the foundation for their life after football. Some athletes do not give it a thought and end up missing the structure and direction that football has given them. The early retirement years can be non-productive."[12]

The NFL is well aware of these realities. A number of years ago, they launched the NFL's Personal Finance Academy, which is designed to help young players gain skills in budgeting, investment planning, and risk analysis. Alok Kumar, chairman of the finance department at the University of Miami (Florida), has served as an instructor for this program. He points out one of the issues that players face: "Everyone might think, well, 'I'm good at one thing. How can I make a mistake in financial decisions?' It's especially dangerous for football players, because they have tremendous skill in one area, and they might think that skill is transferable. It actually is not. People who are super skilled in one area are most likely to make mistakes."[13]

Some colleges have begun helping their athletes learn to handle money. In 2015, Arizona State University professor Glenn Wong began teaching a course designed specifically with future pro athletes in mind. Having taught college students for more than thirty years, he was well aware that most students don't possess much by way of financial knowledge, skills, or experience. But the problem is amplified in the world of pro sports. Wong explained in 2016, "The difference is that certain student athletes are going to be instant millionaires, so the issues they face are much different than the typical student coming out of college."[14]

Of course, not every NFL rookie is an instant millionaire. But many players come from low-income homes or even poverty, and suddenly they are signing contracts worth $600,000 or more. These players have never had to handle any significant amount of money; a half a million dollars is an unfathomable sum to manage. It is not surprising, then, that so many handle it unwisely.

Joe McLean helps pro athletes manage their money, and he says that with these pros, "the commonality is that with great abundance comes less discipline." He adds that, "Athletes don't begin their career with the end in mind. Early on in someone's career, they are just figuring out how to get on the field. And the money is coming, but they almost don't have any time to figure that out. They have to live each contract as if it's their last one. But a lot of athletes initially think there's always going to be another contract."[15]

For fifty-third men especially, their next NFL paycheck might be their last.

Chapter 19

Shaping the Fifty-Third Man

Life in the NFL is hard, and even for the star players entering the league, there's a lot to learn. It's a new level that brings entirely new challenges. A typical high school offensive lineman is between fifteen and eighteen years of age and may not even have hit his growth spurt. In some—not all—schools, football teams employ weight programs, and for many scholastic football players, this is the first experience they've ever had with weight training. Often the training is substandard, as many high school coaches or trainers just don't have much experience or expertise in this area.

The fortunate few that move on to college enter a world where they suddenly are competing against eighteen- to twenty-three-year-olds—the boys have become men, and they have grown substantially. College weight programs are serious, and there's an enormous difference between a twenty-three-year-old redshirt senior and an incoming freshman. The complexity of the game also ramps up considerably.

But then the next level jump is even more severe. Now a twenty-three-year-old rookie is competing against fully grown men with fully mature bodies and years of experience. NFL weight programs are among the very best in the entire world. NFL players are bigger, stronger, more muscular, and faster than typical college players, who themselves are bigger, stronger, more muscular, and faster than typical high school players.

There's a reason why athletes are ineligible to be drafted into the NFL until three years after their high school class graduates. The danger is simply too great.

Ryan Riddle explained the situation this way: "The jump from high school to big-time college football is a substantial one in terms of speed, talent and complexities of the game. But that adjustment period pales in comparison to the jump to the National Football League. In college, you're competing against boys fresh out of high school who are just beginning to

139

fill out their bodies. In the NFL, you are up against the absolute best 2,000 football players in the entire world. This group is strictly comprised of the biggest, strongest, toughest men you will ever see in your entire life, as well as perhaps the best all-around athletes on the planet."[1]

There are all kinds of adjustments that these athletes need to make. They need to adjust to a new schedule, new teammates, a new environment, a new playbook and system, a new city, and a new set of expectations. They are no longer playing against boys or young men who are competing for a spot on the varsity squad. They are competing against grown men who are trying to earn a living and feed their families. That simple fact alone inherently ratchets up the competition level considerably.

Riddle said, "When training camp started and we suited up in full gear, they quite literally separated the men from the boys. The intensity and talent level of college athletes competing for a starting spot is much different from the heat you feel from those who are fighting to feed their families and prolong a career of glory, fame and wealth beyond their wildest dreams. In theory, I was aware of this, but it took experience to finally understand it."[2]

It's difficult in any endeavor to succeed "on your own." Of course, nobody truly succeeds in anything on their own; somewhere along the way we learn something from someone else—a parent, a teacher, a coach, a mentor, a friend, a pastor—and an opportunity was given by someone else that opened the door for our success. The NFL, of course, is no different. Geremy Davis, for example, was blessed by God with above-average size, strength, and speed. He was also given an ability above and beyond his peers to understand the game of football. Of course, being blessed with all that wasn't enough. There are lots of people with great physical gifts that never sniff the NFL or even Division I college football. Davis had to enter into countless hours of hard work. He had to study. He had to hit the weights. He had to take endless reps in practice honing his craft.

The education of Geremy Davis began long before he entered the NFL. It began with his entry into Little League football and the games of Madden with his stepfather. It was there that Davis began to learn about coverages and tactics. It was there that he began to understand how football was played and what role he would have on any individual play. It was there that he began to fall in love with the sport and knew that he would dedicate himself to pursuing greatness. It was there that his dream of becoming an NFL player began to form and take shape.

His high school coaches took this and shaped it further, helping him become a high-level recruit and a Division I player at UConn. His stepfather, at various points along the way, toughened him up mentally and physically, helping him prepare for the rigors of the game.

He arrived at UConn having been recruited by Randy Edsall, but after Davis's freshman year, Edsall left and took over at Maryland, where he would coach Max Garcia for a year. Paul Pasqualoni followed Edsall, and came to Storrs with many years of experience both in college and in the NFL. Pasqualoni coached UConn beginning in 2011, but he endured only two losing seasons as a Division I head coach, as UConn went 5–7 both in 2011 and 2012. When the team got off to an 0–4 start in 2013, UConn fired him and replaced him with T. J. Weist.

Weist arrived at UConn prior to the 2013 season, having been hired as an offensive coordinator and wide receivers coach. Due to his role, he spent long hours with Davis, who by then was entering his redshirt junior season. Davis had a good sophomore year, with forty-four receptions for 613 yards, but Weist knew there was a lot more there to be had.

For Davis, Weist's arrival was a turning point. "He was probably the best receiver coach I ever had in terms of detail, film watching, play breakdown, and just as a person. A great dude, he played a huge role in my life."

Weist helped Davis take his game to a new level. It was during this season that Geremy broke UConn receiving records, catching seventy-one passes for 1,085 yards and becoming a legitimate NFL prospect. Weist would not be retained after the 2013 season, however, and UConn hired Bob Diaco to replace him.

Davis cites Weist as a key factor in his development, and says that Weist even helped out during his draft prep. Davis sent Weist the tape from his workout with the Philadelphia Eagles, and Weist took time to critique Davis's footwork, route running, releases, and technique.

"He was still coaching me from afar even though I didn't have him with me physically," Davis says.

They built up such a great relationship that the two remain in contact to this day. Weist was hired by the Baltimore Ravens as an offensive analyst in 2018, and even worked to get the Ravens interested in signing Davis as a player following his stint with the Chargers.

When Davis reached the NFL, he expected to be mentored by other players, but he was disappointed on that score. He says, "Some guys get drafted like by the Falcons and get mentored by Julio [Jones]. Guys get drafted by Arizona and get to learn from [Larry] Fitzgerald. I always wish I had that. I never got that." It's not that there weren't veterans on the

Giants that he worked with closely. It's that they never took him under their wing.

For Davis, the idea of mentoring wasn't just about learning the playbook. It was about how to live as a man and as a player in the NFL. Moreover, it was how to grow in your faith while playing in the league. Davis explains, "Even in the faith, nobody really took me under their wing. I had teammates in the faith like Prince Amukamura, but I wasn't always in their back pocket. That's why in my third year I had to grow up in the faith and learn more about discipleship. I think that's something the world in general lacks. I needed to be obedient to the Lord who was calling me to start building into other guys."

This lack of mentoring would impact Davis's view of his own role as he moved from rookie to veteran. He would take it on himself to mentor younger players himself, including players who were brought on to take Davis's spot on the team. The competition for those last spots on the fifty-three-man roster is intense and can be the difference between possibly playing on Sundays versus sitting in the stands or at home cheering for your team. It's also the difference between making roughly $650,000 and $150,000 for the season.

It raises the question of how athletes in any sport can support one another when there's a competition for playing time and, more importantly, a roster spot. There are only so many snaps to be had at the wide receiver position in a typical NFL game or season. There are only so many special teams snaps to be had. There are only so many roster spots and only so many active players. People *are* going to be left behind. Players work incredibly hard to make sure that they aren't among those left out.

In 2019, quarterback Joe Flacco—who had won a Super Bowl with the Ravens—was playing with the Denver Broncos. Denver had drafted Drew Lock to be their next starting quarterback, and Flacco was asked about mentoring Lock. Flacco answered, "I'm trying to go out there and play good football. I'm trying to go out there and play the best football of my life. As far as a time constraint, and all that stuff, I'm not worried about developing guys or any of that. That is what it is. And like I said, I hope he does develop. But I don't look at that as my job. My job is to go win football games for this football team."[3]

How do you root for someone who is there to take your playing time from you? How do you mentor someone who has been signed to take your job, take money from you, and possibly end your career? For many professional athletes, this has been one of the hardest aspects of the job.

It's a challenge for any rookie to adapt to the NFL. They all could benefit from mentoring, even as they challenge incumbent players for their jobs. This is particularly true for the wide receiver position, which is one of the hardest positions to learn in the whole game. Former coach Brian Billick explained why transitioning to the NFL from college is extremely difficult for wide receivers: "Wide receiver has become one of the toughest positions for rookies to adapt to in the pros. There are a lot of challenges that factor into this: eluding press coverage, getting separations on a break, running disciplined routes (both in terms of positioning and timing) and mastering the myriad sight adjustments and choice routes that are a big part of the modern pro game. Those are all very difficult aspects of the process. So is gaining the trust of your quarterback. If you're a veteran, like Peyton Manning or Aaron Rodgers, you don't want to throw to someone you hope is going to be in the right place, or someone you think is going to run the correct route. You want the receiver you know is going to make the right sight adjustment. You want the guy who will make the out-cut at exactly 7 yards—not 6 or 8—and who'll tap his toes inside the boundary to complete the catch."[4]

No wonder Davis talked about the value of being mentored by a great veteran like Julio Jones. And no wonder Davis wishes he had that as a rookie. But he didn't.

It wasn't like Geremy didn't get *any* mentoring, though. In fact, he cites one man in particular with building into him like nobody else had before. That man was George Stewart, the assistant head coach and special teams coordinator for the Chargers from 2017 to 2020. Stewart entered the NFL in 1989, serving under Pittsburgh's Hall of Fame coach Chuck Noll as special teams coach. At various stops on his NFL coaching journey, he was the wide receivers coach, including a stint with the 49ers from 1996 to 2002. The first four years in San Francisco, he was the special teams coach but moved to receivers coach for the last three.

One of his star players on those 49er teams was future Hall of Famer Terrell Owens. Owens was a solid receiver his first four seasons, but it was in his fourth season in 2000—and Stewart's first as the WR coach—that Owens broke out, making the first of three All Pro teams while under Stewart's leadership.

In 2018 Owens entered the NFL's Hall of Fame. During his induction, he gave credit to Stewart for his success. "He knew what to get out of me," Owens said. "He became a father figure to me." Owens picked Stewart to be his presenter for his induction—a huge honor for anyone. That's how much Stewart meant to the all-time NFL great.

Davis had the privilege of playing under Stewart many years later. The Chargers' head coach Anthony Lynn hired Stewart, in large part due to his own personal experience as a player under Stewart. Lynn entered the league in 1993 and made his way to the 49ers in 1995. In his second year with San Francisco, Lynn, a running back that mainly played special teams, met Stewart, who had just arrived. Stewart's approach to special teams involved not just the physical skills needed, but also the tactical planning that was missing on other teams.

Lynn had earned Stewart's trust in one particular game against the Ravens, when he made a great play against Ravens' ace Jermaine Lewis. On that play, he did exactly what Stewart drew up, and at that moment he knew that Lynn was his kind of player. For Lynn's part, he similarly had great trust in Stewart. "When a coach makes you better, that's what gets an NFL player's attention," Lynn said. "And he made a lot of us better."

When Lynn became the Chargers' head coach, the one man he really wanted on his staff was Stewart. But he thought it might not be possible. "When I got this job, I didn't think there was any way in hell I could get him," Lynn said. "But I knew I had to try. And I just caught him at a point in his life where he wanted to go back to doing what he loved."[5]

Lynn got his man, and Davis found himself under Stewart's tutelage. And much like Owens and Lynn, Davis found the experience to be one of the best he'd ever had.

"George Stewart," Davis says, smiling. "That man let me come up into his office every day during training camp during my third season. He switched my position from gunner—he said I was too big for that—to wing. He let me come up every day and study the wing position. He said, 'Geremy, I'm going to set you up for success, but it's up to you if you're successful.' Ever since then, I just became a dog on [special] teams. During the season I went up to his office every Wednesday and Thursday. When I mean Coach Stewart never got tired of me, I mean, he wanted me to come up there and learn. Even when I was already established, he liked the routine. People started to follow me. I thank George Stewart so much because he set me up to be in a good position."

Geremy Davis experienced from Stewart a man who combined a no-nonsense toughness with a caring heart. And like Owens and Lynn, he developed a real fondness for the man who took the time to build into him.

"I respect Coach Stewart so much because he gets on people when they deserve it," Geremy explains, talking about Stewart's coaching style. "Some coaches yell just to yell. But whenever Coach Stewart yelled at me or got on me, it's because I actually did something wrong. I want to be coached. Don't pick on me just because I'm a sixth-round draft pick or end of the roster guy and I'm an easy scapegoat because I can't retaliate or stand up for myself without fear of getting cut. But Coach Stew would get on you when you did something wrong, and praise you when you did something right. And I respected his coaching techniques, and honestly, he helped me prolong my career."

Every NFL player needs good coaching and mentoring. This is especially true of a player like Davis, whose NFL career was touch-and-go the entire time he was in the league. People like Stewart enabled him to hone his craft, embrace his role on special teams, and stay in the league longer than the average player.

"I found joy in it," he says. "For the first time, I felt like I contributed to team success. When we beat Seattle [in 2018], I was like, I had three special teams tackles. Or when we beat Cleveland, I had two special teams tackles. When we played the Chiefs and beat them, I had two special teams tackles and played a significant amount at receiver. Phil didn't throw me the ball, but I contributed. It just felt different than being on the fifty-three but inactive. I actually did something. I had purpose."

Moreover, Davis understood the value of mentoring in a young player's life and career, and he took it upon himself to actively help rookies that were signed specifically to challenge Davis for his own roster spot, demonstrating a selflessness and team-first mentality that reflected his faith in Christ.

Chapter 20

Serving

When Geremy became a veteran, he had a choice to make: would he refuse to mentor another rookie who could take his job? Or would he do what he could to help them adjust to the pro level?

Geremy decided that he would give to others what he himself did not receive. Two players in particular received help from Geremy as they entered the league.

Following Davis's rookie year in 2015, the Giants signed Anthony Dablé, a wide receiver from France. Dablé began playing football in France with the Grenoble Centaures in 2007 and, after a few years there, joined the Berlin Rebels of the German Football League. From there he played for the New Yorker Lions in 2014 and 2015, and posted his highlights on YouTube. Giants star Osi Umenyiora discovered Dablé online and encouraged the Giants to sign him. After giving Dablé a tryout, in which he impressed Giants' coaches, they signed him to a contract in February 2016.

Dablé was six feet, four inches, 220 pounds, meaning he was a slightly larger version of Geremy Davis. In fact, he was signed to potentially be an upgrade over Davis on the roster, filling the same role that Geremy did. Davis understood that Dablé, while a teammate, was his roster competition. But Geremy made a decision to act selflessly, for Dablé's benefit and for the benefit of the team.

Davis explains, "When I was with the Giants, one guy who was signed to take my spot was Anthony Dablé. He's older than me, but in terms of watching film and working out, we did all that together and we became really close. He followed me when I would go take extra reps on the JUGS machine. So that was a situation where I knew they signed him to take my spot, but I knew I still needed to serve him."

Despite Davis's mentoring and instruction, Dablé didn't make the team, being released during the final roster cuts on September 3, 2016. Getting cut was something that Dablé didn't see coming. Nor did he understand why, exactly, the Giants released him. When he signed with Atlanta in 2017, he explained his decision: "My agent called me and told me that the Giants and the Falcons wanted to sign me for this year. So I chose the Falcons," Dablé told the AFI Review. "I chose Atlanta because of the experience I had with the Giants. It was not just the way I was cut. They did not give me any reason, they did not tell me what was wrong, what mistakes I had made. I am not mad, I do not want to go back to a place where I can get cut for no reason. I do not have ten years in front of me."[1]

Later in Davis's career, now with the Chargers, he faced a similar situation.

Dylan Cantrell was a receiver out of Texas Tech. Big (six feet, three inches, 220 pounds) and skilled, he put up solid numbers for the Red Raiders in his last two seasons, totaling 129 receptions for 1,491 yards and fifteen touchdowns in their pass-heavy offense. Not a premier prospect, he was selected by the Chargers in 2018 with the 191st overall selection, making him a sixth-round pick, just like Davis. In fact, they were selected just five picks apart (Davis was the 186th pick in the 2015 draft).

When Cantrell made the NFL, teams saw him as more of a tight end than wide receiver due to his impressive size and strength. His NFL career would exemplify life at the bottom of an NFL roster, as he spent time on four pro teams—the Chargers (2018–2019), the Cardinals (2020), the Patriots (2020), and the Washington Football Team (2021). Moreover, he experienced life on the practice squad with three franchises.

Like Davis, when Cantrell showed up with the Chargers, he needed help. But unlike Davis's experience, Cantrell received the help he needed—from Davis, as it turned out.

For Geremy, this was an example of helping out the player who could take your job. Observers recognized the competition for roster spots among a handful of players. Columnist Michael Peterson explained the situation with the Chargers: "The 6-foot-3, 211-pound wide receiver was a standout on special teams in 2018. He appeared in 14 games and collected 13 total tackles. Davis also contributed in the run game by being one of the Bolts' best blocking receivers after being one of the last players to make the final 53-man roster at the start of the season. Heading into the 2019 season, the Chargers will be looking to find out who's going to step up and take the third wide receiver spot. At this very moment, that competition is between Davis, Travis Benjamin, last year's sixth-round pick Dylan Cantrell, and Artavis Scott."[2]

"When I got to the Chargers," Davis says, "there was a sixth-round rookie who was drafted to take my spot before I was established, named Dylan Cantrell [2018]. Obviously he was here to take my spot, but I was still like, how can I help you? My mentality was that I was going to win the spot, but I still wanted to serve him. Him and Dablé are two guys I took under my wing. I wasn't a superstar but I'm knowledgeable about the game and I know what hard work is for sure."

Davis's attitude and approach helped contribute to a special locker room relationship among the receivers. Quarterback Philip Rivers recognized how close the wide receivers group was as a unit. "I think you love to see them compete and see kind of how it shakes out," he remarked. "I think you pull for all of them. You're pulling for us. It will be fun to see that competition throughout training camp and how those guys continue. That's a close room, too. They all pull for one another. It's a neat dynamic. It's one that's probably hard to explain and understand. You have guys fighting for a couple spots, but yet they all pull for one another. It's pretty cool to see."[3]

How did Geremy navigate the dynamic of wanting your teammates to improve, yet not wanting them to take your job? Simply, it was rooted in his faith. That is, he adopted the same attitude as that of Jesus.

He explains, "When I see younger guys, my heart is to be of service to them. That's what Christ did, you know? He came not to be served, but to serve. And a guy like Drue Tranquill, who was a fourth-round pick linebacker [out of Notre Dame, drafted by the Chargers in the fourth round in 2019], was going to come in and play special teams, which is what I played. I wasn't really an established special teams player yet. He asked me how I had the heart to help him when he was coming in and potentially taking my spot. Which was true. I just told him that my heart is to proclaim the gospel and be of service, and then be a football player. I am grateful that the Lord allowed me to have the type of preseason I had, because we both saw a benefit in that. I think if I had gotten cut, I still would have proclaimed the gospel and been of service to him, but I do understand that some people put football over their faith, and I get it because this is how you earn money and support your family. But I just know for me that that was a heart check. Is it more important to be of service to this guy [Drue] and be in community with him, or to push him to the side for the sake of me making the team and getting my money? I can still be of service and work my butt off and leave it all out there on the field. I'm not going to short-change myself on the field because that would be sinful. He blessed me with talents to play this game, so I'm not going to drop a pass for the sake of someone else. No, I'm going to catch this pass, even if it's on this defender who may be a seventh-rounder or undrafted guy. I have to catch this pass. I'm not going to short sell the Lord or my team to better you. I need to be obedient to what he's blessed me with. But in doing so I can still be of service to you."

This encapsulates Geremy's approach to life. Compete hard. Give it all you've got to be the very best you can be. Do everything you can to win the roster spot and earn playing time. But at the same time, do everything you can to help your teammates get better, even those that are in direct competition for your roster spot. It is a very small needle to thread for a lot of players, and as we saw, some simply do not have the time or interest in mentoring players who have been signed to replace them. Davis saw it completely differently. He didn't receive the mentoring from veteran players when he entered the league, and he knew how important it was for others as they became NFL players. He chose to give of himself to help make them better, figuring that that would benefit everyone involved, even if it could cost him his job.

Geremy's servant attitude was even more remarkable given his status in the NFL. Some people are leaders because of their position or title. Others are leaders because of their influence and voice. Still others lead through example and serving others. For Geremy, this last aspect encapsulated the very essence of who he was, and it didn't matter whether he was a star or the last man on the roster.

In fact, at times with the Chargers, he felt invisible. The coaches did not treat the players the same, and this difference was something Davis felt acutely.

"I felt like I could have been a guy to give you two hundred to three hundred yards receiving and still be a core special teams guy. But the grace for you if you make a mistake is very low."

On one occasion, they were in a film session. He and Mike Williams, a star receiver with a similar build to Geremy's (Williams is six feet, four inches, 218 pounds), sat next to each other. On film they showed a clip of a big receiver making a great catch on a back shoulder fade.

"OK, this is a good job by Mike . . . nice catch," said the offensive coordinator.

A voice—not Geremy's—spoke up.

"Oh no coach, that's not Mike. That's Geremy."

"Oh," the coach replied. "Well Geremy, you could have done this better." He proceeded to offer correction on a play that moments before he thought was a wonderful grab—when he believed it to be Williams, not Geremy.

"Why is it different for him than me?" Geremy wonders. "I get it, he's a first-round pick and I'm a sixth-round pick that you signed off the Giants' practice squad. Now I always want to be coached, but if there was something wrong with that route, the same criticism should have been given to Mike or another starter as it was to me."

If there were ten plays and on play number seven, Geremy had a mental error, the coaches would focus on that single play instead of focusing on plays one through six, or on the touchdown he caught on play nine. Players like Williams or fellow star Keenan Allen got more grace when they made mistakes. It wasn't as if their errors were completely swept under the rug, because in the NFL coaches are always trying to make everyone better. But criticism came at players like Geremy much harder than for players with star status.

That created a great deal of stress on a daily basis for Davis. "They [the star wide receivers] have less anxiety because if they make a mistake, the ball is coming back to them. For a player like me, if I don't take advantage of every opportunity, the ball might not come back to me, and I'll only be viewed for that mistake."

On one occasion the team did a walk-through, working on a specific running play. Geremy's assignment on that play was to block the nickel-back to clear space for the running back, but they had to make an adjustment based on what the nickel did. Geremy's responsibility changed if the nickel blitzed on the play instead of playing coverage; instead of blocking, Geremy was to flare out for a short pass called a bubble screen.

"If there's a nickel firing off the edge as the slot calls 'fire, fire, fire,'" the wide receivers coach, Phil McGeoghan, instructed Geremy, "then adjust and run a bubble."

Quarterback Philip Rivers called out the cadence and the ball was snapped. Geremy went to block the nickelback and offensive coordinator Ken Whisenhunt blew the whistle.

"Geremy, what are you doing?" he yelled. "You're supposed to run the bubble!"

Quarterbacks coach Shane Steichen stepped in to point out that Geremy, in fact, did the correct thing.

"Hey, the nickel didn't fire," he said.

"Whatever," Whisenhunt harrumphed.

"I felt like it was premeditated, like he wanted to yell at me," Geremy says, looking back. "He [Whisenhunt] should have seen that the nickel didn't fire. If he did and I messed up, then yeah, I would have deserved getting yelled at. But he didn't and I didn't do anything wrong. It got to the point for me that when I made a mistake, it was like I proved them right of what they expected to see of me. So I played with so much stress, because I had a chance to win that fourth receiver spot. I did my best to play for an Audience of One, but it was so tough when you hear the tangible voice of your coach, while trying to listen to the whisper from the Lord."

It was George Stewart who took Geremy under his wing and made him feel like an important part of the team. For that, Geremy was, and always will be, grateful. The lessons Geremy learned from Stewart, he has tried to pass on to others.

"I always felt like a stepchild," Geremy says. "The only coach who really liked me was George Stewart. I felt respected because I put in the work, but they didn't like me. Only George. He realized they killed me, and he always picked me up in special teams meetings."

That may sound like sour grapes from a player who simply didn't "make it" in the NFL. But the league is littered with such stories. Players are cogs in a gigantic NFL machine, and it's easy for a player on the bubble to feel on the outside looking in, even as he's a part of the team. After all, replacing a Mike Williams or a Keenan Allen is much more difficult than replacing a Geremy Davis.

And though Davis sounds bitter, he really isn't. He understands how things work, and he is thankful for the time he spent with the Chargers. He is just telling it like it is—or was, in this case.

"Don't misunderstand," he says. "It was a great time and I'm grateful to the Chargers. That was the longest I was with any team."

In fact, Davis spent from 2016 to 2019 with the Chargers, playing in a total of twenty-six games. In 2018 they went to the playoffs, and in 2019 Davis had his most productive season ever as a wide receiver, catching three passes for thirty-eight yards. Modest numbers of course, but for a special-teams-only player, any reception was significant.

The 2018 season was special for Geremy. The Chargers went 12–4 and made the playoffs for the only time in Davis's entire football career.

"All my life I was never on good teams," he says. "High school my senior year we were talented but didn't even make the playoffs. And in college, my freshman year, we won the Big East, but I didn't play so I didn't contribute. Then when I started playing, we were terrible. I personally had success, but we were never close to the postseason. We went 6–10 my rookie year with the Giants; 5–11 my first year with the Chargers. Then 9–7 in 2017 but needed help to make the playoffs and didn't get it."

Though the Chargers were beaten badly by eventual Super Bowl champions New England, the 2018 season with Los Angeles was still the most fun Geremy ever had as part of a football team.

"Tyrell Williams and I always talk and say if we could do that 2018 season all over again, we totally would," he says. "It was my breakout year, so to speak. Thirteen special teams tackles, went 12–4 and made the playoffs. Practice was fun, games were fun. If we could redo 2018, we really would."

Part of the joy of that season for Geremy was not only the on-field success, but the relationships he built and the way he was able to invest in and mentor younger players. Despite not being a star, Geremy sought to help others reach their own potential as players and as men, something Geremy has continued to do in the years after the NFL.

Chapter 21

Captain

Leadership can come in many forms, in or out of the NFL. Some men lead by the authority of position. Others lead by influence, whether they have a title or not. Matthew Slater's leadership journey began as a child, under the tutelage of his parents, watching his father, Jackie, ply his trade as a professional football player. The lessons he learned about hard work, dedication, commitment, and character, would shape Matthew the man far beyond Matthew the athlete.

He was not blessed with a perfect NFL body. Certainly he looked little like his father, who was a hulk of an offensive lineman. By comparison, Matthew—an asthmatic—was small and scrawny. If he was to be successful in football, he would have to develop traits that would enable him to compete against much bigger and stronger men.

For years Slater was the quintessential fifty-third man—scrapping and fighting for a roster spot each and every season. Week by week, really, as Matthew saw it. Nothing was guaranteed to him. Bill Belichick has said, "The less versatile you are, the better you have to be at what you do well." Slater was listed as a wide receiver, but in his entire career he caught just one pass. He was drafted to play special teams—to return kicks—early in his career, but he ended up mainly on coverage units in the kicking game. That meant that unless catastrophe struck the wide receiver position, he would only see snaps in special teams situations.

He had become basically a one-trick pony, and by Belichick's reckoning, he had better do that one trick extraordinarily well.

Fortunately for Matthew, he did just that.

As he grew as a football player, he also grew as a man and as a leader. Growing up in a Christian home, faith was important to Matthew. His time at UCLA shored up a foundation that his parents had established in him, and when he arrived in Foxboro, he sought out Christian fellowship.

He found it his rookie year, primarily in the form of three men: tight end Benjamin Watson, running back Heath Evans, and punter Chris Hanson.

Drafted out of Georgia in 2004, Watson earned a championship ring as part of the last Patriots' Super Bowl championship team. He himself developed into a rock-solid player who would end up having a highly successful fifteen-year career with four franchises: New England, Cleveland, New Orleans, and Baltimore. Though he never made a Pro Bowl, Watson was a leader wherever he went, both for his on-field performance and off-field example.

He took Matthew under his wing when Slater arrived in 2008. He helped him understand what it was like to be a Christian man in a decidedly non-Christian professional sports world. For Matthew, this meant everything.

"I can't fully articulate the influence that he's had on my life, on my marriage, on the way that I parent," he says. "The intentionality with which he approached our relationship was transformative for me. You hear all these things about the NFL, and I heard them, but I experienced my dad and the kind of man he was. So I knew there were guys out there like that. But everyone tells you they aren't there. But when you go into a locker room, . . . [there is] some of the strongest Christian leadership that I ever found."

It went beyond Watson, however. The team had been without a chaplain since Don Davis, the strength coach, left before the 2008 season. That left the spiritual leadership role in the hands of the players. Hanson, Evans, and Watson took turns leading team chapels.

Belichick had a favorable disposition on the chapel, understanding the value it brought to various members of the team, for which Slater was grateful. "They're all different guys, unique in their own way," he says, referring to Watson, Evans, and Hanson. "But they're all committed to the gospel, letting their light shine in a dark place, encouraging their teammates, and being Christ-like examples. It set the foundation for me as a young player that I could be my authentic self, because faith is embraced here. I don't know what it's like in other places, but here in New England, it was embraced."

At twenty-two years of age, Matthew was still very much trying to figure out who he was as a man, and how to be that man in the NFL. He had struggles regardless, but they would have been much deeper without the guidance of these three.

"I really felt like . . . between their influence and the adversity that I experienced, that I grew spiritually," Matthew explains. "The Bible talks about how God uses adversity to give us the things we lack so that we can become more like him. I really felt like football was doing that for me. I can't imagine navigating any point in my career, but especially those early years, without Christ as my guide."

At the end of his second season, all three of those men were either gone or getting ready to leave. Watson would depart for Cleveland. Hanson had played his last NFL game and was headed into retirement. And Evans's contract was up, and he would eventually move on to New Orleans for the last two years of his career. That left a huge void on the team—a void of personal and spiritual leadership.

Knowing how important this spiritual leadership role was on the team, Slater approached Watson.

"Who is going to lead the Bible study?" he asked. "Is Coach [Belichick] going to hire someone?"

"No, I don't think so," Watson replied. Then he looked at Matthew with a smile that showed confidence. "I think you should lead it."

No way, Matthew thought. *I'm not ready for this.*

Watson understood the hesitation.

"You need to be a Timothy to the rest of those guys." Watson was referring to the Apostle Paul's protégé, Timothy, whom Paul trained and equipped for ministry. Watson was Paul, and he envisioned Matthew as Timothy.

"There I was, thrust into a position of leading the team spiritually, even before I was leading in the football space," Matthew says. "To be honest, I wasn't thrilled about this because I didn't think I was ready, but I also knew that if I didn't do it, there was nobody else there to lead us that way. So I embraced it."

Needing help, he contacted his pastor, and received resources and guidance in how to shepherd other men spiritually. Along the way, others came alongside Matthew: running back Danny Woodhead, and linebacker Jerod Mayo, to name two. These men understood that they were put in this position like Queen Esther—for such a time as this.

"It was our time," Matthew recalls with a smile.

Growing into a leader of men, Matthew oversaw the team chapel from 2010 through 2013, finding ways to help form the team culture. He resonated with the saying that God prepares the called, He doesn't call the prepared.

"He certainly did that in my case," Matthew says.

He was grateful not only to Belichick, but also owner Robert Kraft, for helping create a space where the men could grow spiritually.

"He [Belichick] provided an environment and a platform for us to have a spiritual outlet on the team, and I'll always be grateful to him and Mr. Kraft for that."

On one occasion, Kraft, a devout Jew, ran into the men during Bible study.

"Do you guys ever study any of the Old Testament?" he asked.

"Yes sir, we do!" they replied. That elicited a smile from Kraft.

Meanwhile, life was coming at Matthew from a number of different directions.

The day before Thanksgiving in 2010, Gary Guyton sat down next to him on the team plane, headed to play the Detroit Lions. Matthew had always been a bit of a homebody, not the party type. His teammates constantly ribbed him for not going out to the clubs with them to drink and meet girls, but that just wasn't Matthew's style.

"I'm looking for a wife," he told them. "Unless you have someone you think I can marry, I don't want to meet her."

Knowing this, Guyton leaned over on the plane.

"I've got a girl you can meet," he told Matthew.

Gary had a best friend who had a pretty cousin named Shahrzad, and she was finishing up her residency as a medical student at Brown University in Providence, just thirty minutes from Gillette Stadium.

"She goes to church. You'll really like her," Guyton said, grinning.

"It's a little more complex than that," Matthew replied. "It's not just if we both go to church. There has to be a connection, etcetera."

But Matthew thought about it for a few moments and figured he had nothing to lose.

"OK, sure. Go ahead. Introduce us," he said.

Little did Matthew know that Guyton had already had a similar conversation with Shahrzad, but she wasn't interested. Not at first, anyway. Eventually they went on a date, but that didn't occur until the end of the season. The date went well, but Matthew wasn't forward and didn't even get her phone number. A month went by without a second date. The season was now over, and Matthew figured he'd give it another go. He asked Guyton for her number, and soon thereafter, they started dating for real.

That relationship wasn't the only thing that changed for Matthew. He still lived at 28 Payson Road, but Ryan Wendell wanted out. He had had it living with Edelman. He told Matthew, "I'm outta here. I can't do it anymore."

"I don't blame him," Slater says with a chuckle.

But he recognized that he had a good situation, and he and Edelman replaced Wendell with running back Shane Vereen. For four years, Edelman and Slater lived as roommates. On the surface, it might seem like an odd mix. Slater—quiet, reserved, spiritual—and Edelman—outspoken, a ball of energy. How did they make it work?

"We lived two very different lifestyles off the field, outside of the building," Matthew explains. "I never infringed upon him, but I never tried to change him, and he never tried to change me. There was a respect there and an agreement that we would not disrespect each other in our common space. It was a good time for the both of us. I don't know that [I'd have had] the type of career that I've had unless I had that time with Julian, because it was formative for me. I learned a lot about people, about myself, about other perspectives in life. I gained an appreciation for things I had never considered before."

Their teammates called them the Odd Couple, and Edelman embraced that.

"Ebony and Ivory, just living together in perfect harmony," he said to Matthew. From that point on, that's what they were.

The first three years of Matthew's NFL career, no place truly felt like home. That was until he roomed with Edelman. The two of them just clicked. Even though the team provided most meals, to Matthew's surprise, it even turned out that Edelman could handle himself in the kitchen.

"Julian was actually a really good cook. But for a lot of us, most of our food came from the stadium. The Patriots provided three or four squares a day, and we were taking full advantage of those meals. Taking milk and juice from the stadium. But yeah, there wasn't a ton of cooking going on." But when there was, Edelman whipped up a mean dinner.

The years went by, and the Patriots experienced terrific success, but not the ultimate success. In 2011, they went to the Super Bowl and lost again to the Giants, 21–17, in another close classic. In 2012 they lost in the AFC Championship Game to the Ravens. In 2013, it was another loss in the AFCCG, this time to Peyton Manning and the Denver Broncos, 26–16. Despite the amazing run of success (three straight trips to the Conference Championship Game), the pressure to win it all mounted.

"To come up short year after year was very painful," Matthew says. "I was in my seventh year at the time, and we knew what it meant to Tom and Bill and Mr. Kraft. Their hurt became our hurt. Their struggle [to win it all] became our struggle. It was something that we all definitely wanted to achieve."

In 2014, however, it all came together for the Patriots. By then, Matthew was a core team leader, a captain, a Pro Bowl player, and a spiritual leader on the team. The Patriots had a typically superb regular season, going 12–4 and making it to the playoffs. In the Divisional Round, they faced old nemesis Baltimore, and the game was an instant classic. It was a back-and-forth affair, with the Patriots coming back from a 28–14 deficit to tie the score at 28–28 late in the third period. During the comeback, the Patriots used little-known, but legal, formations that befuddled the Ravens' defense and Head Coach Jon Harbaugh, who complained vociferously about what the Patriots were doing. New England went on to win, 35–31, and after the game, Tom Brady had this to say: "Maybe those guys gotta study the rule book and figure it out. We obviously knew what we were doing, and we made some pretty important plays. It was a real good weapon for us."

That did not sit well with Harbaugh, who alerted New England's next opponent, the Indianapolis Colts, to be wary of the footballs New England was using. The next week in the AFC Championship Game, in fifty-one-degree rainy weather, the Patriots were found to be using footballs that were underinflated by a little amount. That sparked a controversy over whether the Patriots were deliberately tampering with footballs, and the issue became known as "Deflategate."[1] The Patriots beat the Colts badly in that game and advanced to the Super Bowl, where they would face the defending champion Seattle Seahawks.

In the two weeks leading up to the game, the entire sports world—and even the national news—was caught up in Deflategate. Questions surrounded the Patriots and the legitimacy of Tom Brady's legacy and that of the Patriots. Given that seven years earlier the team had endured the "Spygate" scandal, this new controversy overshadowed what promised to be a great championship football game.

As for the Super Bowl itself, the Seahawks boasted the best defense in the league, the "Legion of Boom," a unit that had been at the top of the league for several years. They had a rising star at quarterback in Russell Wilson, and their coach, Pete Carroll, was the man that Bill Belichick succeeded back in 2000. Could the old dynasty take down the defending champs, or would Seattle establish a new dynasty of their own?

The Super Bowl lived up to the hype. New England came back from a 24–14 deficit in the fourth quarter by scoring two late touchdowns to take a 28–24 lead. Seattle mounted one last furious comeback drive, but the Patriots sealed the victory when Malcolm Butler intercepted Wilson at the goal line at the end. The Patriots had their first Lombardi trophy in ten years, and it gave Matthew Slater his first championship.

Slater looks back on that game, and that season, with obvious fond affection. "Professionally, it was one of the most rewarding things I've ever experienced. From the time I got drafted, we just heard how we weren't measuring up. We were constantly compared to players of previous generations—for me, the comparison was with Larry Izzo. Yeah, you make plays, but Larry won three Super Bowls, and he made all these big plays in all these big games."

For Matthew, though, the actual victory was just part of the joy of the 2014 season. Yes, there was the fulfillment of a dream. Yes, there was finally the overcoming of all the hurdles that stood in their path to become champions. Yes, there was getting the monkey off their backs. But for Slater, the 2014 championship season was about the relationships with the teammates, and the road they took together to get there.

"The thing I appreciate the most with all the teams that won championships was the story, the journey that took place," he says. "For that team, it felt like a seven-year journey. For me personally, I was carrying those guys, like Logan Mankins, who was a great player here but never got to experience a championship then got traded at the end of training camp that year."

In fact, for Slater, those failures—if they can be called failures—in previous years paved the way to make 2014 even sweeter. From 2008 to 2013, the Patriots won an average of twelve games a season. They had made it to the playoffs in five of those six years—the one miss being the 11–5 season in 2018 with Matt Cassel at quarterback for the injured Brady. They had made it to three AFC Championship Games and one Super Bowl. By any reasonable measure, they were wildly successful. Yet due to expectations in Foxboro and in New England, those seasons were seen as crushing failures. Winning in 2014 validated the Patriots organization—from ownership to the coaching staff to the system and culture in place to the players who executed on the field.

"I don't know that it would have meant the same if we had won it my rookie year," Matthew says, reflecting back on that season. "That could have created a sense of entitlement. After all the failures, to get over the hump in 2014, that just made it that much more special. To struggle in that way was fantastic. For our organization to experience down—I mean, we were always very competitive—but to go through that period of doubt, wondering if we were still a championship-level team, to win it in 2014 was very rewarding."

Six days later, Matthew and Shahrzad were married. In the days and weeks leading up to their wedding, Edelman, who caught the game-winning touchdown in the Super Bowl, needed to talk to Matthew about living arrangements.

"Here's the deal," he said. "When you guys get married, what you can do is have Shahrzad just move in with us."

"With us?" Matthew replied.

"Yeah. Here, in our place."

"With you?"

"Sure."

"Nah, man, that's . . . not an option," Matthew said, laughing.

He wanted to get an apartment, but she wanted a house. He didn't want to put down roots because in the NFL, you never really know what your future holds. By then she was making good money and convinced him to move forward with a house. They bought one, and they (and now their four kids) have lived there ever since.

In 2017, Matthew received the prestigious Bart Starr Award, given by Athletes in Action in recognition for exemplary character and leadership, voted on by his peers in the NFL. His father, Jackie, had won the award in 1996, making them the only father-and-son combination to earn the honor.

"I am very aware of Bart Starr's character and the type of man he is, so to be mentioned in the same sentence as Mr. Starr is humbling," Slater said. "I am honored to be receiving this award, not only for what it stands for, but because it is something I can share with my father. I was there when he received his award and to be receiving it myself two decades later is a very special honor for my family."[2]

Matthew had grown into a leader in every sense of the word: elite player on the field, leader in the locker room, family man, and a recognized spokesman and ambassador for the game. But he still had more room to grow.

In terms of football leadership, Slater had become a captain with the full respect of Bill Belichick. Those first few years, Matthew walked around the facility with trepidation, always concerned that he could be on the chopping block. His relationship with Belichick began to change at the end of his third season, as his leadership in the special teams unit elevated his status on the roster.

When the team elected him as one of the captains, a door of communication opened with Belichick that did not previously exist. Now he was part of a weekly captains' meeting with Belichick.

"Now I'm having these weekly sit downs with Coach," Matthew says, "going over the game plan, giving input, hearing from him personally about what we were trying to do. I could make suggestions on how to tweak it, and he's giving me feedback based off that. That started the change in our relationship, and from there we began to have one-on-one conversations about things beyond football."

The years went by, and Matthew took on more and more leadership with the Patriots. He became the voice of the post-game celebrations, giving motivational speeches that ended with, "How do we feel about another Patriots' victory?" followed by the whole team yelling, "Awwwwwwww yeaaaaaaaaaaahhhh!"

Now at the tail end of his career, with so much experience under his belt, Matthew is one of the key voices in the organization. He serves as a liaison between the players and Belichick; he can voice concerns from the players to the coaching staff but also send messages from Belichick back to the players. He is, in a real sense, the go-between, linking the players and coaching staff. In order for that to work, he has to have a good relationship with Belichick.

"At this point in time in my career," he says, "I can go to him about anything as it pertains to the team. It might be an off-the-field issue, or involve someone not in my phase of the game, but there's so much respect there between the both of us, that we're able to sit down and have these conversations."

One thing Matthew has noticed is that not only has he grown as a leader, and not only has his relationship with Belichick grown, but Belichick himself has grown as a man and a leader over these years. The world is different than it was when Belichick and Slater first met. The NFL is different. The Patriots' organization is different. It requires a different Bill Belichick.

"The type of players that he's coaching now," Matthew says, "and the landscape of the NFL now is much different than it was when I came into the league. And to see him address some of the things that guys may be going through off the field, to see him be more open to talk about these non-football things, has been awesome. As he's evolved, our relationship has evolved, and it's been a cool process. I've been fortunate to see that play out over the last fifteen years."

Slater points out that he couldn't coach the new Patriots as he coached the team back in 2001 with players like Tedy Bruschi and Mike Vrabel. Belichick has had to adjust his philosophy, not only of football, but also of how to run an organization. That's not to say that he's a completely different person, but it is noticeable how he's grown.

"The men on the team have changed. Their experience through high school and college is much different than it was. He's had to evolve in order to be able to connect and effectively relay his message to this group. I think that takes a lot of humility and self-awareness and willingness to change. He's certainly done that."

Matthew has had a lot of success in his career, and he is set up for much more after his career is over.

Chapter 22

Platform

As a general rule in the NFL—and this can be applied to the general population as well—people fall into four categories when it comes to serving others in the community. First, there are people who simply don't want to be engaged. They have their own things going on and don't think they have either the time or capacity to give to others. In some cases, it's a matter of interest; many people just have no desire to step out and give of themselves to help others. Second, there are people who want to be involved but don't know how and don't take the initiative to make it work. Third, there are people who get involved but do so with the motive of being noticed. *Look what I'm doing to help!* And fourth, there are people who serve and help others and do it because they love people and don't even care if others are aware that they're serving.

For Austin Carr, serving was a labor of love. He wasn't looking for accolades, and he certainly wasn't looking for compliments. Erica had tried to figure out her own path and had decided to work with Athletes in Action in the city of New Orleans following Austin's signing with the Saints in 2017. She began the work of launching a sports ministry at both Loyola University and Tulane in the city, work that proved to be a challenge to do on her own. Austin decided that this was where he, too, could serve. For Erica, it was a full-time job, but Austin's time was limited. Nonetheless, he volunteered his non-football hours to come alongside Erica and help her with the ministry.

A typical Sunday for Austin during the season would include a game at noon[1] followed by going to the New Orleans Athletes in Action meeting and delivering a message to the student athletes at 6:00.

For Austin and Erica, working with athletes was a joy. They understood the impact they could have on college athletes, having been there themselves not long before. Austin recalls spending time mentoring Luke, a baseball player, Randy, a football player, and others. These were guys who didn't have male spiritual leaders in the home, and Austin had the privilege of helping them learn and grow. Essentially, Austin's second job became one of pastoral ministry to college athletes.

"It's amazing the enormous effect you can have, just consistently showing up in someone's life and being a mentor for them," Austin says. "Meeting with them weekly, talking about life, showing up at their baseball or football games, and being a phone call or text away."

On September 16, 2018, the Cleveland Browns came to New Orleans to play the Saints. Austin received word that he would be getting his first ever NFL start that day. With the score 3–0, Cleveland, the Saints got the ball with a little over eight minutes left in the first quarter. They quickly got three first downs and then, after a seven-yard Alvin Kamara run put the ball on the Cleveland twenty-seven-yard line, the Saints dialed up a play for Austin. Drew Brees dropped back, and Carr bolted down the field. Brees looked to his left and let it fly. Browns defensive back T. J. Carrie collided with Austin, and the ball ricocheted off Carr's hands and fell incomplete. It was a chance for a long touchdown, and Austin came up empty.

A yellow flag flew through the air. The crowd cheered, knowing what the call would be. Pass interference on Carrie, putting the ball at the Cleveland two. An offensive holding penalty would ruin the drive, but the Saints would still kick the tying field goal, en route to a 21–18 victory, thanks to a game-winning kick by Wil Lutz with just twenty-six seconds left on the clock. Austin's first start was a win.

However, he had missed his chance for glory. Yes, he drew a pass interference penalty that advanced the ball twenty-five yards, but he couldn't come up with the catch. After the game, Austin went through the normal postgame routine, and then hopped into his car to make the three-mile drive to the Glazer Family Club at Tulane University, where dozens of student athletes awaited for the Sunday-night AIA meeting. That night, Austin was scheduled to speak out of the gospel of John. He got there and there was all kinds of buzz in the room.

"What's going on?" Austin asked.

"You're trending," a student replied.

At that point, Austin had a sinking feeling. He didn't catch a touchdown. He didn't catch a single pass. He was on the field for thirty-two offensive snaps and was targeted one time. There was only one reason he would be trending on social media, and he knew why. He shouldn't have looked, but he couldn't help it.

"It was all, 'You shoulda f-ing caught that, man,'" he says.

The Saints, like every other NFL team, had a budget to go toward players making appearances in the community. They might pay for a player to speak at a local Boys and Girls Club, or a local school, or a library. They'd fund a player wanting to do a giveaway to help underprivileged kids in the area. But no money came to Austin for serving with Athletes in Action. Any expenditure he undertook for his college athletic ministry came out of his own pocket. Of course he ended up missing out on making a few extra dollars from community appearances, but he was not in it for the money. It was about serving students who were where Austin was just a few years earlier.

Aside from their work with college athletes, Austin and Erica began serving with International Justice Mission.[2] In 2018 they went to the Dominican Republic, and in 2019 they went to Guatemala. The idea was to fight against human trafficking and exploitation. They worked alongside other athletes, like Benjamin Watson and Dodgers pitcher Clayton Kershaw.

The Human Trafficking Institute estimates that there are 24.9 million victims of trafficking around the world. "Trafficking" is another term for "slavery." According to HTI, "The 24.9 million figure includes both sex trafficking, or commercial sexual exploitation, and forced labor exploitation, both in the private sector and state-imposed."[3] Of those 24.9 million, 20.1 million are in the category of forced labor, with 3.3 million of those being children. Some 4.8 are victims of sex trafficking, with more than a million of those being children. Women or girls make up 99 percent of sex trafficking victims.

Such exploitation takes place in every corner of the world, and the numbers are staggering. Yes, the global population is far greater now than it was centuries ago, but still, it's mind-boggling. Between the fifteenth and nineteenth centuries, an estimated thirteen million people were captured and sold into slavery. If you count people in forced marriages, some forty million people are in some form of bondage worldwide today.

Such realities are not often known or understood by the average American, especially those sitting at home watching their favorite football team play on Sundays. But for Austin and others, being in the NFL offered an opportunity to use their platform to see if they could help address this issue.

"By virtue of being an NFL player and having a heart for children," he says, "you're kind of thrust into a nation's spotlight for all the right reasons. The NFL opens so many doors for you to do so much good."

In July 2019 Austin and fellow Saint Geneo Grissom, along with their wives, Erica and Haley, joined Buffalo Bills defensive end Sam Acho and Geremy Davis and spent time with IJM's Team Freedom in Guatemala. They met with the Guatemalan sex crimes unit, called DIDS; an aftercare partner organization that provides safe homes for survivors of sexual violence; and even the vice president and attorney general of Guatemala, advocating for children's rights.

"Being a part of Team Freedom, which is the pro-advocacy group of IJM, was an honor," Austin said. "Joining the Team Freedom group to fight against sex trafficking and human exploitation is an awesome opportunity to love your neighbors as yourself. And when they announced the trip was to Guatemala and there were people in need of rescuing, advocacy in need, it was a great opportunity to use my platform for good and a good opportunity to spread the word about a group that's making the world a better place."[4]

They spoke to children who had endured sexual violence, encouraging them in their bravery. Geremy pointed out that they wanted to do more up-close ministry with these victims of abuse, and not just stay at a distance.

"I'm always quoting scripture, but 1 Peter 4:10 says, 'As each of you has received a gift, use it to be a service to one another using God's greatest grace,'" Davis said. "And I feel like that was just placed in my heart and I want to act off that, too, and not just from a distance."[5]

Aside from the justice work done in the area of child sex trafficking, it was a great opportunity for Austin and Geremy to connect in both service and in their faith in Christ.

It was Ben Watson, though, who really got Austin involved in IJM. Watson had come to New Orleans in 2013 and had played with the Saints through 2015. He spent 2016 out of football due to a ruptured Achilles, but came back in 2017 with the Baltimore Ravens. Then, at the age of thirty-eight, he returned to New Orleans for the 2018 season, which was Austin's second year with the club.

For Carr, the influence of Ben Watson cannot be overstated.

"I shared the locker room with him for one year," Austin says. "He had an impact on the locker room right away. He's not an outgoing guy, despite his social media activity. People might assume he's the life of the party, but I quickly found out that's not the case. He's really chill. He's a kind of quiet, composed, and confident kind of guy."

Ben had led spiritually and in the locker room every place he went in the NFL, whether it was New England, Baltimore, Cleveland, or New

Orleans. A man of high character, he had the respect of players and coaches all over the league.

In October of 2018, Saints veteran Jermon Bushrod and his wife, Jessica, suffered a terrible tragedy, one that would haunt any parent. A week before, Jessica had prematurely given birth to a daughter, Jordyn. But Jordyn was already in dire straits, and on October 18, tragically, she passed away. Jermon posted on his Instagram account, "My heart has been broken. My baby girl Jordyn Lynn Bushrod passed away Thursday October 18th. She was only here for a week, but we were ready to love her unconditionally. We will get through this with faith, family and friends. Thanks for prayers and support."

The camaraderie on a football team can be deep. At the next team meeting, Coach Payton brought the team together to give Jermon support. But Payton found the right words to be difficult. He asked Watson to pray.

"You could have heard a pin drop," Austin recalls. "Everyone was just dialed into Jermon, and to Ben's prayer of blessing and strength over them."

Ben's wife, Kirsten, was heavily involved in the team as well, ranging from giving motherly advice to the young players to supporting the players' wives, to leading a Bible study.

In just the nine months that they played together, Watson filled a significant role in Austin's life. They had a common faith, and they shared the fact that they had both been players under Bill Belichick in New England.

"He had a lot to say about that," Austin says with a chuckle.

The Saints made it to the NFC Championship Game at the end of the 2018 season, but Watson was unavailable for the game due to a bout of appendicitis. He managed to avoid surgery, but missed the biggest game of the year. The Rams beat the Saints 26–23 in overtime to advance to the Super Bowl to face the Patriots.

"One of the hardest things was to watch him have to lead from the sidelines during the NFC Championship Game," Austin says. Watson had won a Super Bowl in 2004, his rookie year in New England, but had only been back one time, during the Patriots' incredible 2007 season that ultimately fell short to the Giants.

Watson would only last one more year in the NFL, playing the 2019 season back in New England, where he started his career.

Meanwhile, in New Orleans, Austin started to experience the life of the fifty-third man in a different way. He played in six games in the 2019 season but then injured his ankle and needed surgery. He was placed on injured reserve in November, ending his season. But during that time, his place on the team had begun to grow in terms of spiritual leadership.

On Saturday nights the Saints had their team chapel. But Austin sensed the team needed something more. He began to invite his teammates to come to his hotel room to share what was in their hearts and to pray for one another. Sometimes just a few guys showed up. Other times as many as ten teammates joined in. It wasn't easy to be consistent about it, but Austin was committed.

"At a chapel, you're all facing the speaker," he says. "But in this prayer time, we were all circled up facing each other. It gave us a great space to really love on one another."

Brees, Watson, and Demario Davis had been the spiritual leaders among the players, and Austin felt a kinship with the other Christian guys on the team. As Watson left, Austin took on more leadership. He began to mentor younger players—rookies especially—because he had in mind the kind of players on the team that tended to feel marginalized due to their status.

"Rookies—they're typically the downtrodden or cast aside on a football team," he says. "It's seniority. That ranged from early draft picks to undrafted guys. I felt like the kingdom was advancing through me, for a veteran like me to just sit with them, ask them how they're doing, hearing their struggles, encouraging them, and sometimes giving them the kind of wisdom that comes from being in the league for a while."

The year 2020 was a crazy one for Austin, one that in some ways he'd rather forget. Of course, the COVID pandemic swept the nation, and the globe, and had a profound impact on everyone in the league. The season began under strange auspices, with intense COVID protocols for everyone involved in the NFL. The league instituted a new Reserve/COVID-19 list to handle positive cases and those in close contact with others who tested positive. Players were tested regularly.

As for fans, the NFL allowed fans, but on the condition that they wore masks. In some cities, however, local COVID restrictions meant that fans couldn't be in the stadium beyond a scant few. For example, the Jets and Giants banned fans because New Jersey's governor, Phil Murphy, set a statewide limit of five hundred people at any large event. In many other places, fan attendance reached several thousand, but so often, NFL stadiums felt barren. It was a surreal experience for everyone involved.

Austin's ankle injury never fully healed—even years later, it still bothers him. More than that, it was the challenge of bouncing back and forth between the practice squad and the fifty-three-man roster.

It began when he was waived following camp on September 5. The next day, the Saints signed him to the practice squad. A month later, on October 12, New Orleans called him up to the active roster, but the very next day he was returned to the practice squad. Three more times, Austin ping-ponged between the two situations: October 24, fifty-three-man, October 26, practice squad. October 31, fifty-three-man, November 2, practice squad. November 28, fifty-three-man, November 30, practice squad.

It was a tough situation, not knowing where he would be, not feeling like a real part of the team.

"I wasn't part of the game plan, you know? Bouncing between the practice squad and the fifty-three-man roster. My ankle was hurting. I'm tired of the team at different points of the season. That's just how it was. But God had work for me to do, and I didn't want to miss out on it."

By the end of the season, he had played in six games, catching three passes for twenty-seven yards, The highlight came in the last game of the regular season, a 33–7 win over Carolina. The Saints were up 26–7 and on the Panther eleven-yard line, and on first down, Drew Brees dropped back and faked a handoff. Austin, lined up on the right, raced up the seam, slicing between three defenders. Brees threw a perfect pass and, leaping, Austin caught it in the end zone, just as Panther safety Tre Boston, a 205-pounder from North Carolina, arrived on the scene. He drove into Austin, spinning him around and sending him sprawling. But he held on for his first and only touchdown of the season, and only the third of his NFL career.

The next week, he was inactive in the Wild Card round victory over the Bears, but the next day, the Saints waived him. On January 13, he was signed to the practice squad again, but the end came three days later, the day before the Divisional Round game against Tampa Bay and old friend Tom Brady, when the Saints released him from the practice squad. Not only wouldn't he play in the game—a 30–20 loss to the Bucs—but he wouldn't even be part of the team when the Saints took the field. It was a disappointing way to end his season.

Though on the field Austin did not see the success he hoped for, he had taken important steps in his leadership in the locker room and in the community, using his platform as a veteran NFL player to influence younger players, college athletes, and even kids in other countries who had been victims of sexual abuse. Austin the player had experienced struggle; Austin the man had experienced great success.

Chapter 23

Victories

There are victories, and there are victories. For Vince Lombardi, victory—winning—was the only thing that mattered. Lombardi famously once said, "Winning isn't everything; it's the only thing." But victory can look different for different people. World-renowned cricket player MS Dhoni said, "I believe in giving 100 percent on the field, and I don't really worry about the result if there's great commitment on the field. That's victory for me."[1]

For fifty-third men, certainly there are games to be won, but for most, there is very little individual glory. David Tyree is one example where a bottom roster player had a dazzling moment that changed the course of NFL history.

Tyree played his college ball at Syracuse and was a solid wide receiver—at the time of his graduation, he was thirteenth on the school's career receiving-yards list with 1,214—but his main contribution was on special teams. Particularly, he was a specialist on the punt return team, blocking six punts in his career.

The Giants drafted Tyree in the sixth round of the 2003 draft (number 211 overall), and, like Geremy Davis more than a decade later, they viewed him as primarily a special teams player.

As a rookie, Tyree played in all sixteen games, starting three of them. He was a demon on special teams, recording seventeen tackles, and he even contributed as a receiver, hauling in sixteen receptions for 211 yards. But he knew the whole time that if his special teams play ever dropped off, he would be cut, because the Giants did not see his receiving skills as being sufficient to occupy a roster spot. His place on the fifty-three-man squad was wholly dependent on his ability to perform in a special teams capacity.

It was more of the same in 2004—a few opportunities as a receiver, but lots of excellent work on special teams, and in 2005 he made the Pro Bowl as a special teams player. While he seemed to be solidly not a bottom-of-the-roster player, Tyree's career always hung on the thread of his special teams work.

In 2007, his play at wide receiver diminished, being targeted just five times and making four catches. Only playing twelve games due to injuries, Tyree recorded just nine tackles for the season. He was still an important special teams player, but one with reduced production and virtually no impact on the offense.

But history would shine on David Tyree. The Giants finished 10–6 that season and went on a phenomenal postseason run, knocking off Tampa Bay and Green Bay en route to the Super Bowl.

Tyree had had a difficult week of practice leading up to the game. Plaxico Burress was New York's star receiver, and one thing Bill Belichick defenses usually did was take away a team's best weapon. That would open doors for other players, including Tyree. Yet his miserable week before the Super Bowl left him and the team shaken. That is, until Friday—the team's last real practice. Tyree turned in his best performance and seemed to finally be in sync. Eli Manning spoke with his brother Peyton and said, "Guess what? David Tyree had the best practice of his life."[2]

The Super Bowl was a tough grind for both teams, and the Patriots held a 7–3 lead going into the fourth quarter. Tyree had made little contribution on special teams, but, per the game plan, he played more than usual as a wide receiver. He caught his first pass in the second quarter, a six-yarder from Eli Manning. But it was his next two catches that served as the biggest moments in Tyree's entire career.

Down four points, the Giants marched from their own twenty-yard line down to the Patriot five. On the second-down snap, Tyree bolted upfield and turned in, and Manning threw a dart that Tyree caught for the touchdown to give New York the lead.

The Patriots would answer late in the fourth quarter, as Tom Brady hit Randy Moss for a touchdown to give the Patriots a 14–10 lead with just 2:45 left in the game. It seemed like New England would indeed complete a perfect 19–0 season. But the Giants weren't done yet. Facing second and five from their own forty-four, Eli threw a pass that was nearly intercepted by Asante Samuel.

"I didn't jump high enough," Samuel said. "Maybe if I'd jumped a little higher. . . . " But he didn't, and the Giants were still alive.

Given a second chance, Eli Manning and David Tyree put together one of the greatest plays in NFL history.

The Patriots' rush swarmed Manning as he dropped back to pass on third down. No less than three defenders surrounded him. Richard Seymour had hold of Manning's jersey and it seemed like he was about to go down. Somehow Manning spun out of it, turned, and flung the ball forty yards downfield toward Tyree, who jumped high for the ball and managed to get his hands on it. Patriot defender Rodney Harrison collided with Tyree and tried to rip the ball free. Tyree pinned the ball to his helmet and, with Harrison pulling at it, the two of them crashed to the ground. Incredibly, Tyree held on, and the Giants had a thirty-two-yard gain and a first down. A handful of plays later, Manning hit Plaxico Burress for the game-winning touchdown in the left corner of the end zone, dashing New England's hopes for a perfect season.

David Tyree experienced the ultimate victory for a bottom-of-the-roster player—or any player, for that matter. He won the Super Bowl. Moreover, he made two enormous plays to contribute to the win. One of those plays, of course, would go down as one of the greatest moments in NFL history.

Not bad for a guy the Giants didn't even think could play wide receiver.

The "helmet catch" was the last pass Tyree would ever catch in the NFL.

"For me, it's this moment that I call the monumental moment," Tyree said of that play. "It's always something that I can go back to and celebrate with fans and teammates. And to be a part of history is pretty monumental. It's amazing."[3]

* * *

Jonas Gray was a classic fifty-third man—a journeyman in the NFL.

For a player who came into college with serious hype and promise, his six-year NFL journey wasn't easy, bouncing around the league, and on and off practice squads and fifty-three-man rosters. Nonetheless, he was drawing an NFL paycheck, and he did suit up in an NFL uniform for two years.

Still, like everyone else in his situation, he wanted his chance.

Let go by the Ravens, Gray signed a futures contract with the Patriots in January 2014. He was cut on the last day of camp, but the Patriots signed him to their practice squad—by now a familiar place for Gray. He worked hard, and Bill Belichick told him, "You're close." Following an injury to starting running back Stevan Ridley, on October 16 the Patriots promoted him to the fifty-three-man roster and activated him for their game against the Jets. He carried the ball three times for twelve yards in a 27–25 victory, playing eleven snaps overall.

The next week he carried the ball seventeen times for eighty-six yards against the Bears, and he was growing into his role. Then came twelve more carries for thirty-three yards against the Broncos. By this point, Gray was clearly part of the running back rotation in Ridley's absence.

Week eleven—Gray's fourth NFL game—was against the Indianapolis Colts. Indy had won six of their last seven contests and thought they were ready to move into the AFC's elite class.

They had no idea what was about to hit them.

Neither did most NFL fans, for whom Jonas Gray was still a totally unknown quantity. Gray, despite getting thirty carries the previous two weeks, was left alone by most fantasy football participants in the belief that he would produce very little in the game against Indianapolis's tough defense.[4]

But Bill Belichick had a plan, and it involved a heavy dose of Jonas Gray. Patriots owner Robert Kraft, told Gray before the game, "I think this is going to be a big week for you."

In the closed confines of Lucas Oil Stadium, Gray carried the ball a whopping thirty-seven times for an astounding 201 yards and four touchdowns. They had no answer for the electric Gray. The Indianapolis crowd had no idea what was happening. Who was this guy?

"I was like a kid in a candy store," Gray said after the game. "It was like nothing I could describe. To get to that point, the dedication it takes, the hard work, it's hard to even describe it to people. I mean, it's a blast."[5]

His performance led to a cover of *Sports Illustrated*, something that Gray couldn't even have imagined just a few weeks before.

Meanwhile, the Pittsburgh Steelers released LeGarrette Blount, a running back with a similar build and game as Gray. The Patriots quickly signed him. Gray, however, was focused on the next game—a home game against Detroit. That Thursday night, Gray worked late into the night studying film. A cardinal rule in the Patriots' organization is never to be late to anything. Gray plugged his phone into his charger and fell asleep. What he didn't realize was that the charging cord wasn't fully plugged in, and the phone never charged.

He woke up suddenly in the morning and looked at his phone. It read 8:30—an hour after the team meeting had started. He saw a text from Vince Wilfork that simply said, "Are you OK?" Gray panicked. The Patriots, worried about Gray, sent Kevin Anderson, their football operations manager, to check on him. Jonas was OK, but by then it was too late to show up to Gillette Stadium. Anderson told Gray to wait there until he was called. Finally he was summoned and made his way to the facility at

5:30 p.m. When he tried to explain to Belichick what happened, Belichick simply said, "We can't have it."

For Gray, this was the beginning of the end. He received just twenty more carries the rest of the season, and was inactive for the Patriots' Super Bowl game against Seattle. He had his chance, he made the most of it against the Colts in spectacular fashion, but one slip-up ended it all. He would play in eight games the following season for two other teams—Jacksonville and Miami—but that was the last the NFL ever saw of Jonas Gray.

Looking back, Gray wondered what his career could have been.

"I don't think I'd still be with the Patriots," he said. "But I'd definitely be in the NFL. I probably would be somewhere with a large contract playing on a team."[6]

He no longer had a place in the league, but he will always have the game against the Colts and the cover of *Sports Illustrated*. There are victories and there are victories.

* * *

For Geremy Davis, there were no Super Bowl moments like David Tyree had. There wasn't even a one-game performance like Jonas Gray's. For Davis, victory looked a little different.

His first success came on Saturday, September 5, 2015, when he survived the final cuts. As one columnist pointed out, "Geremy Davis wasn't supposed to be here. He wasn't supposed to make it to the NFL. He would, maybe, make a practice squad somewhere. Maybe. Maybe is overrated."[7] A week later, Davis took the field against the Dallas Cowboys and his football idol, Tony Romo.

But for Geremy, the first big moment on the field came a month later when the Giants played the 49ers. With the score tied at 20 following a Colin Kaepernick touchdown pass to Garrett Celek, the Giants took over at their own twenty-one-yard line with 11:44 left in the game. A minute later, they faced a third-and-one situation from the New York thirty. Eli Manning connected with Geremy for sixteen yards, a key conversion in a drive that would end up scoring three points, giving New York a 23–20 lead.

Davis recalls the play: "It was third down, and I remember the signal for the play. It was a bubble and a slant, and the signal was like this [holds up his left hand, with thumb and first two fingers extended], and I was like, 'Oh shoot, it's coming to me!' I just said, 'Bro all you gotta do is run a slant and catch it.' I believe it was cover three at the time, and when the guy ran the bubble, the defender went for the bubble, and the slant was open. I caught it. First down. That was like my first real catch that meant something."

Al Michaels had the call: "And that is caught for a first down by Geremy Davis, a rookie from Connecticut, a sixth-round pick."

Cris Collinsworth added, "One thing you always have to know about a receiver—is he gonna be willing to run over the middle here and take a hit. Nice job. Good, clutch play. You come in the game and want to do something good for your team. It's a good start."

Davis would only have the one reception in the game, but it kept the drive alive. New York would keep the ball for another eight minutes, and Josh Brown kicked a twenty-four-yard field goal to give the Giants the lead. Those three points would end up being the difference in the game.

"We came back and won that game," says Davis, "so I feel like I actually contributed."

Three years later, Davis entered his third camp with the Chargers, unsure about his spot on the team. For players on the fringes of NFL rosters, camp can sometimes provide their career highlight. Davis had not established himself as a sure thing with the Chargers, and he needed a big camp to solidify his place on the roster.

On August 11, 2018, they played the Cardinals in a preseason game. Facing a third and nineteen on the Cardinal forty-seven, quarterback Geno Smith heaved a pass deep down the left sideline toward his six-foot-three target, number 11, Geremy Davis. Davis was closely covered by Chris Campbell, a sixth-round draft pick out of Penn State. Davis leapt high and made an acrobatic catch over Campbell's head. He landed in an awkward position but somehow kept his balance, stepping into the end zone for a spectacular touchdown.

Davis smiles when thinking about that catch. "Even though preseason isn't important according to some people, that was the best camp I ever had in my whole career. It was the Arizona play. Third and nineteen, and we call a double move. And Geno throws it up to me. I just take it off the guy's head. I scored my first touchdown. Even though it was preseason, it was still my first touchdown. I think that play established me as the frontrunner to make the team. Every year the Chargers' first four guys were always solidified, but that fifth spot was always a battle."

That play, and that camp, helped Davis make the LA's fifty-three-man roster that year. The previous two seasons he had played a total of five games with the Chargers, spending most of his time either inactive or on the practice squad. At twenty-six, he was approaching do-or-die time in the league.

After being inactive in week one against the Chiefs, Davis was on the active game roster the next six games, but he never played even half of the special teams' snaps. He was on the team and playing (his snap count maxed out at thirteen in week six against Cleveland), but he hadn't really made it yet.

That changed heading into week seven.

Geremy credits special teams coach George Stewart with helping him transform into a top-tier special teams player. Davis explains that "if you're going to be that fifth guy [at WR], you have to do it on special teams. So I was always on and off the practice squad to active. But in 2018, Coach George Stewart changed my position on special teams. I watched film every day in camp. And 2018 was the year where I was like, I'm about to go crazy on special teams, and I did."

The Chargers went on the road in week seven to play the Seahawks in Seattle. Two weeks before, LA played Tennessee at Wembley Stadium in London.

Davis says, "My breakout game as a special teams ace was against Seattle [November 4, 2018]. One player got in trouble in London against the Titans. I was his backup on two special teams. So against Seattle I was going to be a full-time special teams guy—playing all four phases." Davis knew he would get a lot of playing time in the Seattle game—more than he had so far in his whole career with the Chargers.

But there was more—an unexpected twist.

"So going into that game," he says, "the head coach picked me as a captain for this game. I had no idea he was going to pick me." For a player like Davis, being named game captain was quite the honor.

"Yeah, that was sick," he says. "That was real sick. Standing next to Russ [Okung], Philip [Rivers], [Brandon] Mebane, and Mel [Melvin Gordon] and stuff, walking out to the coin toss. It was funny because I was, like, antsy. It was sick. I was like, let's walk and do the coin toss! There's a picture and I'm like three steps in front of everybody, because I'm like so excited to be a captain, which was awesome."

Before the game, however, Geremy's troublesome hamstrings set alarm bells off again. He made it into the game nevertheless, and that's when, for him, the magic began.

"It's funny because as I was warming up I felt a little something in my hamstring, and I prayed, Lord protect me," Davis says. "And on the first kickoff play [of the second quarter, after the Chargers had scored] I ran down there and got the tackle. A couple of kickoff plays later, another tackle. Everyone on the sideline was like, man Geremy is going *off* this game. Later we go out for a punt, and I got another tackle. I had three tackles. So after the game, I got a game ball for being the special teams player of the game, which was sick. I was like, dang, I became a captain that game, solidified myself as a dominant special teams player, and for sure that was the game where I finally felt secure in my spot on the team. I could go into the building and not look over my shoulder constantly."

Davis's spot on the team seemed relatively secure. In the last seven weeks of the season, he would go on to play in the majority of special teams snaps in every game. He even played significant offensive snaps in two of the games. It seemed like he had finally arrived in the NFL. Davis looks back on these moments with fondness, understanding that for his career, they constituted success in the league.

"So all these moments for me," Davis says, "they might not seem exciting for a superstar wide receiver or the common fan, but to me those were victories. It would have been awesome to score a game-winning touchdown, or say I went for seven catches and 150 yards and a touchdown, but I've come to understand that if it was the Lord's will for me to only have nineteen career tackles, and five catches, then I can be content to fulfill the Lord's will, you know? It's not exciting, but I learned to be content with that."

There are victories and there are victories. Geremy had achieved victory in the NFL.

Chapter 24

Done

At twenty-nine years of age, Davis thought he still had plenty of good football left in him. Aside from his nagging hamstring issues, he was in good condition. Plus, he hadn't taken that many big hits over the course of his NFL career. Nobody in the NFL is perfectly healthy, but Geremy thought he was as healthy as one could be for a guy who had been in the league for five years.

The Chargers had let him go following the 2019 season, and at the start of the 2020 football year, the Detroit Lions signed him to a one-year contract worth just over a million dollars. But his hamstrings acted up all camp long, and the Lions—a team that Geremy genuinely believed would finally give him a shot as a wide receiver—had to cut bait. They released Geremy on September 1, on the last day of cuts.

That left Geremy without a football home, and the entire 2020 season went by without an opportunity to play in the league. And so, a few months shy of his thirtieth birthday, having seen his most recent shot at the NFL go by, he wondered what was next. What came next was a trip north.

In February 2021, Geremy signed with the Toronto Argonauts of the Canadian Football League. It was a chance for him to get a new start, in the hopes that he would put it together and another NFL team would come calling. His travel to Canada was delayed due to COVID protocols preventing Americans from moving into the country, but he finally arrived and began working out with the team. It wasn't the NFL, but it was still professional football.

But on Monday, July 19, the day before final cuts, he pulled his hamstring again. Always the damned hamstrings. In a text, Davis would say, "I think I'm done man. I don't know about rehabbing and still trying to play. I don't think God wants me to."

The next day the Argonauts cut him, and Davis's professional football career was over, just like that.

His pro career lasted longer than most. He did not play as many snaps as he wished he could have. He did not get to truly contribute as a pass-catching wide receiver. He never won a Super Bowl. But he was an NFL player for more than five seasons and made several million dollars. He left the game in good health, despite the shaky hamstrings. On the whole, he had a successful pro career.

On his LinkedIn account, he wrote: "My years of being a professional football player did not come easily and those years taught me a great deal about myself and my capabilities. One of my favorite quotes that inspires me daily is 'Do not grow weary of doing good, that in due season you will reap, if you do not give up' by the apostle Paul. I personally walk this out every day. The athletics industry is challenging, and there are times when things might not go the way you envisioned."

For Geremy, the pro football experience featured many ups and downs, as befitting a fifty-third man: three different organizations, spending time on the practice squad, on the fifty-three-man roster as an inactive player, and being active for thirty-six games. He played with some stars along the way—including players like Eli Manning, Philip Rivers, and Antonio Gates. He got the chance to make lifelong friends, and see his high school buddy, Max Garcia, succeed in the league. He led spiritually and mentored younger players, and gave back to others, both in the local community and globally through IJM.

The relationships he began over his time in the league have meant so much to him.

"A lot of us, we still have a group chat," he says. "We still push each other, we celebrate each other."

But it was time to move on, and Geremy sought new avenues. His first step was to launch a ministry called *Obedience Over Religion*, a YouTube channel and Instagram reel where he would talk about a variety of issues related to faith and encourage people whether they are athletes or not. Geremy had gained a deep understanding of God during his time in college, and it grew as an NFL player.

Aside from his ministry, Geremy has gotten into helping others become better athletes. He launched a company called Training 148, based on 1 Timothy 4:8, which says, "While bodily training is of some value, godliness is of value in every way, as it holds promise for the present life and also for the life to come." He seeks to build into younger athletes both physically and spiritually.

Recently he had a conversation with Preston Hale, a defensive back trainer in Arizona, where Geremy lives.

"It's amazing that the Lord has taken me out of football," Geremy said.

Preston shook his head. "Nah, man. It's not that the Lord has taken you out of football. He's just transitioned you to teaching football."

For Geremy, that was a great perspective. He works specifically with wide receivers, teaching footwork, the art of route running, and especially how to play against the defensive backs they would go up against. One hallmark of Geremy's training is a reduced reliance on cones to teach proper route running.

"It looks cute, but it's not football," he says. "You need cones as landmarks, but when I'm training someone, I'm training them how to beat a coverage. It's more important to do things against a body as opposed to a stationary cone. So working against press releases, we will work on press releases versus a corner who's playing a one-robber technique with outside leverage."

Preston had told him, "If you can't do it as a trainer, you shouldn't be teaching it." Geremy has taken that advice to heart, and while he may not be in shape to play a sixty-minute football game, he can still do all the drills and compete with the guys he's training.

"If I'm going to teach guys a certain release," he says, "I have to be capable of doing it myself."

Geremy sees coaching in his future. In 2022, he joined the Philadelphia Eagles during camp, as part of the Bill Walsh Diversity Coaching Internship. The program, which began in 1987, provides training camp opportunities for minority coaches throughout the league. It allows prospective coaches to observe up close how an NFL coaching staff works, the roles that coaches play, and how an NFL training camp is run. Geremy, of course, had firsthand experience with some of this, but his perspective as a player was very different from that of a coach.

More than two thousand people, a mix of former players and coaches at both the high school and college levels, have gone through the program since its inception. Geremy's chance came with the Eagles, and he made the most of it. Several NFL head coaches came through the program, including men like Mike Tomlin, Marvin Lewis, and Lovie Smith.

Davis has taken his experience from his time with the Eagles and turned it into a high school coaching opportunity. Mountain View High School in Mesa, Arizona, has won eight state championships, and been state runner up five more times. Joe Germaine, a former standout at Mountain View, took over the program in 2021 and quickly formed a relationship with Geremy.

"I respect the head coach Joe Germaine," Geremy says, "who was the first coach out here in Arizona that started giving me clients to train. He did right by me in terms of my rates, and then after this internship, I was like, 'If I'm going to start coaching, it'll be with Joe.'"

In the summer of 2022, Germaine hired Davis to be his wide receivers coach, and now Geremy sees the game from a different perspective.

"This internship with the Eagles, I learned so much stuff," he says. "I said, 'What better way to practice it than to start with high school football.' Things I learned in terms of film, in terms of what to look for when coaching on the sidelines. I'm taking a lot of those things I learned from the Eagles and bringing it to the high school level."

Geremy has built his post-NFL life on the foundation of his faith and his desire to impart wisdom to the next generation, both on and off the field. At some point, he hopes the doors open up for him to become part of an NFL coaching staff.

"In terms of aspirations, I do want to coach in the NFL," he says. "Doing this internship, lots of guys get jobs from it."

But for now, he is in a good place.

"I'm very content with where I'm at right now."

* * *

Despite all my success in high school and college and getting drafted in the NFL, I was a bubble guy. Now, just because you're a bubble guy, doesn't mean it's over for you. I mean, I got six years in the league! Find a way to make it work. Write your own story. For guys like myself who are bubble guys, we have to put in a lot more work than the established guys or the superstars to hang around.

So you know I have to throw you some scripture now. In Galatians 6:7 it says, "Whatever one sows, that will he also reap." We have to sow a lot in order to reap the fruit. Sometimes we sow like crazy, and we don't see the fruit that we want to see. However, two verses down in verse 9, we see, "Do not grow weary in doing good, for in due season, you will reap if you don't give up."

Do not give up. I wouldn't say that my career was fantastic statistically. But my role still had value. I mean, I played on scout team where I gave a look for the defense that week. I was a core special teams guy where I made key blocks and made tackles. I went in at receiver to be a blocking receiver that led to first downs and touchdowns. And the very few catches that I did make, which was only five, continued drives and led to field goals and touchdowns. And even with just that, it led to six years in the NFL, which I'm for sure grateful for.

Finally, find the importance of contentment. Not complacency, but contentment. With contentment, you can be at peace in everything you do, if you put in your best effort, no matter what the results are.

—Geremy Davis

Chapter 25

Giving Back

For Marcell Ateman, there is still hope of playing.

"I still love football," he says. "I'm still young. I'm healthy. So of course I'd love to keep playing. When I was out there playing [with Arizona], I still felt that joy."

Given how short the average NFL career is, most players see their careers end like Marcell's—still young enough to play, still with the desire to play, but with the league effectively telling them their time is up. That is always a difficult pill to swallow. But every player needs to come to terms with that reality.

Former Patriots' wide receiver Malcolm Mitchell found life after the NFL to be excruciatingly difficult. Like most pro athletes, Mitchell had connected his sport to his identity in a deep and powerful way. It wasn't just that he played football; he *was* a football player. Virtually every NFL player was a highly successful athlete throughout almost his entire life. It is difficult to disconnect your identity from the sport you were so successful at since you could walk.

"If you don't have a foundation of who you are, outside of that sport, you're going to be shit out of luck," he said in an interview with Tim Layden of NBC Sports. "I guess I knew I would have this breakup with football someday. I just didn't know how bad it would be on my mental health. It's like I've been reincarnated as somebody else. And I don't want to be anybody else."

The same struggle impacts so many former pro athletes, regardless of their sport. Too many football players don't take their college studies seriously enough, perhaps banking on making it in the NFL. But that plan goes awry far more often than it works. For Marcell, it was tough to be released from the Raiders and not be picked up by another team, but he has had to come to grips with the reality that his career is likely over.

"I'm at peace with it now," he says, noting that, nonetheless, he wouldn't say no to another opportunity to join another team in the future. But every day that goes by without an invitation to an NFL camp is another day further from another NFL snap in his future. He knows that possibility grows dimmer and dimmer with each passing week.

"If it gets to the point where it's just not happening, I'll make the decision to just turn the page," he says.

Fortunately, Marcell has other interests. Like Geremy Davis, Matthew Slater, and Austin Carr, Marcell has chosen to use the opportunities the NFL has availed him to invest in others. He launched the Marcell Ateman Foundation[1] to give back to kids in his community. The foundation's mission is to provide students from Wylie East High School—his alma mater—with scholarships that allow them to pursue college.

Timmy is one of the first students to receive such a scholarship. Born in Africa, he grew up in the Dallas area. Tragically, he lost his mother and father at a young age and faced dim prospects for the future. The Marcell Ateman Foundation provided him with two years' worth of tuition to go to college. He is the first in his family's history to continue his education after high school. It's a chance to change the course not only of Timmy's life, but of future generations of his family.

"It was a blessing and a privilege to help him go to school and make maybe a generational change in his life," Marcell says.

Aside from his foundation's work, Ateman has found meaning in developing athletic skills in teenagers. Presently he trains football players and even non-football players in their athleticism. He has worked with a local baseball team not on things like throwing mechanics or the proper swing plane at bat, but rather how to quickly change directions and other body mechanics designed to make them better athletes.

Marcell points out that when he was a teenager, he had to go outside the city to get the training he needed. He finds great joy in providing such training for kids right in the city itself, affording kids the chance to improve in ways that not long ago they couldn't access.

"I want to pour into these kids and give them an opportunity to learn from someone who's been through every stage of it," he says.

The common theme for all these men is the desire to give back to others. They all recognize the gifts they were given, and the responsibility they have to pass those gifts on to others. Each of these men has a faith rooted in the understanding that God has blessed them and that they are called to bring blessing to others.

It is a lesson we can all learn from them, whether we are fifty-third men or not.

* * *

There are three main ideas that I've stood by. Number one, you've got to have a why. Whatever that why is to you, that's what you need to have as your foundation. That's what you need to be grounded in. For me, that's my faith. Anytime things get rocky, anytime something happens, I can always lean on my faith and my family to encourage me in that.

Number two is you've got to be consistent. In anything you do, most people want you to be consistent in what you're doing. And that's true if it's performance based, if it's checking in on people to see how they're doing, if it's community service or other types of service, you have to be consistent.

And number three, it's got to be fun for you. You have to make sure you have fun and have joy in what you do or then you're just working. It just becomes a job, it feels like you want to be directed somewhere else.

So know your why, be consistent, and enjoy what you do.

—Marcell Ateman

Chapter 26

Do Justice

Football isn't over yet for Matthew Slater. At thirty-seven years of age, in his fifteenth season, he continues to play at a high level. And yet he has already begun the transition to life after football.

When he entered the league as a rookie, he was the quintessential fifty-third man, a special teams–only player that every week fought for his place on the roster. He grew into his role and became one of the better special teams players on the team, and then in the NFL. During his first three years, he kept his head down, put his hand to the plow, and just worked on his craft. But as he grew into his captaincy and in his elevated leadership in a spiritual sense on the team, Matthew began to feel the urge to be about more than football.

He started working in the community, a desire that grew out of his faith and upbringing. Having grown up in a Christian home with parents who were invested in their own community, he saw firsthand how an athlete could positively impact others.

"My interest and involvement in the community obviously stems from my faith as a Christian," he says. "The Lord has blessed my family . . . , not just so we can have those blessings ourselves, but I think he wants us to bless others in his Name."

This desire fit perfectly with the Patriots as an organization. Owner Robert Kraft was heavily invested in numerous ventures to do good in the community, and his late wife, Myra, even more so. It was part and parcel of Patriots' team culture for the team—everyone from ownership down— to be ambassadors in the community. He quickly got on board with the ethos of giving back that flowed throughout the Patriots organization.

At first, his involvement stuck to the things the Patriots were doing. Over the years, he built up relationships throughout New England that opened the door to more. Over time, Matthew began to go beyond those efforts. During the COVID-19 pandemic, he and his wife, Shahrzad, started the Slater Family Foundation,[1] which has allowed them to focus on areas they are particularly passionate about: education, health care, and justice. They seek to connect people and resources in underserved communities, particularly in the Providence, Rhode Island, area. Every year they host a Community Jamboree in Providence, which is essentially a resource fair—taking organizations that are active in the city and bringing them to people in the community who need those resources.

They also are involved in helping bring people the health care they need. Shahrzad has been particularly passionate about this aspect of community service, something Matthew knew about when they first met and Shahrzad was still in medical school. Another vision driven by Shahrzad was to help increase literacy. They established a program through a local school to help promote reading and literacy. For Matthew and Shahrzad, education is such a key factor for kids in disadvantaged communities to succeed.

In March 2019, Slater and teammates Duron Harmon, and Devin and Jason McCourty stood before members of the Massachusetts State House to lend their voice in support of a bill that would boost investment in education, something very much in line with Matthew and Shahrzad's passions. It meant a lot to Matthew to have his teammates partner with him in this effort, as all three had been pushing for education reform for several years.

"Do we use the best available knowledge to do our best to improve the foundation of all of our children?" they wrote in a joint piece in 2018. "Or do we tell our children to sit and wait while we do more research? If we are complacent, will our children in less affluent circumstances fall farther and farther behind? All our children deserve an equal chance at success regardless of their economic backgrounds. Shouldn't our policies reflect that?"

Education, literacy, resourcing, and health care all fall under the larger heading of justice, something Matthew has always seen as a bedrock moral principle in his life. It flows out of his understanding of an Old Testament passage, Micah 6:8, which says, "He has told you, O man, what is good; and what does the Lord require of you but to do justice, and to love kindness, and to walk humbly with your God?"

For Matthew, it's not equality of outcomes that he's aiming for, but equal access to opportunity. He sees the disparities that exist between affluent areas and communities with scarce resources. Children, he points out, don't have a choice about which family or zip code or circumstance they're born into. He seeks to bridge that gap and provide opportunities, especially in the area of education, for kids in under-resourced communities.

"I believe every child should have a chance to get a good education," he says. "What they choose to do with it is on them, but it should be afforded them at least."

This is where Shahrzad and Matthew work as a team, together marshaling their efforts, building bridges in the community, seeking ways to use the privilege he has as a professional athlete to make a difference in the lives of those less fortunate. In fact, he says that Shahrzad is the driving force behind their work.

"I can't take credit for any of the work our foundation does," Matthew says. "That goes to my wife, who was bold enough to ask God to provide a way for us to do this."

But it's not just the Slater family. He has tried to model such service to his teammates, especially the younger men on the Patriots. Football for Matthew is not just about winning a Super Bowl or being an All Pro or signing the big contract. It's about the responsibility he has with the platform he has as an athlete, and he seeks to use that platform in a way that can positively affect others. His influence in this area has been telling, as he's seen many of his younger teammates follow suit.

"It's a part of the legacy that this generation has left, that maybe in previous generations past, they didn't have the chance to do it," he says. "When I came into the league, it was like, yeah, we'll do community service, but we don't want to overdo it. You're here for football and that's who you are. But now I feel like the conversations and the access and intentionality is so geared toward the multifaceted player. It's not just him on the football field. He cares about people, he cares about the community, he cares about justice. It's great that we've been able to be a part of ushering that change in."

When his time in the NFL is officially up, Matthew's mind goes back to one of his first loves—ministry. He loves the idea of coaching but then laughs when he thinks about the hours Belichick and his staff put in on a weekly basis.

"Maybe ministry is something I do as a layperson, and I can use my life experience to encourage others however I can. I think my wife and I view ministry as a family—we all do ministry, whether it's in our kids' school or in the community. I'm keeping an open mind, whether it be in business or other arenas. For so long I've said, I won't do this, I won't do that, but God has shown me that I don't know what I'm doing, that he is in charge of it. So my job is to just be obedient to the Lord in whatever he calls us to do."

He would love to stay connected to the Patriots, an organization that has come to mean so much to him. That is, he says with a laugh, "in any other capacity besides coaching."

But that time is not yet for Matthew.

* * *

Before you start thinking about life in the NFL, you need to think about life as being you. I think it's important for young people as they aspire to pursue their dreams that they have a strong sense of self, a strong sense of who you are. This is what I would have told my younger self—that the man or woman you are matters.

As you pursue your dreams, you have to realize there's a cost. A lot of times we don't talk about the cost. We talk about the end destination, which is not guaranteed, but I think you have to learn to embrace the cost that comes with pursuing your dreams, especially in terms of becoming a professional athlete. There's going to be weddings missed, funerals missed, vacations missed, parties missed . . . whatever it is, there's a cost involved in it. You have to make a decision at some point in your life that you're going to pursue A over B, and there will be times when that pursuit is hard and disappointing and can let you down. But if that pursuit is worth it to you, I say pursue it with everything you have.

The Lord gives us very few opportunities in life to do something of this particular nature, and when he does, you should pursue it wholeheartedly. And you should work at it as unto him, with an attitude of gratitude, with a passion. So how you go about pursuing it is about a mindset, a willingness to be selfless and have discipline and a belief in what you're doing. Those things are more important, that's what really separates those that can and cannot do it.

To the young people out there thinking about pursuing your dreams, I say: do it. Believe in yourself. Believe in the process. Enjoy the process. Don't be so focused on the end destination, but enjoy the process.

—Matthew Slater

Chapter 27

A Helping Hand

Following the 2020 season, the Saints approached Austin, looking to sign him to a futures deal,[1] which for Austin was a nonstarter. His agent informed him that there was interest from other teams, and he didn't want to lock himself out of other options.

He knew that he needed to take care of his body. His doctor prescribed injections to facilitate healing in his ailing ankle, but he knew he needed an extended period of time. As a wide receiver relying on quick cuts, and needing to maximize every bit of his speed, he had to make sure the ankle healed. He knew he wouldn't be ready for football activity for a while. That's when the Indianapolis Colts called and wanted to work him out with the idea of signing him. They told Austin that if everything checked out, they would sign him.

"That's as direct as you can get for a fifty-third guy," Austin says. "A team wanting to sign you, coming right out and saying it that way."

But Austin couldn't work out, given the state of his ankle. He told them he needed to wait, and the moment and opportunity passed.

At this point in time, the COVID vaccination had become available, and teams were wanting players to be vaccinated. As in other major sports, and of course throughout society in general, not everyone desired to take the vaccine, especially not right away. A couple of months after his missed opportunity with Indianapolis, his body was feeling better, and he was in much better shape, ready to latch on with another team.

In the meanwhile, Erica gave birth to their first child, a boy named Clive, in April. Of course, a new baby only increased the responsibility he felt to provide. But NFL COVID protocols made it difficult or impossible for an unvaccinated player like Austin to play. Along came the Jets at the start of training camp, but when they found out he wasn't vaccinated, they decided to move on.

"I don't know if they needed a camp body or if they really wanted me," Austin says. "But that day, I decided to go get vaccinated, because this is terrible. I hated just having to wait and not be signable."

He got the Pfizer vaccine, but policy held that he wasn't really vaccinated until two weeks after his second dose, which couldn't come until six weeks after his first dose. That meant that his issue, as far as NFL teams were concerned, wasn't solved. And the timeline essentially removed him from every team's training camp. That didn't stop teams from inquiring, however.

"The Baltimore Ravens tried really hard," Austin says. "They went to the league with my antibodies test,[2] but the league shot it down, and that was that."

At that point, training camps were nearly over, and Austin could see the writing on the wall.

"How bad do I want to chase this dream?" he says, looking back. "How much is all the pain worth? On top of that, my ankle is still pretty bad. Life-changing bad. My ankle doesn't even feel good today [two years later]."

That extended time away from the game made him realize that even if another team signed him during the season, he would never be fully healthy. He figured he would only ever be the 80–85 percent version of himself, and for a player who needed every single bit of his speed, it wasn't enough in the NFL.

Austin thought long and hard about his situation. And things were quickly becoming clear.

"I've got a Northwestern degree. I've got a wife with a Northwestern degree who is ambitious and has dreams for her future. And during that waiting period, I knew I wouldn't make any decisions unilaterally. Erica is dreaming about education reform and what she could do and where we could go, and Chicago kept coming up as the place we needed to be. As that alternative became more apparent, I had more and more peace. I felt like, OK Lord, you're turning the page for me, for us, and that's OK. I've lived a dream, I'm in pain, I've been compensated well, and I trust you with the next step."

In November 2021, the Carr family moved to the Windy City and settled down in Little Italy—"Some people say I even look Italian," Austin says. Erica began her work with By the Hand, a Christian nonprofit that develops afterschool programs for at risk kids.[3] It began in 2001 in the Cabrini-Green area of the city—just a mile due west of Oak Street Beach on the shore of Lake Michigan—with just sixteen kids. Since then, By the Hand has grown to serve more than seventeen hundred kids across Chicago.

The lives of so many people around the world changed in 2020. In the city of Chicago the pandemic wreaked havoc on schools, sports, businesses, and communities. And on May 25, George Floyd was killed in Minneapolis, sparking outrage across the nation. In Chicago, protests turned into looting and riots, and May 29–31 the South and West Sides of the city were devastated, leaving already under-resourced communities without basic necessities.

By the Hand launched their summer programs on July 6, with chapel, small-group Bible studies, field trips, college tours, and other activities, all with proper COVID safeguards. The next day, they began an ambitious project, tearing down an old liquor store they had purchased and opening a fresh food market in Austin, on the western side of the city. Not only did the market provide food, but it also served as a place to teach kids about work and business, giving them jobs and training in the real world.

As Erica joined By the Hand, Austin began work with Intentional Sports, a new nonprofit designed to provide competitive sports opportunities and wellness activities for people in the city itself. Erica gave birth to their second child in the early summer of 2022.

"If you rewind the clock to 2020," Austin recounts, "I was training in Chicago, and the George Floyd riots were going on. A group of Chicago-based athletes led by Sam Acho [NFL player] gathered together. We just wanted to listen to the kids in the inner-city neighborhoods. We went to a neighborhood in Austin, just listening to them, asking them what they need. It was really cool. The kids were there, the police were there. Guys like Mitch Trubisky [then the quarterback of the Chicago Bears], Jason Hayward [then an outfielder with the Chicago Cubs], Jonathan Toews, and other big names in Chicago sports. We heard that they need[ed] fresh food and a safe place to play sports."

The athletes got together and approached the owner of a liquor store in Austin. The store had been looted during the riots and the owner just wanted out. They bought the store and then demolished it to create By the Hand's fresh food market.

"This was my first interaction with By the Hand," Austin says, "and I got to see the amazing work that they're doing in the afterschool hours for inner-city kids. Because after school hours are crucial—you either join a gang or you do something productive with your life. They don't have cars to go drive to the suburbs, to the nice ritzy sports facility. In many cases they're being raised by a grandparent or sibling. Things are stacked against them."

Intentional Sports[4] was born out of these conversations, and the need they exposed. Austin and others had a fresh vision—to build a massive sports complex in the city to give kids a place to play and belong. It wasn't designed to be a for-profit business, but a nonprofit intent on protecting those hours from 3:00 to 7:00 when kids are most vulnerable.

"There's a lot of basketball courts in Austin," he says. "But not places you want to be after six at night."

The youth sports industry is around $23 billion a year, but Intentional Sports has forgone the profit motive and has sought to give under-resourced communities access to competitive sports.

They are currently building the largest indoor turf arena within Chicago city limits. They will have a FIFA-regulation-sized field, and host all kinds of soccer events. Gatorade has joined in as a sponsor, helping provide resourcing. Riot Games will have an e-sports lab in the facility as well.

At the end of 2022, Austin took on the role of overseeing the day-to-day operation of Intentional Sports. It's his heart to give kids who lack resources opportunities that had never existed before in their communities. As a nonprofit, they rely on funding from those interested in helping meet the needs of these kids.

"We think of it as cleats, coaches, and consistency," Austin says. "You need cleats—equipment and a place to play. You need coaches—someone who shows up and helps you out. And you need consistency [in] those things. We don't think that sport solves all the world's problems. Some of these things are way above our pay grade. But we do think that sports will move the needle."

* * *

When I was in seventh grade, I ran into Bubba Paris, who was Joe Montana's left tackle back in the 1980s. I asked him what should I do to make it into the NFL. He said, you know Austin, whatever level you're at, just try to be the best at that. Just be the best that you can be at that level. Then as you advance, try to be the best you can at that level.

They say that comparison is the thief of all joy, and I think the heart behind that is a warning against envy. But the Apostle Paul talks about someone who is excellent at something being a model for us. To do that, you have to compare what they're doing to what you're doing. So I have always tried to look around and see who's good at things, and model myself after them. That's how I kept succeeding at each level. I wasn't a phenom or anything. It took time. But I eventually made it there.

I would also say that it's important to begin with the end in mind, and here's what I mean. It's not only that you become successful, but how you become successful that matters. Beyond the big catch you make that wins the game, your teammates will remember the off-hand comment you made in the locker room, for how much time you took to explain to them the playbook when you're a senior and they're an underclassman, for how you cared for them in their time of need.

I've experienced good teammates and bad teammates. I remember one teammate—Matthew Slater—just how he and his wife served others. One time, Shahrzad picked my wife's family up at the airport before a pre-season game, and Shahrzad was pregnant and her water had just broken! Who you are off the field matters as much, or more, as who you are on the field. As great as sports are, they can become the center of our world, and I can tell you this: the idol of sport is not worth living for. Keep it all in perspective.

—Austin Carr

Notes

PREFACE

1. Rajani Gurung, "Top 12 Most Popular Sports in America," *PlayersBio*, 2022, https://playersbio.com/most-popular-sports-in-america/ (10 Oct. 2022).

2. The top eight are Super Bowls, and the only two other broadcasts to break into the top thirty-two were the last episode of *M*A*S*H* (February 28, 1983) at number 9, and the 2016 presidential debates, at number 32. See "List of most watched television broadcasts in the United States," Wikipedia, https://en.wikipedia.org/wiki/List_of_most_watched_television_broadcasts_in_the_United_States.

3. Nafiz Tahmid, "Why Is the NFL the Most Popular Sport in America?," *SportsZion*, 2021, https://www.sportszion.com/nfl-most-popular-sport-in-america/ (8 Sep. 2022).

4. Austin Svehla, "Why Fantasy Football for Many Is More Than Just a Game," *Norfolk Daily News*, October 2, 2021, https://norfolkdailynews.com/news/why-fantasy-football-for-many-is-more-than-just-a-game/article_1495d0ba-238c-11ec-9175-e78ef965de85.html (7 Jul. 2022).

CHAPTER 1

1. Kamara would go on to become a Pro Bowl player in the NFL.

2. Day one of the NFL draft is reserved strictly for the first round. Day two is for rounds two and three, and day three is for rounds four through seven.

CHAPTER 3

1. Austin's father is Black, and his mother is white.

2. In 2014 the Patriots were embroiled in a scandal known as "Deflategate." The league claimed that Tom Brady was "more likely than not" to have knowledge

of a "scheme to deflate footballs" under the league's proscribed limit of 12.5 psi. After many months of legal battle, the NFL finally penalized the Patriots a first-round pick in 2016, a fourth-round pick in 2017, and suspended Brady for four games. It was, in fact, completely ludicrous, but the Patriots went on to win the Super Bowl in both 2014 and 2016 anyway.

CHAPTER 4

1. Patricia Traina, "Geremy Davis to New York Giants: Full Draft-Pick Breakdown," Bleacher Report, 2015, https://bleacherreport.com/articles/2450513-geremy-davis-to-new-york-giants-full-draft-pick-breakdown (6 Jun. 2022).

2. Ed Valentine, "2015 NFL Draft Results: New York Giants select UConn WR Geremy Davis in Round 6," Big Blue Review, 2015, https://www.bigblueview.com/2015-nfl-draft/2015/5/2/8535331/2015-nfl-draft-results-new-york-giants-select-geremy-davis-uconn-in-round-6 (6 Jun. 2022).

3. "Experts grade Giants pick of WR Geremy Davis," Giants.com, 2015, https://www.giants.com/news/experts-grade-giants-pick-of-wr-geremy-davis-15235908 (6 Jun. 2022).

4. Valentine, "2015 NFL Draft Results."

5. Valentine.

6. Geremy Davis, UConn Pro Day, March 31, 2015, YouTube, https://www.youtube.com/watch?v=DNpAKCybE5o.

7. Zach Kruse, "The Anatomy and Importance of the 40-Yard Dash at the NFL Scouting Combine," Bleacher Report, 2013, https://bleacherreport.com/articles/1537023-the-anatomy-and-importance-of-the-40-yard-dash (8 Jun. 2022).

8. Athletes in Action is an international interdenominational Christian organization that works with pro and college athletes, helping them to connect their faith with their sport. AIA exists on more than two hundred campuses in the United States, and is in more than ninety countries around the world.

9. "Quotes: Day 3 draft picks," Giants.com, 2015, https://www.giants.com/news/quotes-day-3-draft-picks-15233739 (8 Jun. 2022).

10. There were nine compensation picks in addition to the thirty-two regular picks.

11. CB Quandre Diggs and TE Darren Waller.

CHAPTER 5

1. Michael LoRé, "The Life of an NFL Practice Squad Player," The Culture Trip, 2017, https://theculturetrip.com/north-america/usa/articles/the-life-of-an-nfl-practice-squad-player/ (12 Jul. 2022).

2. Ryan Riddle, "The Contradictions of an NFL Practice," Bleacher Report, 2014, https://bleacherreport.com/articles/2172064-the-contradictions-of-an-nfl -practice (12 Jul. 2022).

3. Geoff Schwartz, "NFL Training Camp Is a Mental Grind, Too," SB Nation, 2018, https://www.sbnation.com/nfl/2018/8/2/17642532/nfl-training-camp-2018 -practice-schedule-grind (14 Jul. 2022).

4. Each space ("gap") between offensive linemen has a designation. Between the center and the guard is the A gap; between the guard and tackle is the B gap; outside the tackle is the C gap; and if there is a tight end, the C gap is the space between the tackle and tight end, with the D gap being outside the tight end.

5. Schwartz, "NFL Training Camp Is a Mental Grind, Too."

CHAPTER 6

1. Things have changed since then, as receivers—and players from other positions as well—now regularly wear single digits.

2. "Top Plays from Giants Rookie Mini Camp," Giants.com, 2015, https://www .giants.com/news/top-plays-from-giants-rookie-mini-camp-practice-15266737 (8 Jul. 2022).

3. Desmond Connor, "Geremy Davis Trying to Make Giant Impression in N.Y. Camp," *Hartford Courant*, 2015, https://www.courant.com/sports/football /hc-geremy-davis-uconn-giants-camp-0509-20150508-story.html (12 Jul. 2022).

4. Chris Pflum, "Meet the Rookie: Is Geremy Davis a Sleeper at Wide Receiver?," *Big Blue Review*, 2015, https://www.bigblueview.com/2015/5/30 /8670791/2015-ny-giants-geremy-davis-wr-uconn-analysistraining-camp-pre view (13 Jul. 2022).

5. "5 Standout Players from Giants Training Camp," Giants.com, 2015, https:// www.giants.com/news/5-standout-players-from-giants-training-camp-15586851 (14 Jul. 2022).

6. "Geremy Davis 'Has Lots of Upside,' says Quinn," *Big Blue Review*, 2015, https://www.bigblueview.com/giants-training-camp-2015/2015/8/21/9185707/ny -giants-geremy-davis-has-a-lot-of-upside-says-tom-quinn (18 Jul. 2022).

7. The NFL has since changed that policy.

CHAPTER 7

1. O'Connell would go on to become the head coach of the Vikings in 2022.

2. "Matthew Slater Conference Call," Patriots.com, 2008, https://www.patriots .com/news/matthew-slater-conference-call-4-27-2008-161546 (15 Jul. 2022).

3. Glenn Farley, "Slater's NFL Journey Has Had Twists and Turns," *Berkshire Eagle*, 2021, https://www.berkshireeagle.com/slaters-nfl-journey-has-had-twists -and-turns/article_a3530be8-f96f-11eb-8073-fba9077d3c2a.html (22 Jul. 2022).

4. Patty Leon, "Guyton at Patriots Training Camp," *Coastal Courier*, 2008, https://coastalcourier.com/sports/guyton-at-patriots-training-camp/ (7 Jul. 2022).

5. "Football Memories: Ryan Wendell," Patriots.com, 2014, https://www .patriots.com/news/football-memories-ryan-wendell-195821 (1 Aug. 2022).

6. "Kevin O'Connell battling for No. 2 slot," *Boston Herald*, 2008, https: //www.bostonherald.com/2008/08/04/kevin-oconnell-battling-for-no-2-slot/ (1 Aug. 2022).

CHAPTER 8

1. The special teams coordinator at the time, Joe Judge.

2. Jordy McElroy, "Bill Belichick Admits Emotions from Roster Cutdown Day Weigh Heavily," Patriots Wire, August 30, 2022, https://patriotswire.usatoday .com/2022/08/30/bill-belichick-admits-emotions-roster-cutdown-day-weight -heavily/ (1 Sep. 2022).

CHAPTER 9

1. Richard Johnson, "There's Tons of Other Stuff in Your Football Team's Playbook," Banner Society, August 15, 2019, https://www.bannersociety.com /2019/8/15/20726587/what-is-in-a-playbook-football (5 Aug. 2022).

2. Johnson.

3. Ryan Riddle, "The Truth about Studying Your Playbook in NFL Training Camp," *Bleacher Report*, July 30, 2014, https://bleacherreport.com/articles /2145989-the-truth-about-studying-your-playbook-in-nfl-training-camp (8 Aug. 2022).

4. Brendan Darby, "How Difficult Is It to Learn an NFL Playbook?," *Huffington Post*, 2012, https://www.huffpost.com/entry/how-difficult-is-it-to-le_b _1762657 (12 Aug. 2012).

5. Ben Shpiegel, "Jets Rookie Has Playbook and Notebook," *New York Times*, July 27, 2014, https://www.nytimes.com/2014/07/27/sports/football/jets-rookie -has-playbook-and-notebook-.html?partner=rss&emc=rss&_r=0 (15 Aug. 2012).

6. Zach Koons, "Justin Fields Explains How He Studies the Bears' Playbook," *The Spun*, May 17, 2021, https://thespun.com/nfl/nfc-north/chicago-bears/justin -fields-studying-bears-playbook-flash-cards (4 Aug. 2022).

7. Brandon Hall, "Elite QB Coach Jordan Palmer's Formula for Learning a Playbook Fast," *Stack*, September 6, 2016, https://www.stack.com/a/elite-qb -coach-jordan-palmers-formula-for-learning-a-playbook-fast (3 Aug. 2022).

8. Koons, "Justin Fields Explains."

9. Dan Treadway, "Brain Games: A Top Neuroscientist Explains How Difficult It Is to Master an NFL Playbook," *Sports Illustrated*, August 4, 2014, https://www.si.com/extra-mustard/2014/08/04/how-difficult-it-memorize-nfl-playbook-neurologist-explains (16 Aug. 2022).

10. Elizabeth Merrill, "In NFL, the Playbook Is Sacred," ESPN, 2007, https://www.espn.com/nfl/preview07/news/story?id=2973338 (17 Aug. 2022).

11. Merrill.

12. Mike Florio, "Pettine Explains the Value of Having an Opponent's Playbook," NBC Sports, June 20, 2014, https://profootballtalk.nbcsports.com/2014/06/20/pettine-explains-the-value-of-having-an-opponents-playbook/ (20 Aug. 2022).

CHAPTER 10

1. Patrick Redfored, "Maine Basketball Player Breaks Teammate's Jaw after Fight over Locker Room Music," *Deadspin*, February 23, 2017, https://deadspin.com/maine-basketball-player-breaks-teammates-jaw-after-figh-1792697338.

2. Ryan Riddle, "What NFL Pros Do in the Hours Just Before a Game," *Bleacher Report*, August 8, 2012, https://bleacherreport.com/articles/1289216-what-the-pros-do-in-the-hours-just-before-a-game (1 Sep. 2022).

3. "What's It Like Stepping on an NFL Field for the First Time?," NFL Films Presents, YouTube, https://www.youtube.com/watch?v=U0FImX6obuA.

4. "What's It Like Stepping on an NFL Field?"

5. "What's It Like Stepping on an NFL Field?"

CHAPTER 11

1. Kevin Clark, "What the Brady-less 2008 Season Taught Us about Bill Belichick," *The Ringer*, August 9, 2018, https://www.theringer.com/nfl/2018/8/9/17670364/new-england-patriots-2008-season-tom-brady-injury-matt-cassel-bill-belichick (13 Aug. 2022).

2. Arun Srinivasan, "Moss Recalls Belichick Ripping Brady in Film Room," The Score, 2016, https://www.thescore.com/nfl/news/1212370 (1 Sep. 2022).

3. Tyler Sullivan, "Chad Johnson Recalls Time When Belichick Ripped into Tom Brady," 247 Sports, 2016, https://247sports.com/nfl/new-england-patriots/Article/Chad-Johnson-recalls-time-when-Bill-Belichick-ripped-into-Tom-Brady-48504326/ (1 Sep. 2022).

4. Braden Campbell, "Top Gunner: How Matt Slater Went from No-Name Receiver to Special Teams Ace," *Boston.com*, January 6, 2015, https://

www.boston.com/sports/new-england-patriots/2015/01/06/top-gunner-how-matt
-slater-went-from-no-name-receiver-to-special-teams-ace/ (3 Sep. 2022).

5. Darren Hartwell, "Edelman Reveals What Belichick Tells His Players about
Ball Security," NBC Sports Boston, 2021, https://www.nbcsports.com/boston
/patriots/julian-edelman-shares-bill-belichicks-message-patriots-ballcarriers (1
Aug. 2022).

6. Peter May, "Footballs Fair Game at Bill Belichick's Practices," *New York
Times*, January 25, 2015, https://www.nytimes.com/2015/01/25/sports/football/
footballs-fair-game-at-bill-belichicks-practices.html?_r=0 (9 Aug. 2022).

CHAPTER 12

1. Sean Ingle, "New Orleans Saints Beat Miami Dolphins in Wembley Stinker,"
The Guardian, October 1, 2017, https://www.theguardian.com/sport/2017/oct/01/
new-orleans-miam-dolphins-wembley-match-report (22 Aug. 2022).

CHAPTER 13

1. "Runners Attempt Eliud Kipchoge's World Record Marathon Pace," *Runner's World*, YouTube, https://www.youtube.com/watch?v=SRYtn0j5ccA.

2. Clay Travis, "Reality: You Can't Run a Sub 5.0 Forty," *OutKick*, 2013, https:
//www.outkick.com/reality-you-cant-run-a-sub-50-forty-022414/ (31 Jul. 2022).

3. "Percentage of People Who Can Bench 225 Lbs, 275, 315, etc.," *Fitness
from Ground Zero* (blog), July 13, 2013, http://fitnessfromgroundzero.blogspot
.com/2013/07/percentage-of-people-who-can-bench.html (30 Aug. 2022).

4. "What It's Like Catching a Pass from an NFL Quarterback, Lance
Kearse and Reed Kastner-Lang," YouTube, https://www.youtube.com/watch?v
=qnVemJAJyqU.

5. "What Is It Like Trying to Catch a Pass Thrown by an NFL Quarterback?," Quora, 2020, https://www.quora.com/What-is-it-like-trying-to-catch-a
-pass-thrown-by-an-NFL-quarterback (17 Aug. 2022).

6. Andrew Joseph, "High School Basketball Player Challenges Brian Scalabrine
to 1-on-1, Regrets It Immediately," *For the Win* (blog), March 23, 2021, https://
ftw.usatoday.com/2021/03/hs-basketball-player-challenges-brian-scalabrine-1-on
-1-video (27 Aug. 2022).

7. Alex Kirshner, "How Rare Is It to Be a 5-Star College Football Recruit," *SB
Nation*, January 30, 2019, https://www.sbnation.com/college-football-recruiting
/2019/1/30/18202661/recruiting-stars-rankings-high-school-football (19 Aug.
2022).

8. "Geremy Davis," *274sports*, 2015, https://247sports.com/player/geremy
-davis-3154/ (31 Jul. 2022).

CHAPTER 14

1. Len Pasquarelli, "Bills' Third-Round Draft Pick Could Miss Year," ESPN, https://tv5.espn.com/nfl/columns/story?columnist=pasquarelli_len&id=2051662.

2. Matt Higgins, "Football Physics: The Anatomy of a Hit," *Popular Mechanics*, December 17, 2009, https://www.popularmechanics.com/adventure/sports/a2954/4212171/.

3. Victoria Stern, "Coming in from the Cold: Did Hypothermia Therapy Allow Kevin Everett to Walk Again?," *Scientific American*, September 2, 2008, https://www.scientificamerican.com/article/did-hypothermia-therapy-allow-kevin-everett-to-walk/.

4. Sal Maiorana, "Maioriana's Memories: The Near On-Field Death of Kevin Everett Still a Vivid Scene," *Democrat & Chronicle*, August 8, 2020, https://www.democratandchronicle.com/story/sports/football/nfl/bills/2020/08/20/kevin-everett-spinal-cord-injury-buffalo-bills-tight-end-has-recovered/5616277002/.

5. "Induced Hypothermia May Have Helped Buffalo's Kevin Everett Recover," *Diagnostic and Interventional Cardiology*, September 12, 2007, https://www.dicardiology.com/content/induced-hypothermia-may-have-helped-buffalo-bills-kevin-everett-recover (1 Sep. 2022).

6. Associated Press, "Five Months after Accident, Buffalo Bills Tight End Kevin Everett Is Walking, Standing Tall," ESPN, January 31, 2008, http://www.espn.com/espn/wire/_/section/nfl/id/3224926.

7. Staff Writer, "Everett's Mom on His Improvement: 'He's Like a Miracle,'" *The Ledger*, September 13, 2007, https://www.theledger.com/news/20070913/everetts-mom-on-his-improvement-hes-like-a-miracle (1 Sep. 2022).

8. Staff Writer.

9. Associated Press, "Five Months after Accident."

10. Associated Press.

11. Stern, "Coming in from the Cold."

12. Chris Brown, "Kevin Everett Five Years Later," buffalobills.com, September 7, 2012, https://www.buffalobills.com/news/kevin-everett-five-years-later-8182739 (17 Sep. 2022).

13. Brown, "Kevin Everett Five Years Later."

14. Brown, "Kevin Everett Five Years Later."

15. Allen Wilson and Mike Harrington, "Bills Releasing Kevin Everett Official Move Allows Payment of Benefits," *The Buffalo News*, May 13, 2008, https://buffalonews.com/news/bills-releasing-everett-official-move-allows-payment-of-benefits/article_beb6e201-604c-5590-a606-a396c6b1ddda.html (9 Sep. 2022).

16. On January 2, 2023, in the first quarter of the Bills-Bengals game on Monday Night Football, Bengals wide receiver Tee Higgins caught a pass from Joe Burrow and collided with Bills' defensive back Damar Hamlin as Hamlin brought Higgins to the ground. Hamlin stood, then fell backward and lay unconscious. Medical staff rushed to the field and spent nine minutes performing CPR

on Hamlin, who suffered cardiac arrest. Players from both teams knelt in prayer, stood in shock, and wept openly at the sight of Hamlin fighting for his life. He was taken to the University of Cincinnati Medical Center, and the rest of the game was canceled. Nine days later, Hamlin, whose life hung in the balance for days, was discharged from the hospital, and began the road to fully restored health. This incident was a highly unlikely event, not seen for decades in the NFL. But it serves as a reminder that players are at great risk playing football.

17. Barbara Moran, "CTE Found in 99 Percent of Former NFL Players Studied," *The Brink*, July 26, 2017, https://www.bu.edu/articles/2017/cte-former-nfl -players/ (3 Sep. 2022).

18. Hernandez, a former NFL tight end, was found guilty of murder in 2013 and later took his own life in prison.

CHAPTER 15

1. Reed Ferber, "Usain Bolt and Andre DeGrasse: Hamstring Injuries Explained," *The Conversation*, August 13, 2017, https://theconversation.com /usain-bolt-and-andre-de-grasse-hamstring-injuries-explained-82431 (11 Sep. 2022).

2. Jordan Zim, "Why Do So Many NFL Players Go Down with Hamstring Injuries Every Pre-season?," *Stack*, August 27, 2015, https://www.stack.com/a/ why-do-hamstring-injuries-continually-disrupt-the-nfl-preseason (15 Sep. 2022).

3. Zim.

4. Dan Duggan, "Can Geremy Davis Get One of the Remaining WR Spots with the Giants?," *NJ.com*, August 8, 2016, https://www.nj.com/giants/2016/08/ receiver_geremey_davis_hoping_to_catch_on_with_gia.html (3 Sep. 2022).

5. Duggan.

6. James Kratch, "Giants waive 2015 draft pick Geremy Davis as part of roster cutdown," *NJ.com*, September 3, 2016, https://www.nj.com/giants/2016/09/ giants_waive_2015_draft_pick_geremy_davis_as_part.html (3 Sep. 2022).

7. Gilbert Manzano, "Receivers Geremy Davis, Andre Patton Called Upon during Chargers' Injury Bug," *Orange County Register*, October 3, 2019, https: //www.ocregister.com/2019/10/03/receivers-geremy-davis-andre-patton-called -upon-during-chargers-injury-bug/ (5 Sep. 2022).

8. Samantha O'Connell and Theo Manschreck, "Playing through the Pain: Psychiatric Risks among Athletes," *Current Psychiatry* 11, no. 7 (2017), 17, https://cdn.mdedge.com/files/s3fs-public/Document/September-2017/1107CP _OConnell.pdf (9 Sep. 2022).

CHAPTER 16

1. Andrew Callahan, "Patriots Captain Matthew Slater Reflects on Past Letter from Lions Coach," *Boston Herald*, October 8, 2022, https://www.bostonherald.com/2022/10/08/patriots-captain-matthew-slater-reflects-on-past-letter-from-lions-coach/ (20 Sep. 2022).

2. Bernd Buchmasser, "Where Does Matthew Slater Rank among the NFL's Best Ever Special Teamers? 'It's Got to Be at the Top,'" Pats Pulpit, December 22, 2020, https://www.patspulpit.com/2020/12/22/22196466/matthew-slater-pro-bowl-patriots-belichick (1 Oct. 2022).

3. Chris Mason, "Jerod Mayo Explains How Patriots Captains Devin McCourty, Matthew Slater Have Grown as Leaders," *MassLive*, August 29, 2022, https://www.masslive.com/patriots/2022/08/jerod-mayo-explains-how-patriots-captains-devin-mccourty-matthew-slater-have-grown-as-leaders.html (1 Oct. 2022).

CHAPTER 17

1. The full fight song goes:

> *Skol Vikings, let's win this game,*
>
> *Skol Vikings, honor your name,*
>
> *Go get that first down,*
>
> *Then get a touchdown.*
>
> *Rock 'em . . . Sock 'em*
>
> *Fight! Fight! Fight! Fight!*
>
> *Go Vikings, run up the score*
>
> *You'll hear us yell for more . . .*
>
> *V-I-K-I-N-G-S*
>
> *Skol Vikings, let's go!*

CHAPTER 18

1. Agustin Mojica, "How Long Is the Average NFL Career?," *Sportscasting*, April 6, 2020, https://www.sportscasting.com/how-long-is-the-average-nfl-career/ (7 Oct. 2022).

2. Amelia Josephson, "The Average Salary by Age in the U.S.," *Smart Asset*, December 27, 2022, https://smartasset.com/retirement/the-average-salary-by-age (7 Oct. 2022).

3. Corey Roepken, "Texans Rookie K.J. Dillon Gets Stuck with $16,000 Dinner Bill," *Chron*, December 20, 2016, https://www.chron.com/sports/texans/article/Texans-rookie-K-J-Dillon-gets-stuck-with-16-000-10808555.php (9 Oct. 2022).

4. Amanda Morris and Michel Martin, "Poor Students More Likely to Play Football, despite Brain Injury Concerns," *All Things Considered*, February 3, 2019, NPR, https://www.npr.org/2019/02/03/691081227/poor-students-more-likely-to-play-football-despite-brain-injury-concerns (9 Oct. 2022).

5. Morris and Martin.

6. Abigail Johnson Hess, "Here's Why Lottery Winners Go Broke," *CNBC Make It*, August 25, 2017, https://www.cnbc.com/2017/08/25/heres-why-lottery-winners-go-broke.html (3 Oct. 2022).

7. Hess.

8. Pablo Torre, "How (and Why) Athletes Go Broke," *Sports Illustrated*, March 23, 2009, https://vault.si.com/vault/2009/03/23/how-and-why-athletes-go-broke (13 Oct. 2022).

9. Leigh Steinberg, "5 Reasons Why 80% of Retired NFL Players Go Broke," *Forbes*, February 9, 2015, https://www.forbes.com/sites/leighsteinberg/2015/02/09/5-reasons-why-80-of-retired-nfl-players-go-broke/?sh=b8b849b78ccb (12 Oct. 2022).

10. Colleen Kane, "How NFL Players Approach Their Short Shelf Lives: 'You're Investing in Your Body. Sometimes Those Things Are Priceless," *Chicago Tribune*, September 1, 2018, https://www.chicagotribune.com/sports/bears/ct-spt-bears-nfl-players-shelf-life-20180830-story.html (15 Oct. 2022).

11. American Academy of Pediatrics, "Many High School Football Players Not Concerned about Concussions," ScienceDaily, October 12, 2012, https://www.sciencedaily.com/releases/2012/10/121022080645.htm (9 Oct. 2022).

12. Steinberg, "5 Reasons Why 80% of Retired NFL Players Go Broke."

13. "NFL's Finance Boot Camp Teaches Players to Plan for the Future," Fast Forward Accounting Solutions, https://www.fastforwardaccounting.net/nfls-finance-boot-camp-teaches-players-to-plan-for-the-future/ (12 Oct. 2022).

14. Kaitlin Mulhere, "Meet the Professor Who's Teaching Future Pro Athletes How to Hang Onto Their Millions," *Money*, April 22, 2016, https://money.com/professor-teaching-future-pro-athletes-finances/ (15 Oct. 2022).

15. Barbara Booth, "How This Wealth Manager for Superstar Athletes Helps NBA and NFL Players Protect Their Money," CNBC, February 4, 2020, https://www.cnbc.com/2020/01/30/how-a-wealth-manager-helps-nba-and-nfl-stars-save-money.html (9 Oct. 2022).

CHAPTER 19

1. Ryan Riddle, "The Difference between College and the Pros in the NFL," *Bleacher Report*, September 6, 2012, https://bleacherreport.com/articles/1324537 -the-difference-between-college-and-the-pros-in-the-nfl (12 Oct. 2022).

2. Riddle.

3. James Palmer, https://twitter.com/JamesPalmerTV, 2019 (13 Oct. 2022).

4. Brian Billick, "Toughest Transition? Why Rookie Wide Receivers Struggle in NFL," NFL.com, September 18, 2013, https://www.nfl.com/news/toughest -transition-why-rookie-wide-receivers-struggle-in-nfl-0ap2000000246769 (12 Oct. 2022).

5. Dan Woike, "Chargers Special Teams Guru George Stewart Made Anthony Lynn Better as a Player, so Lynn Hired Him as a Coach," *Los Angeles Times*, May 21, 2017, https://www.latimes.com/sports/chargers/la-sp-chargers-lynn-stewart -20170521-story.html (19 Oct. 2022).

CHAPTER 20

1. Dan Benton, "Anthony Dable Says Giants Cut Him for 'No Reason,'" *Giants Wire*, January 26, 2017, https://giantswire.usatoday.com/2017/01/26/ anthony-dable-new-york-giants-cut-him-no-reason/ (22 Oct. 2022).

2. Michael Peterson, "Breaking: Chargers Re-sign WR Geremy Davis," *SB Nation*, March 19, 2019, https://www.boltsfromtheblue.com/2019/3/19/18273573 /chargers-re-sign-wr-geremy-davis-cantrell-bolts (17 Oct. 2022).

3. Ricky Henne, "Get Ready for Some Intense Wide Receiver Competition," *Chargers.com*, June 17, 2019, https://www.chargers.com/news/get-ready-for -some-intense-wide-receiver-competition (16 Oct. 2022).

CHAPTER 21

1. For a thorough look at the controversy, see: John Vampatella, "A Thorough Look at Deflategate: How Did We Get to This Point?," Patsfans, June 13, 2015, https://www.patsfans.com/blogs/vampatella/2015/06/13/a-thorough-look -at-deflategate-how-did-we-get-to-this-point/.

2. "Matthew Slater Wins 2017 Bart Starr Award," Patriots.com, January 4, 2017, https://web.archive.org/web/20170106192328/http://www.patriots.com/ news/2017/01/04/matthew-slater-win-2017-bart-starr-award (30 Oct. 2022).

CHAPTER 22

1. New Orleans is in the central time zone, so a 1:00 eastern kickoff is a noon kickoff in New Orleans.

2. See: www.ijm.org.

3. Emma Ecker, "Breaking Down Global Estimates of Human Trafficking: Human Trafficking Awareness Month 2022," *Human Trafficking Institute*, 2022, https://traffickinginstitute.org/breaking-down-global-estimates-of-human -trafficking-human-trafficking-awareness-month-2022/ (1 Nov. 2022).

4. Herbie Teope, "Austin Carr, Geneo Grissom Visit Guatemala over Summer to Raise Awareness on Fight against Sex Trafficking," *NOLA.com*, August 17, 2019, https://www.nola.com/sports/saints/article_c1d8d2f2-c0ad-11e9-8007 -27383b56b858.html (2 Nov. 2022).

5. Teope.

CHAPTER 23

1. "If There's Commitment, That's Victory for Me," interview by Siddhartha Vaidyanathan and Nagraj Gollapudi, ESPN Cricinfo, March 24, 2008, https: //www.espncricinfo.com/story/if-there-s-commitment-that-s-victory-for-me -343750.

2. Seth Wickersham, "Book Excerpt: The Passion, Pressure, Profanity, and Near-Perfection of the 2007 Patriots," ESPN, October 6, 2021, https://www.espn .com/nfl/story/_/id/32344433/espn-writer-seth-wickersham-goes-new-england -patriots-historic-2007-run (3 Nov. 2022).

3. John Fennelly, "Retired David Tyree Reflects on Helmet Catch, Eli Manning," *Giants Wire*, July 9, 2020, https://giantswire.usatoday.com/2020/07/09/ retired-new-york-giants-david-tyree-reflects-helmet-catch-eli-manning/ (5 Jul. 2022).

4. He was active in just 1.3 percent of ESPN fantasy football leagues that week.

5. Elizabeth Merrill, "Patriots RB Jonas Gray's Brush with Fantasy vs. Reality, Five Years Ago," ESPN, November 13, 2019, https://www.espn.com/nfl/story/ _/id/28066447/patriots-rb-jonas-gray-brush-fantasy-vs-reality-five-years-ago (5 Sep. 2022).

6. Merrill.

7. "Geremy Davis: 5 Fast Facts You Need to Know," *Heavy*, September 2015, https://heavy.com/sports/2015/09/geremy-davis-new-york-giants-combine-draft -stats-highlights-ucon/ (9 Sept. 2022).

CHAPTER 25

1. https://marcellatemanfoundation.org.

CHAPTER 26

1. https://www.facebook.com/SlaterFamilyFoundation/.

CHAPTER 27

1. A futures deal is similar to a regular contract except that it doesn't kick in until the start of the next football year and locks the player in, not allowing them to pursue deals with other teams.

2. He had tested positive for COVID several months prior.

3. See bythehand.org.

4. See intentionalsports.org.

About the Author

John Vampatella is a graduate of Syracuse University's S. I. Newhouse School of Public Communication. Since graduating in 1991, he has invested his professional life in ministry with college students, presently serving Division I athletes and coaches with Athletes in Action at the University of Connecticut. He is also the director of AIA's Northeast region, overseeing campus chapters across New York and the six New England states. He and his wife, Diane, have been married for more than thirty years, and they couldn't be more proud of their four grown children.

John is an avid athlete, playing basketball and volleyball whenever possible. He also loves to ski and play golf. He and his wife enjoy traveling, whether it is for work or pleasure, and ministry has taken him all over the United States and to places like Germany, Italy, and South Africa.

In his spare time, John loves to write, and aside from articles and contributions to other books, he has written four published books, *53rd Man* being the latest. His first, *The Immigrant*, describes his grandfather's immigration to the United States from Sicily in 1913, and it is set against the backdrop of the Italian-American experience in the twentieth century. His second book, *The Forgotten Game*, tells the story of one of the most remarkable baseball games ever to be played: the fifth game of the 2004 American League Championship Series between the New York Yankees and Boston Red Sox. It features stories of the players involved and dives headlong into discussions about baseball strategy, history, and even discussions about who might be the greatest pitcher of all time. His third book, *For Good Reason*, is more of a professional work, drawing on his three decades of ministry experience, addressing questions pertaining to faith and purpose in life. You may find all John's books wherever books are sold or at his website, johnvampatellaauthor.com.

CPSIA information can be obtained
at www.ICGtesting.com
Printed in the USA
LVHW090047180723
752702LV00003B/6